ON CAMPUS

The Teaching of Drama in the Primary School

THE TEACHING OF DRAMA IN THE PRIMARY SCHOOL

BRIAN WOOLLAND

Longman

An imprint of **Pearson Education**

Harlow, England · London · New York · Reading, Massachusetts · San Francisco
Toronto · Don Mills, Ontario · Sydney · Tokyo · Singapore · Hong Kong · Seoul
Taipei · Cape Town · Madrid · Mexico City · Amsterdam · Munich · Paris · Milan

Pearson Education Limited
Edinburgh Gate, Harlow
Essex CM20 2JE, England
and Associated Companies throughout the world.

Visit us on the World Wide Web at:
http://www.pearsoneduc.com

© Longman Group UK Limited 1993

First published 1993
ISBN 0–582–08906–9 PPR

British Library Cataloguing-in-Publication Data

A catalogue record for this book is
available from the British Library

Library of Congress Cataloging-in-Publication Data

Woolland, Brian, 1949–
  The teaching of drama in the primary school / Brian Woolland.
    p. cm. -- (The Effective teacher series)
  Includes bibliographical references and index.
  ISBN 0–582–08906–9
    1. Theater--Study and teaching (Primary) 2. Drama--Study and
  teaching (Primary) I. Title. II. Series.
  PN2095.W6 1993
  372.6'6--dc20
                                              92-28989
                                                 CIP

Transferred to digital printing 2003

Printed and bound by Antony Rowe Ltd, Eastbourne

C O N T E N T S

ACKNOWLEDGEMENTS

I would like to extend thanks to the following, all of whom have been extremely helpful.

Mary Martyn-Johns, Lindsay Beaton, Liz Pye and the staff of Redlands County Primary School, Reading, who will recognise much of the practical work described in this book.

Alistair Black, David Davies, Dorothy Heathcote – each of whom, in their very different ways has been a positive influence on my drama teaching.

I am indebted to the colleagues and students with whom I have worked over the years, who have influenced and challenged my thinking – in particular my colleagues at Reading University in the Sub-Department of Film and Drama and the Department of Arts and Humanities.

I would like to thank Lib Taylor, always an encouraging and supportive colleague, for her contributions to the introduction to this book and to Chapters 7 and 10.

We are grateful to the following for permission to reproduce copyright material:

The author's agents for the poem 'Whale' by D.M. Thomas from *Selected Poems*, Secker & Warburg 1983. Copyright © D.M. Thomas; Don Campbell & Co. for the 'Smuggling' poster; Kunsthistorischen Museums, Wien for the picture Kinderspiele (Children's Games) by P. Bruegel; Ann Hollaway for the Pied Piper of Hamelin storyboards.

EDITOR'S PREFACE

This new series was inspired by my book on the practice of teaching (*Effective Teaching: a Practical Guide to Improving your Teaching*, Longman, 1982), written for trainee teachers wishing to improve their teaching skills as well as for in-service teachers, especially those engaged in the supervision of trainees. The books in this series have been written with the same readership in mind. However, busy classroom teachers will find that these books also serve their needs as changes in the nature and pattern of education make the in-service training of experienced teachers more essential than in the past.

The rationale behind the series is that professional courses for teachers require the coverage of a wide variety of subjects in a relatively short time so the aim of the series is the production of 'easy to read', practical guides to provide the necessary subject background, supported by references to guide and encourage further reading, together with questions and/or exercises devised to assist application and evaluation.

As specialists in their selected fields, the authors have been chosen for their ability to relate their subjects to the needs of teachers and to stimulate discussion of contemporary issues in education.

The series aims to cover subjects ranging from the theory of education to the teaching of mathematics and from primary school teaching and educational psychology to effective teaching with information technology. It will look at aspects of education as diverse as education and cultural diversity and pupil welfare and counselling. Although some subjects such as the legal context of teaching and the teaching of history are specific to England and Wales, the majority of the subjects such as assessment in education, the effective teaching of statistics and comparative education are international in scope.

Elizabeth Perrott

The Place of Drama in the Primary School

CHAPTER 1

Introduction

The purpose of this book is

1. To consider the importance of drama in the primary school, both as a subject in its own right and as a means of motivating and enhancing learning in other curriculum areas.
2. To suggest a coherent approach to the teaching and use of drama in primary schools.
3. To offer a range of examples of good practice.
4. To look at ways and means of creating successful and exciting theatrical presentations and productions.

The book is aimed at teachers (and prospective teachers) in primary and middle schools. The approaches to teaching drama suggested here should hold good with whatever age group is being taught. There is, however, very little published about teaching drama with children in their first years of schooling (in Key Stage One) and I have therefore included a specific section on working with children in Years One and Two, attempting to show how some of the ideas described elsewhere in the book (which might at first glance appear slightly inaccessible) can be readily adapted for use with this age group.

Hopefully, the book will be of use not only to teachers who have never taught drama (and who, perhaps, feel a little anxious about making a start) but also to those with considerable expertise. The book asserts that drama is an important subject in its own right and should be taught as such; but it also recognises that drama has a vitally important part to play in developing the whole school curriculum.

The book attempts to show that there are many opportunities within the school for sharing drama work; that you don't have to wait for a major School Play in order to develop good presentational work; that the valuable exploratory activities of high quality classroom work need not and should not be threatened by presenting work to an audience; that the School Play itself (too often an annual merry-go-round of fraught tempers and frayed costumes) can be a joyous event.

Using this book

The book is organised into six parts:

Part One examines the place of drama in the primary school:

1. How does drama fit into the National and the school curriculum?
2. What is drama? And what constitutes quality in educational drama?
3. Why we should find time and space for drama.

Part Two, Drama in Practice, looks at the practice and processes of teaching drama. Although each of the four chapters are subdivided into sections for easy reference, it's important not to think of any of the techniques referred to here as self-contained. Good drama is not about having loads of good ideas, but about teasing out the meanings and the significance in what is often one very simple idea.

Here, as elsewhere throughout the book, there are numerous examples given of work in practice. These are all genuine examples of work with children in primary schools (in a wide variety of different types of catchment areas) throughout the country. The examples are given with the intention of providing a stimulus or a framework, as jumping-off points from which it should be easy to develop your own work. If initially, as you're building up your own confidence, you want to use these examples as they appear here, do so – but try not to see them as prescriptive; make them your own.

Part Three focuses on using drama with children in Key Stage One. Many of the ideas and approaches suggested throughout the book can be easily adapted for use with young children. This section picks out a number of activities which are particularly useful, and suggests ways of adapting some of the techniques and strategies suggested elsewhere which at first seem more appropriate for use with older children.

Part Four is concerned with performance and production. What do we mean by 'presentation' and 'production'? What place does this work have in school? How can we create a piece of theatre to be shared with others without losing the benefits of the more spontaneous and exploratory work we do in educational drama?

Performance work should be an educationally productive and exciting part of the work of a school. Whilst educational drama and theatrical presentation are not synonymous, they are usefully complementary.

These two chapters look at all aspects of drama presentation in the primary school – from small group work in the classroom, through Assemblies to the School Play. Good presentations and plays should feed into the work of the school, motivating work of real excellence in all curriculum areas, becoming both a celebration of the work of the school and a driving force behind that work. It is not, however, the intention of this book to suggest that high quality drama work necessarily culminates in presentation or production.

This part includes specific suggestions about scripts, lighting, masks and costumes. It also contains a detailed example of how a drama project could be developed into a major School Play involving every child in the school.

Part Five looks at planning and assessment. It attempts to tackle the 'I've run out of ideas' syndrome. It offers a way of planning drama work which enables you to think ahead whilst avoiding the pitfalls of making the work over-prescriptive; it suggests how to build in links with other curriculum areas at the planning stage. It contains a detailed account of the planning that might go into an extended drama-based project and a section on evaluation and assessment in drama – including self-assessment.

Part Six – the Appendix – comprises a resource bank, offering General Advice.

It contains:

• suggestions of where to find useful resource materials
• suggestions about using video in drama work
• a set of *policy guidelines* which might be adopted by primary schools
• a list of useful story books
• a brief selection of poems which lend themselves to use in drama
• an annotated bibliography
• lists of useful addresses.

THE NATIONAL CURRICULUM

Drama – including role-play – is central in developing all major aspects of English in the primary school.[1]

At the time of writing schools in England and Wales are in a state of considerable upheaval; the establishment of a National Curriculum is one of many changes occurring within the education system. The situation is similar in many countries all over the world where teachers are having to think hard about educational practices and the theory which underpins that practice.

There are some who have argued that drama is in danger of becoming marginalised. It appears neither as a core nor foundation subject in the National Curriculum for England and Wales. Some people have found this omission both worrying and demoralising.

There are, however, some grounds for optimism; the National Curriculum may not recognise drama as a core subject, but it does contain numerous references to it. Whereas before the advent of the National Curriculum it was possible (if not sensible) for a headteacher to argue that an individual teacher should not be teaching/using drama, it is now clear that any school which is genuinely delivering the whole of the National Curriculum would have to be using drama; and I would argue strongly that it should be taught both as a subject in its own right and used as a learning medium for teaching other subjects.

There is substantial evidence that active participation in drama can enhance learning in most curriculum areas.[2] The very fact that we have specific Attainment Targets for Speaking and Listening should encourage many hitherto reluctant teachers to make time and space for drama, or at least for drama-type activities. It is difficult to see how much of the work required by the Programmes of Study in the statutory Order for English can be achieved without using drama.

The great value of using drama to motivate and enhance work in other curriculum areas is underlined by the various curriculum documents – for Maths, Science, Technology, History, Religious Education, Geography – all of which refer directly or indirectly to the usefulness of role play or drama.

The National Curriculum Council has published a large poster entitled 'Drama in the National Curriculum'[3] which identifies specific references to drama in the Statutory Orders for English, Science, Technology and History; it also indicates where these elements are explored further in the Non-Statutory Guidance documents for English, Science, Mathematics and Technology. So long as you don't view the poster as indicating that drama is primarily a service tool for these other subjects it can be useful.

Teachers who have used drama as a learning medium, a way of deepening understanding, as a means of delivering other aspects of the curriculum, will not need specific clauses in curriculum documents to encourage them in their work; but the clauses are there – and the National Curriculum Council poster referred to above points out some of the more interesting specific references.

Chapter 5 deals with drama and the whole curriculum in depth, offering specific examples of how drama can be used in the teaching of history, science, technology and maths.

Drama as a subject

Drama deals with fundamental questions of language, interpretation and meaning. These are central to the traditional aims and concerns of English teaching . . . We would stress, however, that the inclusion of drama methods in English should not in any way replace drama as a subject for special study.[4]

However successfully we can use drama in teaching other subjects we should never forget that it is also a subject in its own right.

Dramatic fiction is the form of fiction with which children are most familiar. Very few children arrive in school without a wealth of experience of drama on television; many act out simple, but important, dramas in their own play. A number of children come to school without having ever been read to: their vernacular knowledge of drama and dramatic fiction is far greater than of written forms – but it is also very uncritical. Drama, in one form or another, is an important part of their lives; we should give children opportunities to understand and make their own dramas as well as simply enjoying it passively.

Drama in schools is a practical artistic subject. It ranges from children's structured play, through classroom improvisations and performances of specially devised material to performance of Shakespeare.[5]

The Arts Council's *Drama in Schools* booklet[6] offers some excellent advice on drama in the National Curriculum, including a curriculum model. The booklet includes suggested programmes of study and end of key stage statements. Every school in the country should have received a copy. If you would like your own copy the address to write to is given in the Appendix. The booklet asserts that 'the three activities which constitute the subject of drama in schools are making, performing and responding'. Although I have not used the same format in this book, the classification is a useful one and the suggestions in this book should be seen as complementary to the programmes of study suggested by the Arts Council.

Throughout the book I argue that presentation and performance work (of various kinds) is complementary to good classroom drama work, and indeed that drama and theatre are inextricably bound up with each other.

But all of this begs one vitally important question: What do we mean by drama?

What do we mean by drama?

For too long the subject has been surrounded by vagueness; attempts to evaluate drama have been shrouded in a veil of subjectivity. Of course there are extraordinary personal, subjective benefits to be had from being involved in good drama; but this should not invalidate attempts to look objectively at the skills involved which are unique to drama. Many of the claims made for drama have tended to be along the lines that

- it encourages self-expression
- it makes people more sensitive to others
- it promotes an awareness of the self
- it encourages co-operation and collaboration.

It may well do all these things, but many teachers would claim that similar intentions underlie all their work in the primary school. If we are to argue strongly for drama to be given its place in the curriculum, it is essential to ask the question 'What makes drama *uniquely* drama?' If we are to convince colleagues, parents, governors and (most importantly) children themselves that drama is not just 'worthy' but essential, we really have to think very carefully about what drama *is*, how it works and what it does.

If in music the 'building blocks' are *pitch, melody, harmony, tempo, rhythm* and *texture*, what are the raw materials of drama?

Role or Character

- acting *as if* you were someone else; or
- as if you were yourself in another situation.

Narrative

- ordering a sequence of events or images in such a way that their *order* creates meaning. This is not necessarily the same as story telling and plotting, which are examples of the ways in which narrative can be used.

Language

- verbal
- non-verbal (including, for example, body language, facial expression, the use of space).

There is a danger of over-simplification (non-verbal language can range from facial expression to symbolism and ritual) but by seeing these as the basic building blocks we do get a clearer sense of dramatic activity as a continuum: from pre-school play to professional theatrical performance.

When pre-school-age children successfully engage in dramatic activity they are using these 'building blocks'. When a young child says: 'This is my shop', she is pretending to be a shopkeeper, turning a chair upside down to become the counter, making part of the kitchen into a shop and playing with a narrative sequence. The grasp of cause and effect narrative may be only tentative (a young child might well pay the customer for the bag of sugar!), but part of the purpose of the child's dramatic play is to work out possible sequences of events and their consequences. Furthermore, the adult who joins in with the play can challenge it and give it focus: 'I wonder if you could help me. I've forgotten my shopping list.'

Whether the specific dramatic activity is imaginative pre-school play about shopping, or performing at the National Theatre (or indeed watching that same performance) the drama is primarily dependent upon all parties agreeing to the pretence.

By focusing on an imagined, fictional world of make-believe, the drama (whether it's in a large theatre or in the classroom) draws our attention to aspects of the 'real' world; it helps us to recognise a sense of our own reality, and understand it better.

Drama is essentially a social art form; it is concerned with how individuals relate to the world they live in; how individuals interact with each other and with society in a wider sense.

It therefore becomes the drama teacher's central task to find ways and means by which s/he can encourage as broad an understanding as possible of these various interactions – between the fictional world of the drama and the actual world; between the personal and the social.

In any dramatic activity there is some shared, tacit understanding of the rules of the make believe, although there is of course enormous variation in the way these rules are set up. The child playing shops declares the rules simply by saying 'This is my shop . . .'; in the school hall during a drama lesson the teacher might explain – 'I shall be playing a part in what we are going to do today . . .'; and in the National Theatre the Battle of Agincourt is represented without a drop of blood being shed. We learn to 'read' the rules, to understand the conventions remarkably quickly.

When we are working in educational drama with children we have to consider *role, narrative* and *language*; but all of these are dependent on *context*:

- Where does the action of the drama occur?
- In which historical period?
- What are the political and social conditions?
- What is the setting; and the specific situation prevailing at the time of the action, the 'back story'.

This context offers the characters a background against which to make decisions and provides motivations for their actions. Context is crucial in understanding the interactions which take place in the imagined world.

Perhaps we are doing a drama with Reception children about trying to find out if a dragon is friendly. Whether we tell the children the context or ask them is very much a matter for the individual teacher; but if the drama's going to be successful we'll need answers to the questions:

- *When and where*   Does the action take place today, in the here and now, a dragon hiding somewhere in 'Our Town'? Or is our story set long ago with Knights in Camelot?
- *Political and social conditions*   Who makes the decisions? The local Mayor, the townspeople, the children, King Arthur? Who do we go to for help – or who comes to us for help?
- *The 'back story'*   And how did this dragon get here? Has it woken from a long sleep? Hatched from an egg discovered in the school pond?

Chapter 2 contains detailed examples of practical work approached in this way.

Narrative

This is the means by which the drama is propelled forward. In a drama lesson the teacher uses various devices to create dramatic tension (Chapter 4 includes a specific section on this), effectively holding the children's attention and interest by ordering events, enactments, meetings, scenes, etc. in such a way that information is withheld or released to tantalise and intrigue as well as to inform.

The narrative of a drama lesson can function in all the ways that it can in the theatre; and the range of possible narrative effects is just as diverse. As events are revealed and explored (not necessarily in chronological order – drama lessons frequently have most unusual time structures) so understanding deepens: of the fictional world, of the characters which populate it, of the 'real' world, and of ourselves.

Language

In drama we use a variety of different and varying forms of language, both verbal and non-verbal. We can use our voices in a huge variety of ways. We can communicate through body language or sign language, developing physical, visual forms of theatre which do not require words. This spectrum of language ranges from 'talking heads' in a radio play (in which sound and music play a very important part) to mask work, mime and dance/drama.

Even in verbal language, there is a range of possibilities open to us (in spontaneous exploratory work and in performance):

- naturalistic dialogue, day-to-day speech
- formal heightened style of language, perhaps to indicate the beginning of a ritual, or a regal proclamation
- direct address to an audience
- characters in a play talking to themselves
- choral speech.

Non-verbal language

In addition to the more obvious use of non-verbal language in drama – mime, masks, sign language – we also use props, costume, set, lighting, sound and music. They are all part of what might be defined as a non-verbal sign system; using them effectively is part of the language of drama.

We establish and develop the drama by working with and manipulating:

- symbols
- body language
- space
- ritual.

Symbols

Even the simplest dramatic activity involves the creation of symbolic meanings at some level. The child who uses an upturned chair as a shop counter is using the chair to represent the counter; when the counter becomes significant in the dramatic play it begins to function as a symbol.

Props are often invested with symbolic qualities. The particular choice of props is what shapes the contextual world. A large set of keys, for example, might in different contexts signify imprisonment or freedom. No object is symbolic on its own. The context in which it is used gives it its meaning.

Symbolic meaning has to be relevant and readable to the group you are working with; the richer the symbolic meanings you create for a group – either as participants or as audience – the richer the dramatic experience.

Use of space

In any dramatic activity the space in which events take place, the space between people and between objects, should itself be significant and meaningful.

Any movement based activity uses space as one of the elements to explore, create and communicate meaning. Simply ordering the space in the school hall during a drama lesson – so that part of the hall represents a well, another part a dried up-river – is making the space itself articulate: the space itself is used to communicate meaning in a simple but effective way.

Ritual

Finally it is worth considering the relationship between ritual and any dramatic activity (be it improvisatory work, rehearsal or presentation). Ritual is a distillation, encompassing all the above rules and elements in a condensed and highly stylised form. In ritual the roles adopted, the props used, the costumes, the use of language, movement and narrative is all reduced to essentials – in which each of the elements becomes deeply significant and thus takes on a prominent symbolic quality.

The value of ritual for the drama teacher lies in its ability to encapsulate the central focus of the play at any one moment; it can function effectively on both an emotional and an intellectual level for participant and spectator alike.

In practice all these elements become inextricably interwoven. For example, the use of certain types of sound and lighting in a theatrical performance could well signify malevolence, but their use would also increase the dramatic tension at that moment, thereby driving the *narrative* forward. Similarly, in a classroom drama, heightening the style of your verbal language might:

- create expectations of the role you are playing
- create a narrative interest
- imply an element of ritual.

Spoken language itself is a form of symbolic interaction.

It is the moments of high theatricality which give drama (in the intimacy of the lesson or the public arena of the School Play) an excitement, an exhilaration that is unique to the subject. And it is where you recognise most clearly that drama and theatre are indistinguishable: good drama is intensely theatrical; good theatre intensely dramatic!

MYTHS OF TIME AND SPACE – FINDING TIME FOR DRAMA

Alright then, I'd like to do some drama; I can see that it's useful, but . . .

'The hall's always in use. There's just no space.'
'The timetable's so full; and with all the pressures of the National Curriculum, I simply can't find the time.'

There are four big myths surrounding drama in the primary school:

1. *You need to be a good actor* You don't. Many of the best drama teachers I have worked with are quietly spoken and would never want to take an acting role in a theatrical production. (The issue is dealt with more fully in Chapter 3 in the section on 'Teaching in role'.)
2. *You need to be creative and arty and inventive and have lots of wonderful ideas* Most of us would love to be more creative than we are. And most of us are much more creative than we think we are. Good practice in drama (on the part of both teacher and child) is characterised far more by the abilities to listen, to be responsive and to focus attention on a key issue than by being cleverly creative. I hope the chapters on *planning* in Part Five will help scotch the myth of creativity and convince the doubters that by tackling problems task by task they have plenty of *appropriate* ideas.
3. *You need time on the timetable put aside for drama* I think this is desirable, but it's not essential. When you're first starting out with teaching drama it's a good idea not to be committed to a long period in the school hall, which can be nerve-racking and confidence draining. Good drama can take place in five or ten minutes, providing these short sessions are on a regular basis. Infant teachers will be familiar with the idea of focusing and challenging children's play by joining in with it. Older children can equally benefit from the opportunity to work on something for a short period in small groups *in the classroom*. This approach is discussed in detail in Parts Two and Three.
4. *To do good drama you need the school hall* No, you don't. What you do need is to ensure that there is adequate and *appropriate* space when it's necessary. What is appropriate? Certainly, there are times when it is right to work in the hall, but the size, the cold floor, the echo, the noise from an adjacent kitchen, the use of the hall as a throughway – all these factors work against you. In many primary schools there are other spaces which are better suited to drama: the TV room, the library, a music room, an unused classroom. And there are plenty of occasions when the everyday classroom is a *better* place in which to do drama than the Hall (in which concentration can quickly be lost as children somehow

expand to fill the space). This book contains many suggestions for such work.

If you are going to use the hall, try to make sure you're not going to be interrupted. One of the other great myths of drama is that it's always noisy. There are all too many occasions when I've been teaching a lesson and somebody has come in and apologised, saying they didn't know we were there! Quiet, rapt attention is as much a characteristic of good drama practice as invigorating (and loud) discussion.

Drama is important. It deserves an allocation of time and space which communicates that importance to children and parents. The Appendix of this book includes a short section, entitled 'The drama room', where I discuss how such a space might usefully be equipped.

It is all too easy to find excuses for not doing drama. Working in a primary school is very demanding and extremely hectic. But it really *is* worth finding time for it.

At the end of a short series of lessons with a class of five and six year-olds I asked them what they thought drama was. One child said acting, another making plays – and then a rather shy child (who had clearly enjoyed our work together without ever pushing herself forward) said, with a beaming smile: 'I don't know what it is, but it's tickly.' It may not be a definition, but it's a pretty good description of what it feels like when it's good.

Notes

1. English for Ages 5 to 16. Proposals of the Secretary of State for Education and Science and the Secretary of State for Wales, June 1989. DES, HMSO.
2. For further reading about the usefulness of drama in developing language: Parsons, B. et al. 1984. *Drama, Language and Learning*, NADIE, Tasmania; Fines, J. and Verrier, R. 1974. *The Drama of History*, New University Education, is an excellent account of the benefits of using drama to teach history. See also, for a more generalised account: DES 1990 *Aspects of Primary Education: The Teaching and Learning of Drama*, HMSO.
3. National Curriculum Council, March 1991. *Drama in the National Curriculum*, DES.
4. English for Ages 5 to 16. op. cit.
5. HMI. 1989. *Drama from 5 to 16 – Curriculum Matters 17*, HMSO.
6. Arts Council of Great Britain. 1992. *Drama in Schools – Arts Council Guidance on Drama Education*, ACGB.

PART TWO

Drama in Practice

Starting out

Drama and Story
Using photographs and paintings as starting points
Using poetry in drama

Example: *'The Island'* – based on D. M. Thomas's poem, 'Whale'

If you have never taught drama before, where do you begin?

This chapter suggests ways of using stories and poems, photographs and pictures as useful starting points that provide a strong stimulus for the teacher and the children. It concludes with a detailed account of a drama which I developed by using a poem – 'Whale' by D. M. Thomas – as a starting point.

Picture books are often excellent resources for drama. Not only do they usually have a good narrative, but they also give us strong images we can work with. We can take one of the pictures from a book and use that as a starting point. We can use pictures (whether they originate in children's picture books or on the easel of a famous artist), photographs, posters or objects to start our drama sessions.

Chapter 9 on *planning and assessment* deals with how to go about 'finding ideas' for drama. But a good starting point is often the only 'idea' you will need. If this sounds worryingly simplistic, remember that the key to good drama lies not so much in having 'good ideas', but in working with ideas, finding significance, helping children to examine the consequences of the ideas that they have. We do, however, need good beginnings; we need to find starting points which will grab the attention of the children.

One of the most wasteful aspects of seeing drama in education as somehow separate from other forms of dramatic fiction is the sheer wealth of material that one throws away. We can learn a great deal about *dramatic structure* by looking at other dramatic forms. Drama lessons need a dramatic structure just as much as plays and films. A good movie, TV play or piece of theatre hooks its audience within moments. If you can do the same in a drama lesson you will have the children with you, they will want to collaborate with you.

In the drama lesson we are not performing for an audience,

certainly, but if we can find a starting point or an opening image which intrigues, startles, mystifies, is above all *dramatic*, you are well on your way to a drama session which at least has rich potential.

The practical work and the suggestions given here should be read in conjunction with the next two chapters (on *working methods* and *organisation*) where many of them are amplified and discussed further.

DRAMA AND STORY

Many people start teaching drama in the primary school by getting children to take on roles from stories they know and acting them out, following the original narrative. This is a valuable and worthwhile activity if it brings the story to life for the children and gives them a personal stake in it.

Drama and story are closely interlinked. They are not the same thing; but without a strong narrative it is difficult to sustain interest in a drama.

If you choose to use existing stories as starting points the work can be much more exciting if the drama develops from the story you're using rather than illustrating it. Drama can create excellent opportunities for learning when the participants are given responsibility for the action. If the children can make key decisions and then live with those decisions the opportunities for learning are likely to be far greater than if their actions in the drama are decided for them by an existing narrative.

One of the problems of 'acting out' a known story is that the children already know how it ends. And we thereby not only miss out on valuable learning opportunities, but can also lose the dramatic tension of not knowing what will happen next. If the tension of not knowing what happens next is lost, we have to replace it with some other tension. When we go to the theatre we often do know what's going to happen to these people (seeing a Shakespeare play, for example); what keeps our interest is the exploration of how and why they get where they do.

If we use a known story as a starting point, we should think how we can explore it, open it up, keep some dramatic tension alive. We can, for example:

- Stop the reading of the story before the end (as written) and work with the children to create their own ending.
- Explore what happens before the written story starts.
- Explore what happens after it ends.
- Look at what's going on elsewhere while the well-known story's taking place.
- Consider how we can move people from 'offstage' in the known story to the centre of our 'unknown' drama.

Thus, with the story of the *Pied Piper*[1], our drama could explore the following:

• Where did the Pied Piper come from?
• How did the mayor become mayor?
• How can we get rid of our corrupt town council?
• What was life in this town like before the rat plague?
• How can we persuade the Pied Piper to return our children to us?
• What are the children doing while they are held prisoner? Could it be that they prefer the company of the Pied Piper? Or are they planning an escape?
• Suppose they do escape. How will we now deal with the Pied Piper? Should we put him and the mayor on trial?
• What is happening in a neighbouring town where they hear the Pied Piper of Hamelin story as a rumour; but they have their own plague of rats, and don't know what to do about it.

In this last suggestion we would be *using* the story directly, perhaps the children would retell it in their own words. The drama might also be exploring how stories get changed in the telling.

If we start on the drama *before* reading the story, the teacher can set up a situation similar to that in a story and read extracts from it to the children alongside their own drama, or after they have finished their version. The drama described in Chapter 5 in the section on 'Writing in role' – 'The Giant Awakes' – is inspired by Roald Dahl's *BFG* and Ted Hughes's *The Iron Man*, but most of the Reception-age children did not know either of these stories. After the drama had finished, the teacher read both stories to the children, and they were fascinated; they had a stake in them, it was as if the stories had in some way become their own.

This concept of 'ownership' of material is important in all teaching, but especially in teaching drama. Anyone, child, adolescent or adult, who learns enthusiastically and willingly will learn far faster and at a far more profound level of understanding than if coerced into something. Of course children should be numerate and literate from an early age. But there is something more important than learning to read, and that is *wanting* to learn to read. Imagine a child going home at the end of school and saying, 'We're reading *The Iron Man*; it's great, it's just like our drama, only in the book he . . .'

Telling and reading stories is a vitally important part of a child's education. What I'm suggesting here does not replace that, it enhances it. And I also aim for children to value their own stories, to feel that their own stories, the ones they create in drama, are also important.

The teacher as narrator

Most children respond positively to story. A story which is read to them has a certain status. It's useful to be able to capitalise on this. The teacher can take on the role of a narrator in the drama. This can sometimes take the form of the teacher leading the children through a series of activities with them acting out what she says:

And then they came to a river, so they put on their boots . . . and they tried to walk across . . . but it was too deep . . . and they all drowned . . .

The strategy lends itself to parody, but there is a serious point. If we are trying to use drama to create learning opportunities for children we're not doing them any favours by making all the key decisions for them. If we're teaching maths we might demonstrate how calculations are done, but we can't expect the children to learn how to do them for themselves if we do all the sums in their workbooks. This strategy of teacher as narrator can be extremely effective if used to support children's work rather than to prescribe it.

Suppose the class are on an expedition through the rain forest in search of plants for medicines. They come to a river. Far better to ask them 'How are we to get across?' than to simply tell them your solution to the problem. This allows us to move into Science and Technology – they can make models and build bridges, test materials for breaking strengths – as well as exploring the highly dramatic nature of the moment: 'How do these people deal with their disappointment? It looks as if their journey has come to an end.'

Having made their way across the river (it might have taken them a couple of weeks of drama time, and might, for example, have involved them in negotiations with indigenous people), the teacher might *now* act as a narrator, summarising their actions and giving significance to the work:

The expedition came to a river, where they found that the equipment they'd brought with them was inadequate. They tried making a bridge out of ropes made from lianas; but they couldn't make it strong enough. They tried to make small boats from fallen trees. And time was running out, their supplies were getting low; they had heard from their guide that the river could soon flood – so two brave girls set out on their own to find the people who lived in this part of the forest, to beg their help . . .

Telling the story thus is a way of recapitulating, reminding the children what they have been doing, but it is also a way of giving coherence to what can sometimes seem rather tangled.

Narrative tension and slowing down the drama

It is worth making a point here which will be picked up again later: the importance of a strong narrative in drama cannot be underestimated – you have to 'hook' the children into the work – but the really valuable learning takes place when you intervene in the action to slow it down, to examine what's going on between people at the moment of high tension, not when the narrative is flowing quickly. The children want to rush on and find out what happens next; you hang on tightly to the reins and stay where you are and explore that moment in detail. It's been said that drama is simply about people 'in a mess'. We need to use strong narrative in order to create the tension that will keep the children locked into the drama while they examine what are often difficult and challenging areas. The book contains several examples of this strategy in action.

USING PHOTOGRAPHS AND PAINTINGS AS STARTING POINTS

In the introduction I argued that the key building blocks for drama are:

- role
- narrative
- verbal and non-verbal language.

I then went on to develop the need for these to be seen in specific contexts. When we're working from existing stories, much of that work has been done for us. We know the characters and the situation. Certain key questions have already been answered for us. At its most basic those questions are:

- Who is involved in this story?
- What has happened up to now?
- When and where is it taking place?

In each of the following examples, a way of using the stimulus is found by expanding on those simple questions:

- *Who* is involved in this drama? What are the roles? What groups of people are affected by it?
- What is the *frame* through which we view the story/image, i.e. from whose point of view do we see it? This idea of the *dramatic frame* is one which will be expanded upon in detail in Chapter 4 – Organisation.
- *What has happened* immediately prior to the start of the drama? In film and TV scriptwriting terms this is sometimes called the 'back story'. In drama it's often unproductive to ask: 'What is going to happen'? That is what we are going to find out in the drama itself.
- What is *the key issue*? This will help us maintain a clear focus.

A SHIP HAS BEEN SIGHTED
in this quarter
ENGAGING IN THE UNLAWFUL ACT OF

SMUGGLING

whosoever can lay information leading to the capture of this ship or its crew

will receive a reward of

£500

From His Majesty's Government

This 19ᵗʰ day of October 1782

Fig. 2.1

Some suggestions:

Using a poster

Example: The 'Smuggling' Poster (opposite)[2]

Possible roles/groups of people involved

- the smugglers
- unwilling smugglers
- family of smugglers
- crew of a Navy ship
- the people/person who put up the poster
- a community which relies on the smugglers
- a community which is terrorised by the smugglers
- a film/TV crew making a documentary about the smugglers.

The frame

- The class are the smugglers confronted with the consequences of their actions. An adventure story.
- We are trying to find out what really happened all those years ago. An investigation.
- Others are trying to find out from us what really happened.
- We see the actions of the smugglers through the eyes of those who have to stay at home and live with the fear of what will happen to them. A family drama.
- The class as people who have lost their livelihood, offered the opportunity to become smugglers. A social drama.
- Navy personnel who have friends and relatives amongst the smugglers. A moral dilemma.

The 'back story'

- The smugglers have been bringing in contraband for several years. It is a way of life for the community. The Customs and the Navy are beginning to crack down as the loss of income from taxation makes it difficult to finance the Navy against the growing threat of invasion from France.
- A small coastal community – long ago famed as a haunt of smugglers. Everybody in the village has some connection with the smugglers of old. Everybody can tell some story. Maybe they even have things in their attics which will bring back old stories.
- This same community, back in 1782, has just heard what has happened to a neighbouring village, where relatives have been

imprisoned for withholding information about their own family, thought to be smugglers.
- A group of smugglers, who have been involved in this 'trade' for a long time, are on the point of deciding to 'go straight'. But it is difficult. How do they get rid of their smuggled goods without incriminating their families?

The Key Issue/the unanswered question

- How do people survive when they are outside the law? What sort of pressure does that put on their families?
- How do we deal with the stress that results from family loyalties being in conflict with the law of the land?
- How does a small self-sufficient and self-contained community deal with an invasion of its privacy?
- How do people stand up for what they believe is right when they are under enormous economic pressure to do otherwise?

Possible starting points

- The poster is pinned up in the school hall before the children come in. They find the teacher looking at it. She turns to the class in role and says: 'We're done for. We're outlaws now. We can't return to our families.'
- 'This poster, which is now kept in the Maritime Museum in Liverpool, used to be displayed on the wall in this Inn. I'm sure that everyone in this village has some story to tell about the events all those years ago.' This could then lead into a whole group drama in which the stories were acted out for a TV crew, or be a stimulus for small group work and/or written work in which the children worked alone and in groups to produce the stories and enact them for each other. The *frame* of the investigation giving us a good reason for looking at each others' work and drawing conclusions from it – 'If it's true that some of that treasure is still hidden in that cave, should we go looking for it? What should we do with it if we find it?'
- The poster shown to the class by the teacher: 'This was nailed to the tree on the village green. I've taken it down. I'll not have anyone informing on my son.'

Using a painting

The same sort of questions can be used equally productively with paintings. We can add – in what circumstances might this painting have been made? Who painted it?

The painting can be used as part of the dramatic fiction (as in the 'Smuggling' poster example) or it could be a stimulus for drama about the contents of the painting.

Example: Children's Games by Pieter Bruegel[3] (see overleaf)

- In groups, create a still image of one of the groups from the painting. Bring it to life. Add dialogue, add thoughts. What do they feel about each other?
- Move it forward in time to later that day. What would they all be doing?
- Having created the still image, instead of moving forward in time, go backwards. What led up to this moment?
- The class as the children in the painting, but twenty years forward in time. They recollect what was happening in their lives when Bruegel painted the picture.
- The teacher-in-role as Bruegel. 'I visited this town twenty years ago and I was paid to paint this picture. And now, at last, I am able to return and give it to you. But things have changed so much. What's happened in the meantime?'
- Our drama could focus on the strangeness of the painting, trying to answer the question 'Why are there so few adults in it?' 'Where have they all gone?'

Using a photograph

We can use a photograph in very similar ways to those already discussed. We could also ask the question: Who took the photograph? What was going on outside the frame of the photograph? Why was the photograph taken?

We could, of course, make a *still image* (see Chapter 3 – Working Methods for a detailed description of this strategy), a representation of the photograph, bringing it to life, moving forward or backwards in time.

We could again use the photograph as it is, as part of a dramatic fiction:

- Teacher-in-role as photographer: 'I've taken this photograph. It's the best I could get.' The drama begins in the newspaper editor's office.
- Or as picture editor: 'We've been using our own photographers up to now because it's cheaper that way. But we're not getting the results we want, so we're hiring you as a team of freelancers. I expect the best. . . . Now, what are you going to need to take with you on the expedition?'

Fig 2.2 P. Bruegel's Children's Games

Objects and artefacts

A few brief examples of the way one might use these as a starting point or stimulus for drama:

- *A large empty picture frame* With older children an investigation into the stolen picture. What the picture might have been. Who might have stolen it.

Or, with younger children, it could become *The Magic Mirror*:

'I found this in my attic at the weekend. It seems very strange and powerful. Do you want me to take the cloth off it?' 'I need your help to find out about its powers.'
Maybe we will walk through it to a magic land, maybe it will enable us to see things we cannot otherwise see. In any event we'd begin by trying to find out about the dangers and limitations of its magical powers.

- *An item of clothing*
'Can you help me find my little girl. We were at the funfair together and she was wearing this when I last saw her.' This could take us into a drama about the dangers of public places.
On the same theme, if the teacher wanted to be a bit more adventurous with it, she could play the lost child: 'Can you help me find my Mum and Dad?'

In the examples given above, the resource is used as a starting point in itself. Resources like this can, however, be used at any time in the drama. The quality of the work is always enhanced by good quality artefacts and visual stimuli.

USING POETRY IN DRAMA

Thus far we have looked at the way these various stimuli can be used to get us going; but the practical examples have all been simple, undeveloped suggestions. The example that follows is intended to show:

1. How a poem can be used to initiate a drama.
2. How that drama might then be developed in practice.
3. How we might use drama to stimulate the writing of poetry.

The strategies referred to will all be examined in detail in Chapters 3 and 4.

Example: The Island

Consider this poem: 'Whale' by D. M. Thomas[4]

WHALE

A whale lay cast up on the island's shore
  in the shallow water of the outgoing tide.
    He struggled to fill his lungs,
    he grew acquainted with weight.

And the people came and said, Kill it, it is food.
And the witch-doctor said, It is sacred, it must not be harmed.
And a girl came and with an empty coconut-shell
  scooped the seawater and let it run over the whale's blue bulk.

A small desperate eye showing white all round
  the dark iris. The great head flattened against
    sand as a face pressed against glass.

And a white man came and said, If all the people
  push we can float it off on the next tide.
And the witch-doctor said, It is taboo, it must not be touched.

And the people drifted away.
And the white man cursed and ran off to the next village for help.

And the girl stayed.
She stayed as the tide went out.
The whale's breath came in harsh spasms.
Its skin was darkening in the sun.
The girl got children to form a chain
of coconut-shells filled with fresh water
that she poured over his skin.

The whale's eye seemed calmer.

With the high tide the white man came back.
As the whale felt sea reach to his eye he reared
on fins and tail flukes, his spine arced
and he slapped it all down together, a great leap
into the same inert sand.
His eye rolled
in panic as again he lifted and crashed down,
  exhausted, and again lifted and crashed down,
    and again, and again.

The white man couldn't bear his agony and strode away
  as the tide receded.
He paced and paced the island and cursed God.

Now the whale didn't move.
The girl stroked his head
and as the moon came up
she sang to him
of friends long dead and children grown and gone,
sang like a mother to the whale,

Continued

Example continued

and sang of unrequited love.

And later in the night
  when his breaths had almost lost touch
    she leant her shoulder against his cheek

and told him stories, with many details,
of the mud-skipping fish that lived
  in the mangroves on the lagoon.

Her voice
and its coaxing pauses was as if fins
were bearing him up to the surface of the ocean
to breathe and see,
as with a clot of blood falling on her brow
the whale passed clear from the body of his death.

D. M. Thomas

Who are *the people* in the poem?

* islanders with an elaborate set of taboos and sacred rituals
* a witch-doctor
* a girl
* a white man, an outsider to this community

A very simple narrative summary

A whale beaches itself on the shore. The islanders want to use it for food, but the witch doctor says it must not be touched nor harmed. An outsider comes to the island people with what he considers to be superior knowledge. A girl responds to the whale and cares for it as best she can, daring to go against the authority of the 'witch doctor'.

At this point, having read the poem and thought about its dramatic content I need to ask myself a couple of key questions:

1. If I'm not going to ask the children simply to re-enact the narrative of the poem, what roles can they take on?
2. What decisions can I ask them to make?

The detailed account which follows is of a series of lessons which were part of a drama/poetry project. In each case I began with the same starting point – and rapidly diverged as the children began to take on the ideas and make the drama their own. The classes involved were Years Four to Six from a variety of different catchment areas, all with at least thirty children in them.

'The Island' as drama
The poem was not be read to the children until after the drama. It is the *situation* described in the poem which provided the stimulus for drama.
  The children played the islanders. I decided that I would refer to the 'witch doctor' of the poem as the 'Wise Man' or the 'Healer'.
  I took on the role of the chief of the tribe (not mentioned in the poem) and used that role to present the key issue – 'What shall we do about the whale?'

Continued

Example continued

If the teacher is to be the chief, however, it is better for the chief to be weak and nearly blind, unable to walk far, frightened of the Wise Man and ready to give up power. The Wise Man, to whom the chief would refer (but would be an off-stage character in the drama) can then retain ultimate authority, as in the poem. (The reasoning behind this decision is discussed in detail in the section on 'Teacher-in-role' in Chapter 3.) Put simply, it allows the teacher both to use the role to set up the drama and to hand over responsibility to the children for decision-making at an early stage. If the chief had all the power the decision-making would be limited to 'Do we do as we're told, or not?!' Common enough in real life, but not very productive in drama.

'Shut your eyes. Imagine . . .' The island described by the teacher (out of role) as it would have appeared before the storm. The impression given is of a tropical paradise. 'I'll go away from the circle; when I come back I'll be playing a part in the drama. When I speak, open your eyes.'

Teacher returns in role. 'The gods are angry. In my long years the storm last night was the worst I have ever witnessed. I know that many of our dwellings are damaged beyond repair, fences have been blown down and I have heard that trees in the forest have been uprooted. Tell me what other damage there is. I cannot see it for myself. My eyes are weak, and I can no longer walk distances.'

Time for children to respond to this. The teacher-in-role draws meaning and significance from their suggestions.

'The Wise Man, the Healer, came to me at first light. He said that now more than ever, we must keep to our customs. It was he who told me of the damage. He also said that he had walked to the centre of the island and from there – where it is possible to see the bay, the lagoon and the beaches – he could see many of your fishing boats smashed like crushed coconuts; but, worst of all, he told me that a whale lies cast up on the island's shore, in the shallow water of the outgoing tide; and that it is still alive. It is a warning from the gods.'

'We shall meet again here at the setting of the sun. Between now and then go about your business. Repair what you can. And go down to the shore. Look at the whale, but do not touch it. Act as my eyes, not my hands.'

The language is formal, almost ritualised, and precise but much is still left open to the children, e.g. the word 'dwellings' is used rather than the word 'huts'. It is up to the children to construct their own village.

The children play at repairing the village, rescuing animals and going down to the shore to see the whale.

Meeting at sunset. The teacher-in-role asks what they should do about the whale. The chief passes on information that the Wise Man, the Healer says 'It is taboo . . . it must not be touched.' Out of role the teacher asks the children what they feel about the whale. About the Wise Man, the Healer? About the chief? This is not a discussion. The children are asked to internalise their thoughts and feelings and then, briefly, to jot them down on a sheet of paper.

Continued

Example continued

They then represent their feelings through still images. The teacher then comments (out of role) on their images, e.g. 'I can well understand your anger. I wonder when it will be sensible to express it? The chief is still very powerful.'

Teacher (out of role) – reflective narration: 'As the islanders went about their work the following day, they talked with others to find out what they wanted to do about the whale.'

The 'play' is now more dramatic. Further discussions may take place either as they are at work (miming) or sat down in-role in a circle.

An opportunity to share these ideas at a meeting. The suggestions could be simply discussed verbally or they could be summarised through still image work, with the teacher either interrogating each of the images herself, or asking the class to do the same – or they could be enacted.

We also need to consider with the class how they might represent the whale itself. Do we make a large class painting of the whale's head, or perhaps, using a roll of paper, a mural of the whale on the beach? Do we drape the gymnastics vaulting horse with cloth and pin a painting of the whale's eye to it? Do we chalk the outline of the whale's body (or head) on the floor of the hall? To an audience which had not taken part in the making of this representation it could look gauche, clumsy, fatuous even. But if the children have actively made the decision of *how* to represent the whale and then made it themselves, it will considerably enhance their commitment to the drama.

The ideas they expressed were:

1. keeping the whale wet
2. building a wall round it to make a pool and floating it off to sea
3. making medicine and taking it to the whale
4. disobeying the Wise Man and trying to push the whale back out to sea.

That last suggestion occurred only once, but it's exciting and dangerous. And it's these dangerous areas which are often the most productive dramatically. Drama has been described as taking place in a 'No Penalty Zone'. When we're taking part in a drama we can make mistakes, we can try out difficult decisions and see what happens; we don't have to impress our friends, we can afford not to be streetwise. We live with the consequences only for the duration of the drama.

If the children choose to disobey the Wise Man, they will have to deal with the consequences – *in the drama*, where it is safe to take such dangerous decisions. Role-playing the chief, I felt I had to resign: 'If you will not obey me, I can no longer be your chief. I am too old and sick to command your respect.'

This increases the stakes – and shifts the focus. The whale has been dealt with and the drama is now about power struggles within this non-technological community, about how the new chief is to be chosen and about the relationship between the chief (whoever it is to be) and the Wise Man, the Healer – who by now (in nearly all the different dramas that this poem initiated) had become a sinister off-stage figure.

Continued

Example continued

> *What to do when you have a number of conflicting suggestions?* We can act on each of the suggestions in turn, we can write them down on a piece of paper, according status to each. There are times when we can turn the choice of what to do back to the children: 'Can we put both of those ideas together?' But it's best not to get bogged down in lengthy discussions which may well alienate the less articulate members of the class.
>
> ## How to conclude?
>
> The sessions described above took place over several weeks. In the following chapters I shall suggest ways of ensuring continuity and coherence when the work extends over a long period of time. But whether the drama lasts for an hour or several weeks, we do eventually need to draw it to a close; and when we do we need to find ways of *reflecting* on the experiences of the drama – what has happened, what we've learned from it, what it all means. One way is for the teacher to become a narrator, as described earlier in this chapter.
>
> In this case all the sessions concluded with the children being asked to find a space on their own with writing and drawing materials. The teacher asked questions, to which children were asked to give an *individual* response:
>
> 'I'm going to ask a lot of questions. I don't expect you to answer all of them. Some of them may not interest you. You don't need to remember the questions. Start writing when you want to and use my questions as if they were your own thoughts. Write one word for your answer – or fill a page. Try to answer the questions in your head, and see if they make you ask more questions yourself.'
>
> The questions included:
>
> - What colour is the whale?
> - What does it feel like to touch?
> - What does it smell of?
> - What do you see in its eyes?
> - What do you feel about it?
> - How big is it compared with other things on the island?
> - When you stand close to it, can you hear it making any sounds?
> - If you could talk to the whale, and it could understand, what would you say?
> - What does the whale dream of?
> - What do you think the chief feels about the whale?
> - What do you think he feels about the Wise Man, the Healer?
> - Why do you think it is that the Wise Man, the Healer is so certain that it's wrong to touch the whale?
> - Why do you think the Chief, the Wise Man, the Healer, and the islanders think that the gods are angry?
> - What did you feel about the storm on the night when the whale came ashore?
>
> Over the next few days the children were given opportunities to return to their writing and rework it until they were satisfied with it.
>
> When they had completed their own written work the original poem was read to them – as an example of another response to a similar situation.

This section has focused on a detailed description of the way a drama can be developed from one poem by using the basic principles outlined earlier in the chapter. It is not intended to be prescriptive. There are other ways of working with poetry.

1. You might ask yourself – Who is writing the poem? Where is s/he? Who is s/he writing for?
2. Use the poem to develop movement or mask work, and develop the dramatic situation from that.
3. Use the poem to create sound pictures, or Choral Speaking.

We shouldn't forget that poetry grew out of dance and song. Certainly, when working towards performance these are elements to which we should give careful consideration.

The Appendix contains a list of published stories and picture books which I have found useful for drama.

Bibliography

Davies, G. 1983. *Practical Primary Drama*, Heinemann, contains a good chapter on story and topic.

McCaslin, N. 1990. *Creative Drama in the Classroom* (5th edn), Longman, New York, Ch. 9 – Building plays from story; Ch. 11 – The Possibilities in Poetry (includes a section on choral speaking).

Notes

1. The best known telling of the story of the Pied Piper is probably in Robert Browning's poem. There are, however, a number of other versions. I would particularly recommend a recent edition (which also includes a fascinating historical note discussing the historical basis of the legend) by Sara and Stephen Corrin, with illustrations by Errol le Cain: Corrin, S. and S. 1988. *The Pied Piper of Hamelin*, Faber and Faber. Chapter 7 of this book contains two alternative storyboards for dramatisations of The Pied Piper story.
2. This poster is one of several reproductions of early posters published by Don Campbell & Co. of Poole, Dorset.
3. Although not all Pieter Bruegel's paintings are suitable for use with children in the primary school, many of them are rich in detail and give a fascinating insight into medieval life. They offer rich stimuli for starting drama work, and for historical research. Look particularly at: *The Hunters in the Snow, Peasant Wedding (The Wedding Banquet), The Peasant Dance, The Tower of Babel* and *Hay Making (July)*. Several books of reproductions are available. Particularly recommended is: Roberts, K. 1971. *Bruegel*, Phaidon Press.
4. 'Whale' appears in *Selected Poems* by D. M. Thomas, published 1983 by Secker and Warburg.

CHAPTER 3

Working methods

This chapter starts by examining *small group work*, then looks in detail at four particular strategies:

*   forum theatre
*   still images
*   games and exercises
*   teaching in role.

For the sake of clarity each of these is dealt with separately. They should, however, be seen as interactive working methods.

The second half of the chapter proposes that *whole group work* is a working method which develops out of *small group work* and gives greater coherence to it.

SMALL GROUP WORK

There are frequent occasions in a drama session when children are divided into groups and asked to work on a task. Here are some simple guidelines on the organisation and monitoring of small group work.

The nature of the task

They can be asked to:

*   *Improvise spontaneously* – in which, for example, they are given a starting point and asked to develop a scene in role.
*   *Prepare a short play, or scene from a play* – during which the children will be working both in-role, as the people in the play, and out-of-role, discussing how they are going to tackle the task.
*   *Create a still image* – in which they work out of role to create an image like a statue or three dimensional photograph.
*   *Do some written work* – such as writing in role.
*   *Discuss in or out of role* – with the results of the discussion later fed back into the whole group.

Organisation of the work

In setting up the work you need to pre-plan:

Time limits

How long are the groups going to need for the task? If no time limit is set the work tends to be unfocused. For many tasks they will need no longer than two or three minutes, and frequently as little as 30 seconds. If, as you're monitoring the work, you think that all the groups are engaged in the tasks and working well, you can give them a little longer. But it's important not to say they've only got two minutes for something, and then let them go on for ten. Children learn the 'hidden' curriculum very quickly – in this case that you don't mean what you say!

If possible, it's a good idea to build a time limit into the dramatic narrative itself – something has to be accomplished before time runs out. This increases the urgency of the task, and raises dramatic tension.

Group size and allocation

It must be appropriate for the task. Do you let children work in 'table' groups, with friends in groups of their own choosing, or do you select the groups?

There are no hard and fast rules here. In some classes friendship groups are very productive, but there are times when you might want to keep certain children apart because they frequently distract each other, or maybe you want to make sure that boys and girls work together. It's often easier for children if you make the choice on their behalf, and it saves time if they know the groups they're going to work in before they get to the hall or drama space.

One way of allocating groups quickly and randomly, ensuring a good mix, is to ask the children to sit in a circle, allowing them to sit where they want, and then counting round the circle, giving each child a number – one to eight, then starting again. 'All ones here, twos here, threes here etc.' Thus, with a group of 32 children you'll have eight evenly balanced groups of four.

What if you have a class of 32 and you want them working in groups of four, but today there are only 30 in school? Five groups of four and two of five, or six of four and two of three? Or seven groups of four and two doing something different? The answer will depend on the nature of the work, but have it ready before you divide them into groups.

Setting up the tasks

Pre-requisites for spontaneous improvisation

Clarity is all important. The task should be specific, interesting and within the group's capability. With experience and goodwill it's remarkable what people of all ages can achieve in drama, but remember that a good many children will be anxious. 'Fooling around' in drama is often symptomatic of misunderstanding and embarrassment.

As with still image work, aim for gradual progression. And as in any drama, make sure that the context for the drama is clear. When you give out the task clarify Who? What? Where?

1. *Who* is involved in the situation? What roles are they to take on?
2. *What* is the situation? What has happened, what is the 'back story'? What's the problem? What's at issue?
3. *Where*, and when, is this happening?

The first and the last of these are relatively straightforward but the 'What?' is more complex. It's often more exciting not to preplan what's going to happen in the scene, but we do need to know what has happened up to now. It's also very important for there to be a problem of some kind, an issue which needs to be resolved, otherwise there's no sense of the outcome mattering.

This 'issue' could range from –

'How do you teach your little sister to tie her shoelaces?'

through –

'How will you persuade the Pied Piper to release our children?'

to –

'Can you encourage this reluctant old man to give a radio interview about the way the community used to be 60 years ago?'

Examples

1. *The Castle Banquet*
    Year One. Four per group.

    *   *Who?*
        All of the group are cooks
    *   *What?*
        The King and Queen (who like very special and unusual food) are returning to the Castle. A banquet is needed; the cooks have to prepare a menu and the food. *Issue*: Will it be ready in time?
    *   *Where?*
        In the Castle kitchens

2. From *Arabel's Raven* by Joan Aiken – see Appendix
    Year Two. Three per group.

    - *Who?*
      Arabel (a seven year old child)
      Arabel's mother and father
    - *What?*
    - Arabel has found a very friendly and very mischievous raven.
      She wants to bring it home. Her mother and father are worried
      about the mess it will make in the house, how to look after it,
      etc. *Issue*: Will Arabel persuade them to let her look after it?
    - *Where?*
      In the kitchen – with the (imaginary) raven on the window sill
      tapping at the window outside.

3. *The Borrowed Bike.*
    Year Six. Three per group.

    - *Who?*
      Three school friends: *A, B* and *C.*
    - *What?*
      A has a new bike which s/he thinks has been 'borrowed'by *B*
      B doesn't know anything about the bike
      C does know who borrowed it (it is not *B*) – but is frightened of
      being bullied if s/he says anything about it.
      Issue: Can *C* be persuaded/encouraged to tell the truth.
    - *Where?*
      After school, in the playground. They have to sort out the
      problem before the caretaker locks the school gates.

This information – the Who/What/Where – can be conveyed to the
children in a number of ways:

1. They can all be divided into groups and the whole class can be
    told 'All A's are . . .; all B's are . . .', etc.
2. Information can be given to each child separately (either verbally
    or in writing), so that no-one knows what the others' information
    is. (This would work well with the third of the examples above.)
3. They can be told some of the pre-requisites, and have to work out
    the others out-of-role before starting – perhaps they are told who
    they are and what has happened, and they have to agree where
    and when the situation is taking place.
4. Every group can be tackling the same problem, or different groups
    can be working on different improvisations.
5. As is indicated in the chapter on teaching in role, it's possible to
    set up the pre-requisites through carefully chosen opening lines.

For example, 'Mum, can I go out to play?' indicates that the two people in the improvisation are mother and child and that the issue is whether or not the child is allowed out. This could be made much more complex, but there's certainly enough to get started if at least one of the participants has some previous experience.

The problems of small group work can be summarised as follows:

- Organisation. The groups themselves need very careful organising if the work is to be anything more than structured play.
- It is difficult to work for development and progression in the tasks at a level appropriate to each group.
- Control can be difficult if there is a range of different tasks being undertaken at any one moment.
- It is difficult to offer positive and constructive feedback to groups without ignoring others. Only a limited amount of reflection is possible.
- Competitiveness tends to creep into the work in ways which frequently blind the participants to the real issues being worked on. There is sometimes a tendency for one or two children to dominate the work and this can be destructive and intimidating for others.
- Audience. It is difficult to share the work without each group showing what they have done – which can be unproductively time consuming.

These are serious problems, which need to be addressed carefully.

We can deal with most of these problems, however, by examining and tackling the central problems of monitoring, intervention and audience/performer relationship.

Monitoring and intervention

1. Warn the children that you will be going round and 'freezing' work in progress, looking at it as it's happening – sometimes called 'spotlighting', so that the group doesn't show what they have done, but continues with their spontaneous improvisation from where they are.

    This enables you to comment on the content of what they're doing. With the Castle Banquet, for example, you might say, 'Look at this wonderful cake they're baking over here. I never thought you could get icing in so many different colours of . . .'

2. Instead of performing the whole of their improvisation for the others, one child can report back on what has happened – either in or out of role.

3. The teacher can enter the small group improvisation in role, using the role to focus and challenge the work. This technique of working in role with a group (however large or small) is discussed at the end of this chapter.
4. The teacher can work in the classroom with one group at a time while the rest of the class are engaged in something needing minimal supervision. This allows you to monitor the work very carefully and help a group with a task that they might find very difficult if unsupervised.

Audience

1. Find an overall fictional context for the creation of the small group 'plays', so that the audience are encouraged to comment on the *content*, rather than the lack of specific theatre skills.

   This might, for example, be that the overall drama is about the making of a television documentary (with a real video camera or an imagined one), in which people are being canvassed for their opinions about a new relief road. When we look at each of the small group 'scenes' we can accord them much higher status; instead of commenting on the changing position of the door handle, we can discuss which moments from each of the 'interviews' we will keep in the documentary; we have an informing context in which to discuss what each of the interviewees said.
2. Develop a sense of the audience having a responsibility, not simply being passive. Still image work is particularly useful for encouraging an audience to become active (see also the discussion of 'Forum theatre' which follows, and Chapter 7 – 'Developing the work towards presentation').
3. Set up situations in which there is a larger place within which the small group work takes place: a castle, for example, within which there are various small groups, each involved in different activities – cooking, cleaning armour, building new fortifications, growing food, etc. Now when you 'freeze' and 'spotlight' the work the groups have an interest in other people's work, they want to know what's happening. This is what we should be working towards when work is being shared: creating a desire to see other people's work because it matters within the drama; because everybody's work affects everybody else's in some way.

This strategy of setting up interactive and interdependent small groups is effectively what is happening in *whole group drama*.

FORUM THEATRE

Forum Theatre[1] can usefully be seen as *small group work* which involves the whole group as active spectators.

As we have seen, three of the commonest problems associated with small group work can be summarised as follows:

1. Difficulties for the teacher in providing appropriate and useful feedback to individual groups.
2. Difficulties in showing or sharing the work. How do you ensure that those children who are watching are actively engaged in the 'performance', and not simply whispering about the scene they have prepared?
3. Difficulties experienced by the children in commenting on the work of their peers in a constructive way. So often this can tend towards 'It wasn't very good, Miss. They all opened the door different ways!'

At its simplest two people (or a small group) enact a scene or a drama while the rest of the group watch. The spectators, however, become interactive participants in the drama. This can be done in one of three ways:

1. The spectators can become advisers to one or more of the performers.
2. The spectators can take over the performers' roles.
3. The scene can be 'replayed' in ways suggested by the spectators, as if the spectators not only have access to the rewind button of a video recorder, but can also change what is enacted before them.

The initiative to stop the scene and try it in another way can come from spectators, performers or the teacher. The strategy gives the audience a stake in what is going on.

Here is a simple example of it at work in practice.

Class divided into threes. A, B and C in each group. As are to play the Pied Piper, Bs the Mayor of Hamelin and Cs the parent of a child held captive by the Pied Piper. Each group is to try to negotiate for the release of a child. It might help in advance to give certain additional information to each of the three groups independently of the others (see above section on small group work): perhaps the Pied Piper is prepared to let the children free if s/he can get a good deal; perhaps the mayor is unwilling to use any public funds to buy off the Piper.

The groups play out their scene for themselves in small groups, but only for a couple of minutes. The teacher should intervene before the children reach their own resolution to the problem.

A volunteer *A, B* and *C* (not from the same original group) are then asked to play out the scene centrally. All the other *A*s (i.e. the Pied Pipers) position themselves behind their 'representative' (with *B*s and *C*s similarly arranged). The three now play out the scene.

The teacher stops the scene as soon as it looks as if any of the 'performers' are finding it difficult. But instead of simply struggling in embarrassment they can turn to their advisers and ask for help: 'What do I say now?', 'How do I react to that?' Once the children are familiar with this method of working they can manipulate it for themselves – e.g. the performers can ask for advice whenever they need it; the performers can 'Tag' an adviser to take over from them.

Strict parameters and rules do need to be built into the system early on, whether it is the children or the teacher who sets them.

In particular consider time limits – both for enacting and for advising, perhaps the performers have to spend at least a minute improvising before they can request advice.

One of the great joys of forum theatre is that it is extremely flexible. Once children have seen it at work they often suggest ways of adapting it.

Remember that the *principle* is that the audience is given a stake in what is performed; they are an interactive part of the drama.

Here are some further ways in which the method can be used:

1. The teacher, introducing a drama which is going to be based on the Pied Piper story, might ask the class *how* they want the Pied Piper to be played. The teacher (in role) will be the Pied Piper, but s/he wants the class to have a say in the characterisation – so the children 'construct' the character: perhaps

   Teacher: In the drama I'll play the Pied Piper, but I need your help. I want you to tell me how you want the Pied Piper to be. What does he look like?
   Class: He's rather shifty.
   Teacher: How do you want me to do that?

   Child demonstrates.

   Class: He's very clever.
   Teacher: Does that mean he shows people he's clever, or does he keep quiet about it?
   Class: He keeps quiet about it.
   Teacher: Tell me some other things that will help me play him.

2. Perhaps this has now developed as a whole group drama, with the children playing the townspeople of Hamelin. Instead of having the children go through the small group work suggested above,

the teacher remains in role as the Pied Piper and the children are asked to elect two or three representatives who will seek out the Pied Piper and try to bargain with him/her. As they bargain they can now stop the drama and turn (out of role) to their peers and ask for help. The teacher could come out of role, saying 'This doesn't seem to be going very well for you. Would you like to start again and try a different way?'

Children seem to have little difficulty accepting this convention because it is so like the action replays they will frequently have seen on television. When first introducing the idea it might be helpful to refer to television.

Chapter 7 contains two storyboards of the Pied Piper story, showing how the story might be told from very different view points.

GAMES AND EXERCISES

Many teachers begin their drama lessons with a game and then an exercise, arguing that this warms the children up, shifts them from thinking in set ways, encourages them to collaborate, to concentrate, to trust each other.

There are others who insist that games and exercises per se have no place in the drama lesson, that the best way to learn about drama and to learn how to use it is by doing it, that if the drama itself is powerful and effective there is no need to prepare children for it by doing something else.

There is a danger of becoming too dogmatic. Whilst games are not of themselves drama, many do contain important dramatic elements: ritual, role play, narrative, symbolic action and symbolic use of space for example. If you want to use a game it's important to give careful consideration to its purpose and/or function.

The advantages of using games

Games can

- be non-threatening
- be fun to play
- indicate clearly to the children that a different kind of thought process is going to be required of them in the drama session
- introduce collaborative ways of working
- focus and channel energies which might otherwise become distracting
- create useful opportunities for the teacher to assess the mood and interests of the class.

In my own drama teaching I rarely use games with a class that I know well, but when I'm working with a class that I've not met before I often begin the session with a short concentration exercise and then a simple game. Certainly, the activities do focus concentration and energy, but I also use these activities diagnostically, to give myself time and space to assess the class, to learn about their social health; they help me feel comfortable with the class, and that is important. We need to challenge ourselves, to move ourselves on, but we need to give ourselves a safe framework in which to do so.

The disadvantages and dangers of using games

1. Playing an active game can over-excite children to the point that all they want to do is play the game. Playing the game takes over the drama session and becomes a means for the children (and sometimes the teacher) to avoid the drama.
2. There is frequently a hidden agenda in the use of games. If we come up with a different game each time we do drama, what are we teaching the children? Among other things that it is the teacher who has all the good ideas, thereby making it difficult to hand over responsibility for decision making to the children.
3. While games may be useful, and it may well be that there should be time in school devoted specifically to playing games, games are not of themselves drama. And it is important that children do not get the impression that they are.

Trust games

There is also a danger of overestimating and misperceiving the value of a game per se. We should be clear, for example, that what people learn from a 'trust game' is that they can trust the person/people they are working with at that moment. There is no magical osmosis whereby children somehow become more trusting and trustworthy as individuals through playing a game – nor simply by the action of doing drama, it should be added.

Although we would want the children we work with to become more trustworthy, it is dangerous to teach children to become unquestioningly trusting. We might, however, usefully make 'trust' the focal point of a drama in which, for example we examined when it is appropriate to trust someone, or how we might learn to trust someone in difficult circumstances, or how we can gain someone's trust – but this is very different from the worryingly naive claims sometimes made for 'trust games'.

Using games productively

If you do want to start your drama sessions with a game, *don't* feel you have to come up with a different one each time. You are not an entertainer at a children's party. If there is a game which you find effective, use it on a regular basis for a short period, perhaps five minutes at the beginning of each session. Whatever games you use, give children the opportunity to get better at them. You don't need a vast repertoire of games in order to be a highly effective drama teacher.

Games don't have to be the starter or warm-up activity. They can become part of the drama itself – 'Keeper of the Keys', for example (described in detail below) can be used as a test of skill, part of the dramatic fiction, as a preparation for a great quest.

If you are using a game or an exercise at the start of a session, choose something appropriate. If they've had to stay indoors for a wet break they'll want to do something physically very active. A game of tag (see below) may well be just the thing; but if they've just come in from the playground and that's what they've been doing for the last fifteen minutes, it would be a bit of a waste of time.

Ask yourself:

- Do they need warming up? Mentally or physically? The idea of a 'warm-up', as practised by professional actors is as much to get blood flowing to the brain, to get energised mentally, as to limber the body.
- Are they already very excited? – in which case they'll need something calming.
- What sort of activities are they going to be involved in during the session? A lot of verbal discussion? Non-verbal communication? Movement work? Something involving ritual?

Choose a game or exercise which leads into or complements this work.

- Is it appropriate sometimes to finish the drama session with a game or an exercise which calms and focuses?
- It's possible to use a game as a way of demonstrating to children how they can begin to take responsibility for their own learning. How can you give them the opportunity to make alterations to the rules to give them 'ownership' of a game?
- Games can be used very productively by thinking about the dramatic elements within them and using the game to lead directly into other work. What are the dramatic elements in the game you are using?

...ntinued

...y has the mission landed on this planet? Do the crew want to
...?
...y does the alien want to get into the spaceship?
...uld an alien have human feelings?
...w can we find out if the aliens mean us any harm?
...at benefits might there be from establishing a friendship with
   aliens?
...at do the friends and relatives of the crew feel back on earth as
...y await news?
...e teacher might add the information that we need help from the
...ens ourselves, or that the aliens look much more gentle than we
...d feared.
...e teacher might play an alien who could not communicate at all
...th the crew members (children) and wanted to learn their
...guage.
...uld it be that the alien does not want to steal the spaceship, but
...nts the key for some other purpose?

...he above is a detailed examination of ways of developing a
... not comprehensive. 'Keeper of the Keys' can also be used
... ritual; it can be used to teach about the nature of dramatic
...d dramatic structure (see Chapter 4).

...nes

...g out one's own name, each in turn, going round in a circle.
...g out one's own name plus one person to the right, then
...ree, etc.
...ng the circle, calling own name. When you are approached,
...t off for someone else, calling your own name.
...ng the circle, calling the name of the person you are
...aching.

... numerous different versions of tag. All of them contain
...ments of role play, narrative and ritual. The following
... useful to give children the opportunity to channel excess
...verybody is in action for the whole time it is being played.

... When B is caught, s/he freezes, eyes closed, counts to 5, then
...he game continues for as long as you want – or to a pre-set time
...en somebody is caught three times, for example.

...me can be developed, rapidly turned into a form of role play
...er and Hunted' situation – by asking, 'Who are you?' 'Where
...'Why are you running away?'

Developing games and exercises into drama

A lengthy description of how one game can be developed into drama
follows together with a couple of brief indications.

Example: Keeper of the Keys

This illustrates how one might use a game:

1. To create a 'back story' as a basis for drama; and as a stimulus for
   creative writing.
2. To demonstrate dramatic tension.
3. To introduce ideas of symbolism.
4. To encourage and develop listening skills.
5. To develop roles and narrative within a game and expand them into a
   drama.

This account of the various uses of the game also gives several
examples of starting points with teacher in role.

'Keeper of the Keys' is one of many games which have been used by
drama teachers over the years. It is sometimes known as 'Hunter and
Hunted'. There are many versions; and, as with any game, the rules can be
changed or adapted to suit the participants.

Description of the game

Children all sit in a circle. Two volunteers (A and B) are blindfolded, or are
trusted to keep their eyes shut. A set of keys is placed in the circle by the
teacher. A, the 'Keeper of the Keys' is in the circle, armed with a rolled up
newspaper. B has to try to find the keys and get them out of the circle
before being hit by A. If the Keeper hits B s/he wins. If, on the other hand
B succeeds in removing the keys from the circle without being hit, B wins.
   Simple variations include:

- Neither A nor B knowing the whereabouts of the keys.
- B allowed to continue if hit, but without the use of that part of the
  body – i.e. if hit on arm – cannot use arm; if hit on head – dead!
- A has keys tied very loosely on a string to his/her foot.
- A sits on a chair with the keys beneath. Only A is blindfolded. B has
  to remove the keys in a given time limit.

Playing the game is not in itself drama, though a great deal of dramatic
tension arises when it is well played. The following questions, which
effectively treat the game as if it were a ritual, can turn it into drama:

- I wonder who the 'Keeper of the Keys' is?
- And who, or what, is trying to get the keys?
- Neither of them can see. They are blindfolded. If we are making up a
  play about the 'Keeper of the Keys', why do you think that neither of
  them can see?
- So what does the blindfold represent?

Continued

Example continued

> - What does the circle mean in this play? What does it represent?
> - What is the 'Keeper' looking after? Who is the 'Keeper'?
> - What does the newspaper represent?
> - Who, or what, is *B*, the thief?
> - And why does the thief want or need to take the 'keys'?
>
> Providing the teacher retains an open mind, an extraordinary drama can evolve from this. Here are two examples of the beginnings of stories which evolved from questions like the above:
>
> 1. *Class of Year Three children*
>   The 'Keeper' is a guard who has been blinded to stop him ever setting eyes on the magic jewels. He is armed with a silver sword, and spends most of his life in the dungeon beneath the castle where the jewels are kept (the circle of children being the walls of the dungeon). The 'thief' is the rightful owner of the jewels who wants to get them back in order to free the prisoners in the castle.
> 2. *Class of Year Six children*
>   People take it in turns to guard the key to the spaceship. If you are the guard you have to wear a blindfold because you are armed with a laser torch which is so powerful that it would blind you if you could see it. A clever alien wants to steal the spaceship, and knows about the laser torch, so it puts on a blindfold as well. The keys to the spaceship are kept in a cave with only one entrance (the circle of children).
>
> What we have now is much more than a game: an exciting story to which we do not know the end; and a visual image which will lead us to an exciting starting point for a drama, an image which we know has engaged the children. If I had tried to impose either of the above on another class I doubt the drama would work. The stories were their own, so they could see that the drama would be theirs. They started the drama with ownership of the material, with a commitment which comes from the game and the questioning.
> *It is also worth noting that the questioning has opened up a new area of exploration – that of* symbol *and meaning.*
> The rolled-up newspaper represents a sword, and the sword is itself a symbol of dangerous power. The teacher now needs to ask how best to engage all the children actively. What roles are the children to play? If the teacher-in-role strategy is to be used, what role will the teacher play? What is likely to be an engaging and appropriate issue?
> It might help at this point to ask the children a further question: 'What might happen if the thief (the rightful owner of the jewels/the alien in the above examples) does or does not (depending on the drama) manage to steal the 'keys'?'
> This might be termed the 'worst case syndrome'. Whatever answer the children provide also creates the fundamental tension behind the drama: 'If we don't manage *X*, then *Y* will occur.'
> Note that the children have seen that the outcome of the game cannot be pre-planned, and are likely to take this understanding with them to the

Continued

Example continued

drama itself. The teacher can now s
can never know what exactly will ha
Here are some ideas showing how c
to the age range for each of the abov

1. *Prisoners in the Castle*
   (a) Children are workers at the
       opens with teacher saying
       about to say to you . . . C;
       secret? . . . I've already los
       guarding the jewels any mo
       help me?'
   (b) Children as villagers, teacher
       be a wizard with great pow;
       stolen. Can you help me get t
   (c) Teacher as the guard, the ch
       once the drama has started.
       you're all there. What do yo
       good.'
   (d) The teacher simply says: 'Wi
       brother out of prison?'

   Some other questions which might |

   - What powers do the magic jew
   - Who has put the people in pris
   - What sort of life does the guar
   - Could we try to talk to the gua
   - Are we sure the jewels rightfull
   - If we do get the jewels, what sl

2. *The Stranded Spaceship*
   (a) Children as crew of spaceship,
       asking for help: 'I admit that v
       That was wrong; but we despe
       Will you help us?'
   (b) Children as crew of spaceship,
       the guard on duty. Drama begir
       aliens have stolen the key; and
       How are we going to survive on
   (c) Children as aliens, teacher as c
       know you want to steal our spac
       you will tell us all about yourselv
   (d) The reverse of the above, so
       marooned on the alien planet, th
       them passage back to earth prov
       way of life on earth.

   Other questions, and ideas, which mig

   - Why has the key to the spaceship
   - Are the aliens as frightened of us

Example c

> - W
>   si
> - V
> - C
> - H
> - V
>   ti
> - V
>   ti
> - T
>   a
>   h
> - T
>   v
>   l
> - C

Although
game, it
to explor
tension a

Name g

1. Calli
2. Calli
   two,
3. Cro:
   you
4. Cro:
   app

Tag

There a
strong (
version
energy –

A chases
chases *A*
limit, or

The
– a 'Hu
are you

From there it can become an adventure yarn told in movement, with *B* miming climbing a cliff face, going through tunnels, crossing rope bridges, etc. *A* has to follow wherever *B* goes.

This, in turn, can move into still image work. Three still images to encapsulate the key moments in your story.

Blind

Again, there are numerous variations of these blind games/exercises. The following involves everybody at the same time.

Everybody stands in a circle. One person directed across the circle. When s/he gets to the other side of the circle s/he is gently redirected across again. This continues until s/he feels confident enough to close his/her eyes. Then a second and third person introduced to the circle. The 'game' is one in which the people on the outside are given responsibility for those on the inside, crossing the circle with their eyes closed. The class is competing with itself.

This can be developed thus (in pairs):

1. *A* leads *B* to a number of different textures.
2. Control your partner without words.
3. Control your partner without touch.
4. 'Blind' person is a Robot.

The role play can become more interesting, and more complex – if, for example *B* becomes the blind parent of a sighted child being shown round the classroom or the hall by *A*, a teacher in that school.

Two concentration exercises

When I introduce myself to a class that I am working with for the first time I frequently begin by asking them to sit close by me on the floor and listen with their eyes shut to the sound of a pair of Indian bells struck together. They are asked to open their eyes when the sound stops.

I have a colleague who never uses games as such. But she often takes a rather beautiful candle into the hall when she teaches drama. At the beginning of the session she lights the candle, the children sit round it in a large circle and she asks them to watch the flame, to concentrate on the flame and nothing else. For me, as a 'warm up' activity there's nothing to beat it!

STILL IMAGES

The idea of the still image is one which has already been mentioned several times both in this and in the preceding chapter. It's a very useful technique – not least because it is so adaptable.

Just as children are very familiar with drama itself through the dramatic fictions that they see enacted on television and on film, so too they have encountered the idea of still images in other contexts: their own family snapshots, freeze frame on the video recorder, sculptures, waxworks and comic strips.

As with all techniques, it's important to be clear about why one is using it. At its simplest the participants use their own bodies to create a three-dimensional still photograph. But it's a technique which can be used in many different ways, for example:

- As a control device.
- To initiate a drama.
- To focus on a particular moment.
- As a means of reflecting on the significance of a given moment, of developing an understanding of the depths and layers of meaning any given moment or image might carry.
- To open up a situation, to broaden thinking which has hitherto been from a limited viewpoint.
- To develop understanding of the significance of eye contact and body language.
- To develop understanding of narrative.
- To select the key moment(s) or the key stages in a narrative.
- To develop understanding of the articulate use of space.
- To recap on previous work.
- To represent photographs taken, so they can be examined within a fictional context.
- To make it possible to deal with very fast moving, or potentially violent, events.
- To shift the children away from thinking about drama in straightforwardly naturalistic ways and into more stylised modes in which, for example, emotions and ideas are given physical representation.

Still image work has the additional advantage of being easily repeatable. We are not concerned about spontaneity, but with accuracy and detail – setting the tone for what we hope will follow. We can return to a particular image at various points in a lesson, noting the way our understanding of a given image changes as we understand more about the broader situation.

Introducing the idea

Because the audience can take such an active part in still image work it is something which can easily be tackled in the classroom, which might be the best place for introducing it to a class who are unfamiliar with it.

1. A movement exercise – moving round the room without bumping into one another – and at a given signal everyone freezes. 'It's as if I'd just taken a photograph.' You could even use a polaroid camera, show them the photo, ask them to recreate that moment.
2. Using herself, the teacher creates a still image. Children guess what it is: making a cup of tea, turning on TV, reading the paper. They do similar actions, creating a still image from their own lives – cleaning their teeth in the morning, eating a packed lunch, etc.
3. The teacher 'moulds' a volunteer to create a still image. The children then do the same with a partner.
4. Teacher shows photographs of statues. Can they make themselves into a statue of, for example, Anancy playing a trick?[2] Somebody who has just had a trick played on them by Anancy? Put the two together?

As with all drama work, it's important to move forward at an appropriate pace, to aim for gradual progression. There's a neatness and conciseness, however, about Still Image work which makes this easier to achieve than in other areas of drama.

I'll now examine three different ways of using the technique of Still Image – to initiate a drama, to develop understanding of narrative, to focus and reflect on a particular moment.

Using still image to initiate a drama

*   A photograph (or picture) is given to a group(s). They then take up positions as if they were the people in the photograph. When they are satisfied with what they have produced they are asked to bring the image to life – for a very short time, perhaps as little as ten seconds – and/or say one line of dialogue each. From there the groups can be questioned further – either by the teacher or by other children – to establish what is going on.
*   The class work in small groups to 'mould' each other into still images which will function as waxworks or statues in the drama. The making of the images becomes the first part of the drama, in which (for example) the work is inspected by the teacher in role as new Mayor, who commissions a statue to commemorate the return of the children of Hamelin!
*   The teacher will be taking on a role in the drama; the class help to construct the role by using the teacher to create a still image of the role. When they are satisfied with the image they have created they take up their own positions in relation to the image, positions which indicate their role and attitude.

Example

The teachers reads part of a story to the class – about a merman caught in a fisherman's nets. The class create an image of the merman at the moment he is brought to land, surrounded by humans. The teacher will take on the role of the merman, but asks the children: 'How do you want me to look? How should I express fear? Show me how to do it.' When ready each child can then join in the still image, remembering their position and expressions so that it can be recreated later, and so that half the group can move out of the image to examine the other half.

We can then move backwards or forwards in time. What led up to the merman's capture? What do each of you feel about it? What does each of you want to do now?

• The class make an image of something which is then put into a fictional context as photographic evidence.

Example

The children are to be in role as time travellers. They are asked to create still images of an incident they saw on one of their journeys back in time, as if these were holographic, three dimensional pictures. The rest of the class then use these pictures as evidence, discussing the implications of what they are shown in order to plan for their next journey back in time.

Using still image to develop understanding of narrative

• Having been working on a drama spontaneously, the class (either as a whole group, or in small groups) are asked to consider the most important moment in the story so far, and to represent that moment as a still image.

This activity develops skills which are important in other areas of the curriculum as well as in drama, namely the ability to analyse, to edit, to condense and to focus.

• The activity can be taken further by asking them to represent three key moments in a story line (either one they have heard or one they have themselves developed through drama). This opens up possible discussion about dramatic structure. Choosing three images should give us 'beginning', 'middle' and 'end', i.e. what is stable, how that stability is disrupted and how the disruption is resolved.[3]

This task of considering key moments can be a very valuable way of recapping from one session to the next when the drama extends over a long period, as it usually does once it becomes part of a project or topic work. It's more interesting for the children than being asked 'Can you remember what we did least week?', it makes them immediately active, it reminds them what they were doing and can be very informative for the teacher, who can see clearly what the children are finding most engaging about the work.

• Having made a sequence of images, ask them to put them into a different running order. Changing the sequence of a series of images invariably affects the meaning of a narrative. This exercise could be used in conjunction with image sequencing exercises we might do in Media Studies.[4]

The examples given above imply fairly naturalistic images or representations. But we can also ask children to create more expressive images which are more like pictures of a state of mind or of an idea.

Example

The children are in role as islanders who have decided to abandon their homes because a volcano is becoming active. We could ask each child to say (or write) what they are feeling as they leave the island, but we might first want to focus on the leavetaking in a more active way. Suggest that in small groups they make an image to show what it's like to experience conflicting feelings – of sorrow, loss, relief, excitement, hope, expectation.

Using still image to focus and reflect on a particular moment

Whatever kind of image the class have created, we now have an opportunity to deepen and clarify their thinking. While one group holds their image still, the rest of the class briefly become spectators, an audience. The teacher can comment on the image, trying to deepen commitment to the work and draw out the significance of what has been made. At the same time she can take the opportunity to try to build the esteem of those class members who lack confidence and are finding the work slightly embarrassing.

Example

The children are involved in a drama about the construction of a railway (described in detail in Chapter 5). They have been working in small groups to show the lives of a small rural town as yet unconnected to the railway. One small group of children have decided to be miners. They have created a still image showing work down the pit – but one child can't stop giggling.

The teacher says: 'I see work which is backbreakingly hard; I see people in very cramped conditions; I see people working together, needing each other. And I see one of these miners managing to stay cheerful in these very tough circumstances.' You, the teacher, are taking the work seriously even if they're struggling with it. In my experience this is one of the quickest and most effective ways of drawing children into the drama; you are helping them to make sense of what they're doing, you're showing them clearly that what they're doing matters.

The teacher can comment on the images, as in this example; but with a large part of the class functioning as an audience we have an opportunity for involving them actively in the process and developing the sense that in educational drama the 'audience' should be active and responsible. The class can be asked to:

* Move around the image and look at it from various points of view. How does this change your impression of what you see?
* Give the image a title or caption.
* Who is most important in the image? Who do you think they want us to look at? Who's the person we're meant to focus on?
* What might that person (or others) be thinking? What are their hopes and fears in this situation?
* What does each person want to happen?

This not only opens up what is going on, but takes us forward as well. The 'thoughts' given to the characters in the image are those which will lead to action.

* You can put one question to anybody in the image, who has to answer in role – or out of role (but be consistent!).
* Suggest a line of dialogue for each character.
* A spectator group can copy a particular image, and then animate it – with dialogue if appropriate.
* If the image represents a still photograph we can frame it by using an overhead projector as a light source, as if the image is a photographic transparency. This takes us into some very interesting work about point of view.

Example

The 'photographs' have been rescued from the wreckage of a plane crash. What do they show? What do they not show? What is hidden from us? Where do you think the person who took the photograph was when s/he took it.

Above all else the guiding principle is to tease out the meanings inherent in the images; to ask: 'What's important here?'

There are several examples in the book where still images are used at key moments in the drama as part of the dramatic fiction, notably 'The Giant Awakes' (Chapter 5), where the images are used as photographic evidence.

TEACHING IN ROLE

Teaching in role is a strategy which a great many teachers have found extremely useful. It is most often used in whole group work, but it is also very productive in *forum theatre*, particularly if the role you take on functions as an *obstacle* which the class (or representatives of the class) have to find their way round by argument, persuasion and compromise.

It is also useful on a one to one basis, or with a small group – either in front of the class or discretely. Teaching in role is a *strategy*, a means to an end; it is not an end in itself. The purpose is to offer a way of intervening which challenges and focuses the work, which moves it on, which creates learning opportunities and deepens the understanding of the participants.

Teaching in role requires the teacher to play a role in the drama with the children for a specific purpose. The role itself should provide some focus for the drama. This could be as simple as entering the drama as a messenger and passing on information. If you've never tried the strategy before this is a good way of beginning: the messenger doesn't have to stay in the drama.

One reason that many teachers find the idea of teaching in role worrying is that they feel that once they have embarked on a role they will have to stick with it for the rest of the lesson. This is to misunderstand the strategy, which demands that the teacher moves out of role occasionally to reflect on the work.

To take the *example* of the messenger, consider this simple sequence:

1. The children are in role as the townspeople of Nazareth; *out of role* the teacher has established with them the nature of their work, their commitment to their land, families and places of work.
2. *In role* the teacher enters as a traveller to tell them that she has come from a neighbouring village, where Roman soldiers are

delivering a decree that all will have to pay a new tax; the traveller has to go on her way.

3. *Out of role* the teacher asks the children about the traveller – what did she say, what does it mean for them? They might then be asked to consider their response if the soldiers arrive in Nazareth.

More adventurously, the teacher might choose to play the role of the Roman Centurion who reads out the decree. This is a confrontational role. Always remember, however, that at any time the participants in the drama can come out of role to consider what is happening. Indeed it is vital that they should do so from time to time. If the confrontation between Nazareth and Rome looks like it's becoming unproductive, the teacher can come out of role and ask the children to reflect on what has been happening – perhaps through discussion, perhaps through a short piece of writing (a diary entry, a letter to a friend, a sketch representing how the townspeople feel about the power relationship, or – shifting the perspective – the report that the Roman has to make to his commanding officer).

Types of role

We can classify roles in terms of their *function* and in terms of their *status*.

The messenger role, for example, has the function of bringing information; but that information could be brought by a beggar or a King. When we're using role we need to consider both function *and* status.

The following lists are not exhaustive, and many of the categories overlap; they do give an indication of the vast range of possibilities open to you:

Possible functions of a role:

- *To seek help and/or advice*: 'I've inherited a circus and I've no idea how to look after the animals.'
- *To seek information*: a traveller looking for a lost companion, a curious stranger.
- *To co-ordinate*: an investigator trying to co-ordinate the enquiry into an air-crash.
- *To obstruct*, to provide an obstacle which the class has to overcome, *to challenge*. For example, the mayor who doesn't believe that the damage in the town is caused by a giant. 'Can you get me some proof?'

The teacher playing the Pied Piper, with whom the class has to negotiate for the release of the children.

- *To assist the class with their tasks*: the teacher as the learner, someone taught by the class, an apprentice, a deckhand, a new recruit.
- *To be the Devil's Advocate*, to enable/provoke the class into clarifying their feelings and articulating what they believe to be right:
  'I don't see why we should share the proceeds.'
  'We should leave the whale alone; that's what we've been told.'
- *To bring information*, the messenger: 'I'm getting a message through from an alien life form.'
  'I've been asked to tell you that we all have to fill in a census return.'

Classifying roles by status

1. *High status*: King, Queen, Captain on a ship (or spaceship), leader of the expedition, leader of the village, headteacher, team leader, athletics coach, managing director, etc.
2. *The second in command*: The chief in awe of his Adviser (cf 'Whale' in 'Using Poetry', Chapter 2), Monarch's dogsbody, Deputy, go-between:
   'I can't do anything about it, but I'll tell her how unhappy you are about it.'
3. *Equal status* (on the same level as the class): one of the team, a member of the gang, villager, crew member.
4. *Low status*: beggar, traveller seeking help, plague victim, shipwrecked sailor, refugee, apprentice, etc.

Any role has both a function and a status; it is effectively a combination of the above. Some of the combinations seem to go together automatically – e.g. the apprentice will be low status, somebody who needs to be taught – but often it's useful to think beyond the obvious. Consider, for example, the different challenges posed to the group by the Devil's Advocate who is high and low status.

Responses to the status of the role

When planning to use teacher-in-role consider what *sort* of responses to the role are possible. Put yourself in the position of the children. If you were encountering a tyrannical overlord, what would *you* do? This may not, of course, be what they decide! Ask yourself what are the possible and likely responses? This should not defuse the dramatic tension.

You should think *why* you're choosing a particular role. Think through the likely *focus* it's going to create in the drama, the problems and dilemmas it is likely to introduce.

High status

The advantage of this type of role is that it's similar to the traditional teacher role; you're retaining control. This can be productive, but there's a danger that it prevents the children from taking any real responsibility for the drama.

In an encounter with a high status role the options are few – they can agree to do as they're told (in which case you, the teacher, end up doing all the decision-making) or they can refuse; it's a battle of wits and wills: you remain in control or they overthrow you. That *might* make for excellent drama – but be prepared for it.

When used in conjunction with the *function* of Devil's Advocate you can push the children to a point where they refuse to take orders; they have to *persuade* you that what you are proposing is wrong.

You are, perhaps, the captain of a pirate ship, proposing to take on a cargo of slaves because it's easy money.

Second in command

A much more versatile position. You can always defer to the 'off-stage' higher authority (which means you're less likely to have a revolution on your hands!); you can seek assistance; you can still play Devil's Advocate; you can co-ordinate; bring information and, importantly, transfer responsibility to the children. One of the dangers of the position, however, is that it's very easy to slip into full authority – which is a 'con' that children can see through all too easily.

Equal status

Enables you to ask very open questions of the 'What should we do now?' variety. If the children are unused to the teacher taking on a role, however, they will want to push you into an authority role. Providing you resist, this can in itself provide useful learning opportunities: 'I'm not in charge; I can't make decisions for you.'

The traveller or stranger can be of equal status; this allows you to ask particularly useful questions in role: 'How do you organise your meetings? How do you make sure that everyone doesn't speak at the same time?'

Low status

This needs a good deal of confidence on the part of the teacher, but is very productive as real responsibility for decision-making is transferred to the children. It raises the status, and esteem of the children.

Although the Devil's Advocate role is traditionally associated with high status roles, you should remember that someone in a low status position can still have opinions, can still provoke.

I have sometimes taken on a role where I have been injured, a plague victim, and used the role to become Devil's Advocate, suggesting that one of the more aggressive boys in a class 'Finish me off.' Risky, certainly; but it hasn't yet failed to get the class – and the child concerned – to argue strongly that while there's life there's hope!

How to prepare children for the strategy?

Teachers often have more problems with the concept than children: pre-school children will often play with adults, asking them to assume roles (the shopkeeper, the bus conductor); children who play in this way are used to moving in and out of role, are quite happy for an adult to be *in* their play one moment and to be themselves the next. Infant teachers who go to the play corner and take part in domestic or shopping activities are already using a form of teacher-in-role

With older children there can sometimes be difficulties. The easiest way to introduce the strategy is to give a few simple demonstrations:

1. Role play the beginning of a very simple scene on your own – e.g. 'Why are you late home? You've not been in trouble with your teacher again?!'
2. Then ask – 'Who was I pretending to be?'
3. Ask for a volunteer to join you. Improvise a short scene with a simple but clear beginning: 'Can I go out to play now, Mum?' Try several on this one to one basis. Then try working with a small group, doing the same thing. From there it is a comparatively small step for you to take on a role in a piece of forum theatre, and then on to working in role with the whole class.

Forum theatre

If you are working in forum theatre the class can help in the creating the role for you: 'How should I play this character?'

'Do you want to meet someone who's going to be helpful or who's going to make life difficult for you?' This is a useful question because it also takes the class towards an understanding that drama is often far more enjoyable if the problems that are raised are not easily solved.

Negotiations with a difficult character (e.g. the Pied Piper holding the town's children in the mountain caverns) are better conducted with the teacher taking on the problematic role because the teacher can judge just how difficult to make the task, and can allow the children success when they need it.

Moving in and out of role

Always make sure the children understand how you are going to signify moving in and out of role. As you, and the children, become increasingly familiar with the strategy you can make the boundaries less clear; but initially clarity is all important.

- You might use a cloak, scarf, cardigan which you put on to signify that you're in role. When you take it off again you're back being the class teacher again.
- What props can you use that help *signify* the role – a brief case? A bunch of keys?
- Another simple, but effective way is to say 'I will be playing a part in this drama unless I'm sitting in this chair. And when I sit here it means two things: first, that we all stop playing a part at that moment and second, that I'd like you all to come over and sit down to discuss what we've been doing.'

Further considerations and suggestions

We've already discussed the status and power of the role. How much *knowledge* does the role have? Be careful not to use 'superior' knowledge to intimidate. Releasing knowledge slowly not only enhances the drama, it also increases the likelihood that the children will want to get involved in research.

Use the role to defy expectations. Let them find, for example, that authority has clay feet. Use their expectations and then confound them. The book *Drama Structures*[5] contains an excellent example of this in the 'Starship' project. The teacher takes on the role of an alien, who says that the crew of the Starship must be lying when they say their leader is a man. She knows very well that male creatures are incapable of such responsibilities. She wants to speak to a female, the real boss!

Thinking beyond the starting point

As a starting point the role can create highly dramatic moments, but be careful not to choose a role which then limits you. Think ahead. How can the role continue to be used?

Example: The Roman Census

The *initial* function of the role is to pass on information that the Nazarenes will have to leave Nazareth for the Roman census. This can be done by:

*   A Roman centurion giving fearsome orders (*high status*).
*   A town elder passing on information and advising them to do what the Romans say (*second in command*).
*   A weak member and infirm townswoman who has heard rumours (*low status*).
*   A traveller who has come from a nearby town, where the Romans have already given out their orders (*low to equal status*).

Having given the information, where do you go now? Is that all the role is good for? The Roman centurion can return and enforce the evacuation but he can't open up responses. Each of the other roles is more productive:

*   The traveller is a stranger whose curiosity can enrich the sense of community.
*   The infirm townswoman will need to be helped on her own journey.
*   The town elder can help organise the necessary preparations (or resistance), can ask all manner of questions about families and journeys which will help deepen the commitment to the project.

There are several examples in this book of the use of the teacher-in-role strategy, notably:

'The Construction of a Railway' in 'Drama at the centre of the curriculum', Chapter 5.
'The Island' in Chapter 2.
'The Crashed Space Ship' and 'The Giant Awakes' in Chapter 5.

WHOLE GROUP WORK

When I first started teaching drama I accepted the prevailing dogma that you started by getting children to work individually, then in pairs, then in small groups and eventually (when they were really good at drama) in larger groups! It was an appealing idea because it at least seemed to offer some sort of progression to the work at a time when there was little or nothing written about coherent development in drama. But the great strength of whole group drama is precisely that it gives context and coherence to small group work; it makes it easier for the teacher to monitor work, to make it highly dramatic and keep it tightly focused.

What is whole group drama?

The image I had of whole group drama when I was first introduced to the idea was of a large crowd scene in which everybody was acting as a group. I assumed whole group drama had to be about football hooligans on their way to a match or passengers in an aeroplane about to crash; that there might be shades of difference, but that basically everybody would be doing the same thing at the same time. How wrong could I be? Whole group drama in fact offers individuals great opportunities for personal decision making.

Whole group drama is best seen as an organisational strategy, a way of organising all the small group and individual work which takes place within a unifying fictional context.

Suppose we set up some small group scenes about neighbours arguing, trying to resolve a dispute (it could be open-ended, up to the children to sort out the 'back story' or the teacher could prescribe it – a barking dog in one house and loud music late at night in the other). A problem arises when the groups come to share their work – when for long periods children will be passive.

We could still make our drama about disputes between neighbours, however, and organise it as a whole group drama – simply by setting each of the improvisations in a single street. The drama might be unfocused, but we can now ask each group to look at the others' work as examples of what's going on elsewhere in the street. The advantage of this is that it enables us to start focusing on content. We could make a plan of the street, we could ask each of the groups to find a reason to go to someone else's 'house'; we could perhaps ask other people in the street to try to help resolve some of the disputes other people are having.

But the drama is still not very exciting, and the unfocused nature of the work is likely to continue to create organisational problems. We need something dramatic to focus it, either to introduce something which will create a potential for change in this situation (which will potentially destabilise the situation) or pick up on something going on in the groups which will have the same effect; we need to focus on an issue.

In this instance, for example:

- The corner shop is to be closed and knocked down to make way for a multi-storey car-park.
- The street is preparing its contribution to a town pageant.
- An empty warehouse is to be converted into a leisure centre – the inhabitants of the street are actively involved in the planning.
- People in the street are asked to prepare for an influx of refugees who will be looked after in the local church hall.
- A big hole has suddenly appeared in the street! What are we

going to do about it? (This starting point is described in detail in Chapter 5, 'Writing in Role' – 'The Crashed Spaceship'.)

We can introduce this issue in a number of ways:

- The teacher can act as a narrator, telling the story thus far.
- The information can be given in the form of a poster, letters, tape-recorded message (as if coming over the radio), video-tape (TV news), or on a computer screen.
- The teacher can take on a role and introduce the information in role – as a messenger, as a member of the group, as an outsider, as someone giving orders.
- The teacher can present the class with an image which intrigues, mystifies, challenges.

Where to start? Slow build up or in at the deep end?

This unifying issue can be presented at the beginning of the drama or at a later stage, after the children have taken on roles and started on small group work. The advantage of presenting the issue at the start of the drama is that the work is focused from the beginning. The danger of approaching whole group work by letting children first improvise in small groups and then presenting them with an issue which you hope will give them a focus is that they remain more interested in what's going on in their group than in the supposedly unifying issue: 'Why should I be interested in the corner shop being knocked down when I never use it, and anyway we've just been burgled?!'

The advantage, however, of first letting them improvise more freely in small groups is that with careful monitoring you can see what's interesting them, what they want to explore in their drama. It may well be that several groups have had a burglary, in which case the teacher could use this as the focus: 'How are we going to deal with it? How are we going to stop it happening again?'

Interdependence

So far we've concentrated our attention on this one imaginary street. It exemplifies a group of people who have separate lives, ideas and attitudes, who are united because they're in a common space and (if the drama is working) because they now share a common concern: something has happened which they have to deal with by working together.

In creating whole group dramas we should be aware of the need to ensure that every child feels they have a stake in what is happening and that they can genuinely influence outcomes.

One way of doing this is to establish, within the whole group framework, small groups with common interests, which depend on each other. This means that when they watch another group's work they are affected by what they do, they're all working within the same fictional context.

To take the example of the island community (described in 'The Island', Chapter 2), these small groups might be:

- hunters
- boatbuilders
- fishermen and women
- net makers
- builders
- farmers – those who tend crops and animals
- woodcutters
- woodworkers – carpenters and carvers.

We can use the technique of spotlighting, focusing attention on one group's work: 'Look what's happening on the farms.' If the crops have been destroyed by the storm or animals have got loose, it will affect every group. As children become more experienced they establish their own interdependent relationships, but initially it requires careful questioning by the teacher: 'You're a woodworker. Who do you get your wood from? How do you help the builders?' We can then establish the way group members interact amongst themselves and with other groups. This type of work, in which the children are playing at their roles, is frequently a necessary stage in the process of building commitment to the drama; and it's one which adults find as useful as children. It can, nevertheless, get out of hand and we should always bear in mind the need to intervene, to challenge, to focus the work, to use this period of 'dramatic play' to provide learning opportunities.

One simple way of deepening the 'play' is to ask each group to consider what very special skills each individual brings to the group. In the case of the woodcutters, for example,

- Who knows those parts of the forest where the best trees grow for boatmaking, for furniture making?
- Who is best at climbing trees?
- Who makes the tools?

Every child is special, every child should feel they have a special role in the drama, that their presence or absence will affect what happens in the drama.

If we can achieve this it will make it much easier to keep the children engaged in the work throughout, even when they are watching what others are doing.

Working in this way, setting up a whole group which functions as a community, frequently leads drama teachers towards work which is set either in villages or small towns or on islands. It's not just that drama teachers are nostalgic romantics who hanker for a simpler way of life (though there may well be an element of truth in that); it's that these self-contained communities cannot easily call upon outside forces to solve their problems. The problems of the drama remain within the group. Good drama is very much about dealing with the mess we find ourselves in, not calling up some outside agency to solve all our problems.

Bearing that in mind, we find ourselves setting whole group dramas on spaceships or sailing ships, in medieval castles, on expeditions; and what all these have in common is that within the setting it is comparatively easy to ensure that each participant has an essential role; we can easily create a chain of dependency, to ensure that each child feels they have a stake in the drama.

Allocating roles

How do we ensure that every child has a role?

If the dramatic starting point is strong and the situation is clear, children will usually find roles for themselves. But there may be occasions when you want to be sure that every child has an appropriate role. This might be because it will give you, the teacher, more confidence in what you're doing, in which case the simplest way is to discuss the likely roles and ask for volunteers before the drama proper begins.

This will not, however, solve the problem of certain children taking on what appear to be menial roles. We should never allow the drama to reinforce any child's feeling of poor self-esteem, so the problem needs to be tackled. The simplest way is to ensure that once the drama is under way these roles become highly significant in the drama.

Many of the organisational procedures that we use with small groups can easily be adapted, for example giving out cards with relevant information.

A slow but dramatic way of allocating roles is to come to the children (probably gathered in a circle) and ask them who's who in role: 'I'm a stranger here. Where can I buy bread? And who supplies you with flour? Who works with you?' Each person goes in turn to one or more other(s) in the circle, saying who they are and what dealings they have with them.

The problem with this approach is that it can become rather competitive and nerve racking for those children who don't get 'chosen' early on. When I use it I ensure that I have some 'special' roles 'up my sleeve' as it were, so that the children who are approached last are allocated roles which, at least potentially, are the most important.

Breaking out of the community based drama

Basing whole group work on a community is a relatively simple way of organising a drama project. It is, however, by no means the only way of organising whole group work.

The class can take on the role of any group of people unified by a common concern or problem, so long as we ensure that every child has an active role to play.

The class can be, for example:

1. Detectives investigating a crime. The children go into the hall and find a frame with the picture cut out of it; an empty cash box; or a desk and chairs overturned, papers strewn all over to give the impression of a ransacked office.
2. Archaeologists exploring a Roman settlement.
3. Architects or builders preparing to build a new leisure centre.
4. RSPCA officers who have to deal with the animals in a badly run zoo.

In each of the above examples the children have been asked to take on the role of 'people who know'; and it is this which gives them their stake in the drama.

The work could be enhanced by the teacher working in role alongside the children; but it is not essential.

Building belief, involvement, engagement, commitment

Do we want children to believe in what they're doing? Do we want them to be involved?

The words are used frequently in connection with drama.

I very much hope that they are engaged in the work and committed to it, but I don't want them to believe it's real; and the word *involvement* to me implies an inability to stand apart from the role-playing. It's an important issue, and has led to some serious misunderstandings about the teaching of drama.

It is in periods of reflection that the real learning occurs in drama, when people are given the chance to think about what they have been doing. Children, remarkably, often understand this better than many adults. Even very young children have little difficulty in the notion of moving in and out of role. Frequently in whole group drama we need to stop the drama and move out of role to think about the situation;

without these periods of reflection whole group drama can become indulgent and aimless.

The problem with the word *involvement* is that it seems to imply a single-mindedness, a deep identification with character which is not only unnecessary, but often counter-productive. It is as if involvement in 'character' is the highest goal. Professional actors are very much aware of the need to stay detached from the roles they play night after night; similarly, children taking part in a drama project need to keep their wits about them, to be thinking about meaning and implications in what they say and do and make.

When outsiders watch a drama class they frequently comment on how 'involved' the children seem. I think what they mean is that they appear so intent on their work that they don't seem to notice onlookers. What I hope (and would like to think) is happening is that the children are aware of the onlookers, but that they're making a choice to stay in role; that their engagement with the issues and the problems of the drama is what is keeping them intent on their work.

So how, in whole group drama, do we build commitment to the work and engagement in the issues? How do we shift the children from the glib superficial, mocking comments (which are usually symptomatic of nervousness and insecurity) to deeper, considered responses?

There is no single, simple answer. We use a range of strategies:

• Raising the status of the children, making them important in the drama.
• Careful questioning.
• Periods of reflection.
• Teacher in role to challenge, to redirect and make sense of glib responses.
• Encouraging research.
• Developing intercurricular work, which itself enhances the drama.
• Developing the drama beyond single lessons into extended projects.
• Making the work as visual as possible, trying wherever possible to create visual images and symbols rather than simply talking.
• Above all, the teacher needs to take the work seriously – which means that whenever possible we ensure that drama time is not interrupted.

Discussions and meetings

One of the criticisms sometimes levelled at the whole group drama approach is that it always seems to involve lots of meetings and discussions, and that this disadvantages those children whose grasp of language is uncertain; that this 'type' of drama can rapidly become nothing more than a heated discussion involving only the teacher and the more articulate members of the class.

Whole group drama, however, is not a *type* of drama, but an organisational strategy; as with any strategy it can be well used or misused. There are occasions when the strategy demands whole group discussions and it's all too easy to be lulled into thinking the drama is going well because a group of very articulate children are thoroughly engaged in the work and able to vocalise their very imaginative ideas, while other children are left out of the real decisionmaking processes.

Here are some pointers to how we can make meetings and discussions more dramatic and accessible to all the children in the class:

- Establish in advance the *purpose* of the meeting – both for yourself and for the children. Is it one at which they will simply be given information by the teacher in role? A way of heightening the formality of language? If the intention is for the group to reach a key decision they should know this.
- Establish the *rules* of meetings. Who can speak and when? It is sometimes useful to encourage meetings to be set up as a form of ritual. Perhaps people can only address the meeting when they hold a certain talisman (which is passed from speaker to speaker).
- Wherever possible try to bring in *physical and visual elements*, so that the meeting is about much more than group discussion. When setting it up, for example, ask 'Where do our meetings take place?' so together you and the children can organise the space in a way which is visually meaningful. Sometimes we'll all be sitting in a circle on the floor, but not always. How do we organise the RSPCA offices or police headquarters?
- If the whole group has to make its decision through verbal discussion it is often better to first present the issue or problem to small groups, then ask each to report back to the whole group. This way everybody has a chance to air their opinions and *everybody's voice is represented* at the meeting.
- *Voting.* Don't assume the children know what is meant by democracy. *Before* putting something to a vote you need to negotiate (usually out of role) what it means. You'll need to get agreement from everyone that if they end up in the minority they will bide by the majority decision.
- When you ask for *volunteers*, or opinions, be prepared for the 'Me me me!' syndrome. If we're asking for somebody to persuade the giant to leave us in peace, ask those whose hands are highest: 'What qualities are going to be needed here? What *sort* of person would be best suited? Somebody who's cunning? Clever? Or perhaps someone who's 'brave'.' And then we can explore,

through the medium of drama, what those words *mean*. Does being brave mean being strong or overcoming our fears? Then we can return to the problem of persuading the giant to leave us alone and ask who *in the drama* has those qualities?

• Remember that the essence of drama is acting out 'What if?' situations. In any subject we can discuss 'What might happen if . . .?' In drama we can try things out, we can find out what happens. As a general rule try it, do it and *then* talk about it. *Don't avoid the drama* (as exemplified in the 'Construction of a Railway' project documented in Chapter 5).

What next? What does a whole group drama look like?

We've had our meeting, we've all got our roles, what do we do now?

If the dramatic frame is an enquiry or an investigation the children might well be creating still images, which they can then bring back to the whole group. What differentiates this now from uncontextualised still image work is that the audience are now looking at these images in role; they are interrogating the images as if they were detectives looking at photographic evidence.

Prepared small group work can similarly be viewed in context as if it were video material, or plays acted out – showing, for example, the bravest thing they have ever done.

There will also be spontaneous small group work, with the teacher maybe intervening in role, or staying out of role, commenting, spotlighting work for others to see. Occasionally, the teacher will make use of Forum Theatre techniques; and there will certainly be times when a small group of children will be working in front of the class in a spontaneous improvisation.

There is no set model. The problems within the dramatic fiction are dealt with as they arise; the teacher tries to keep the focus, intervenes as necessary and ensures that there are periods of reflection when everyone can consider carefully the meaning and significance of what has happened.

Whole group drama – the myths and half truths

• *'It's very demanding in terms of organisational skills.'* Providing you understand clearly the rationale for whole group work, it is often much less complex than small group work; a simple narrative thread can keep the drama alive.

• *'It only really works if you are prepared to work in role alongside the children.'* Working in role definitely helps; it's an economical and effective strategy. But it's not an essential part of the process. And if you do choose to use teacher-in-role there are going to be many occasions when you'll have to step out of role to reflect on the work.

- '*Whole group work and small group work indicate quite different ideological approaches to the teaching of drama.*' It's difficult to imagine whole group work which doesn't also involve small group work at some point, but with the advantage that whole group work gives the small groups a focus, a purpose and a context to their work.
- '*There are teachers who do whole group work and there are others who do small group work, and their approach is very different.*' For those who have never tried whole group work this might seem true, but it's a half truth at most. The two approaches should be seen as complementary.
- '*Whole group work is all about process, never about performance.*' For some this is true; but I would contend that the best way to develop performance work is by using the whole group approach. Part Four of this book offers specific examples of plays developed in this way.
- '*Whole group work is all about endless meetings and discussions and is therefore intimidating to children whose grasp of language is uncertain.*' Be very careful of this one. It's all too often true. Guard against it, see the discussions as ways of reaching decisions. It's the decision-making that's important; it doesn't always have to be tackled verbally. Make sure that every child contributes to the decision-making process.
- '*In order to run a whole group drama effectively you have to be not only very experienced, but also very charismatic.*' People who ooze experience, self-confidence and charisma appear to find most aspects of teaching easy; many of the best drama teachers I've seen working, however, are quiet and self-effacing, and I've seen relatively inexperienced young students running very successful whole group drama sessions.

To summarise

When we're using whole group drama:

- We must give the class a clear focus to the work.
- Dramatic play is an important stage which people need to go through to build up their commitment to the work, but don't expect learning to take place without teacher intervention.
- We need to structure in periods of reflection.
- All the strategies referred to elsewhere in this book (such as forum theatre, still image, small group drama) can be used within the context of a whole group drama.

- If the class is working in small groups as part of the whole group, try to ensure these groups are interdependent, that they can see how their work relates to that of others.
- Try to ensure that every child feels they have an essential role in the drama, that they have opportunities to make decisions and influence outcomes.
- Establish that once an idea has been accepted it is not to be denied.
- Negotiate with the group to agree on decision-making procedures; don't assume they understand the workings of democracy!
- When involved in discussions and meetings consider the needs of the children who are less verbally articulate.
- It is this form of drama which best lends itself to topic work and intercurricular project work.

This book contains several detailed examples of whole group drama projects:

1. 'The Island' in Chapter 2.
2. 'Construction of a Railway', 'The Giant Awakes' and 'The Crashed Spaceship' in Chapter 5.
3. 'The Donkeyman's Daughter' in Chapter 8.
4. A 'Toxic Waste' project planned in detail in Chapter 10.

Bibliography and recommended reading

Boal, A. 1979. *Theatre of the Oppressed*. Pluto Press.
Boal, A. (translated by Jackson, A.) 1992. *Games for Actors and Non Actors*, Routledge.
Berry, J. 1988. *Anancy–Spiderman*, Walker Books.
British Film Institute. 1988. *Picture Stories*, BFI Education.
British Film Institute. 1989. *Primary Media Education: A Curriculum Statement*, BFI Education.
Opie, I. and Opie, P. 1969. *Children's Games in Street and Playground*, Oxford University Press.

Teacher in role and whole group drama

Fines, J. and Verrier, R. 1974. *The Drama of History*, New University Education.
Morgan, N. and Saxton, J. 1987. *Teaching Drama*, Hutchinson Education, pp. 38–66.
Davies, G. 1983. *Practical Primary Drama*, Heinemann Educational Books.
O'Neill, C., Lambert, A., Linnell, R. and Warr-Wood, J. 1976. *Drama Guidelines*, Heinemann.
Wagner, B-J. 1976. *Dorothy Heathcote: Drama as a Learning Medium*, Hutchinson.

Notes

1. 'Forum theatre' is a term first coined by Augusto Boal, a South American Theatre Director, who was inspired by the work of the educationalist, Paulo Freire. Boal's work on Forum Theatre, which was first used as part of a literacy project in Peru, is described in his book *Theatre of the Oppressed*, published by Pluto Press.
2. *Anancy* is the extraordinary spider hero of West Indian folk tales who has the unique ability to change from man to spider and back again. There are several excellent collections of Anancy stories available – see appendix.
3. Concepts of dramatic structure are discussed further in *Part Four, Performance and Production*, as are the associated skills of editing, condensing, selecting and shaping. Note particularly the storyboard diagrams (pps. 158, 9) illustrating different points of view in the Pied Piper story.
4. The British Film Institute publish an excellent resource pack for teachers who want to start teaching the media: BFI. 1988. *Picture Stories*, BFI Education.
5. O'Neil, C. and Lambert, A. 1982. *Drama Structures*, Hutchinson.

CHAPTER 4

Organisation and development

This chapter starts by looking at the issue of control and discipline, and the related skills of questioning and reflection. This discussion then moves on to examine specific ways of developing, deepening and enhancing the work, looking in particular at narrative and non-verbal language. The chapter concludes with a discussion of collaborative teaching.

*   control and discipline
*   reflection
*   questioning skills
*   narrative: dramatic tension and the dramatic frame
*   non-verbal language: the use of space and symbols
*   collaborative teaching

CONTROL IN THE DRAMA LESSON

I believe that the two prime requisites for good control are careful organisation and clarity. The teacher does not need to know exactly what will happen and cannot usefully plan a story line very far ahead, but should give a great deal of thought to the organisation of the lesson:

*   How will groups be divided?
*   How will the situation of the drama be introduced?
*   Are props/costumes (for children or for the teacher in role) needed?
*   Are suitable writing materials easily available if the children are likely to need them for reflective work?
*   How will the space in the classroom/hall be used?
*   What resources are needed?
*   What register of language do you intend to use?

As the drama develops remember that if each child feels s/he has a clear responsibility within the drama control problems are far less likely to arise.

The children must be quite clear from the outset about the task in hand; what is going to be expected from them during the course of the lesson? We all mess about when we think that what we have been asked to do is silly or pointless. Build into the drama periods of reflection; they give significance to the drama itself and to individual contributions.

Ground rules

Always establish good ground rules at the beginning of each session. Keep the rules clear and simple and to the point. If possible try to frame them in a dramatic way – because this is a further pointer for the children showing *how* you are going to work together. It is productive to *agree* these rules with children rather than dictate them. If you explain that in the drama lesson you are going to be working *together*, that you will need their help, that you cannot create the drama on your own, you are raising their status, making them important. This sense of collaborative work – within agreed parameters – is a key to good control and good drama.

These ground rules might include how we make sure we can hear each other, who talks and when, how we organise meetings, whether or not children are allowed to use PE equipment, do they have access to chairs?

Stopping work

Perhaps the most important ground rules to establish are those about silence and stopping work. You should make quite clear what signals you'll use to indicate that you want them to stop what they're doing. Remember, however, that if you're asking them to become engaged in a problem in any depth, simply clapping your hands and asking them to stop what they're doing can be quite destructive. You need at least two different signals:

1. One that indicates *stop* at once (something's going very wrong and you need to draw everyone's attention to it).
2. One that effectively says stop what you're doing and come over here when your concentration is wavering.

The signal for (1) could be clapping your hands or banging a drum or tambourine. I prefer to use a set of Indian bells – very small cymbals which produce a quiet but high pitched and very pure note which can be heard above all sorts of other noise. (See also 'Games and exercises' in Chapter 3, where the use of Indian bells (p. 49) is described in another context.)

For (2), simply sitting in a chair can be very effective. 'When you notice that I'm sitting here it means I want you to stop what you're doing and come round.' This may sound rather wishy-washy, but it can be extremely effective. The hidden message to the children is that you value their engagement in their work. Another way might be to raise your hand – a bit more tiring if some are so engaged in their work that they don't stop what they're doing for a couple of minutes.

Having established the ground rules, explain to the children *how* you will be working – e.g. if you are going to play a role yourself *tell* the children, and tell them what signals you are going to give to indicate that you are going to move into role.

One of the great advantages of working on a drama project, rather than on single, self-contained lessons, is that one can not only choose the duration but also the location of the drama lesson; the work becomes integrative. When the children begin to perceive drama as part of the curriculum and not as something separate they value it more highly.

The child's point of view

If there is a problem try to see it from the child's point of view. *Why* is the child 'playing up', misbehaving or distracting others? Here are some common reasons:

- *Are they themselves distracted?* It is hardly reasonable to expect the children to concentrate on sharing out the last of their emergency rations if the dinner ladies are putting out tables for lunch. Make sure there are as few interruptions to the work as possible. Drama makes difficult demands on the participants. Interruptions are distracting and embarrassing. I once worked with a teacher who was called out *six* times in an hour to deal with comparatively trivial problems (certainly trivial compared with the slaying of the Minotaur). The hidden agenda could easily appear to be that 'our drama is the least important thing in the school'. Maybe the children could make a notice to hang on the hall doors – STRICTLY NO ADMITTANCE EXCEPT TO THESEUS AND ADVISERS (adapted as appropriate, and put up with staff agreement).
- *Do they properly understand what is required?* Think how you would feel if you were asked: 'I'd like you to be slaves in the hold of a sailing ship.' What would you do? Perhaps sit and do nothing at all – or perhaps be revolting? What else could you do if you'd been given no further guidance? Suppose, however, the children have to secretly plan an escape which the crew of the ship are to know nothing about . . .

- *Are they embarrassed by the situation or task in hand?* This may come from the content of the drama or from its organisation. Whilst it is productive to ask boys and girls to work in small groups together, it is often very embarrassing for them to be asked to choose a partner of the opposite gender. Don't let organisational oversight get in the way of the work. Children find it embarrassing to work on something they feel they have outgrown.
- *Do they want to be the centre of attention?* There are some occasions when it is educationally valuable to offer such a child the 'centre-stage' for a while through the drama itself. The class may learn a great deal about tolerance from such a strategy. There will be other times when it may be necessary to ask: 'Do you want to take part in this drama, or not? Are you behaving like that to make people laugh or because it is what you honestly believe to be right.' In most cases asking a child to sit out for a while is sufficient 'discipline' providing the drama is interesting enough to draw them back in.
- *Are they bored?* Perhaps the task in hand is too easily achieved or is pitched at an inappropriate level.
- *Are they unable to tackle the problem?* Perhaps it is beyond their intellectual grasp; or maybe the language it is couched in is too complex.
- *Are they unwilling to tackle the problem?* Maybe it opens emotional wounds. Any teacher is constantly having to make difficult value judgements. Here the key issue is the extent to which the child is likely to benefit by tackling the problem through drama.

If, after taking all this into account, the drama lesson begins to go wrong, it is often a good idea to ask the children to help in analysing why. If this means stopping the lesson, so be it. Do something else. Try not to feel too bound by the timetable. As you gain in confidence you and the children will probably soon find that there is never enough time to do all the things you want to do.

REFLECTION

It is vitally important to create periods of reflection within a drama when the participants can consider what they have achieved as individuals and as a group; when they think about the significance of their work and examine the implications of any decisions they may have taken. Reflection is one of the keys to good control and organisation in the drama session; it is largely through reflection that children learn to value what they are doing.

Reflection can take place in or out of role; during a lesson (as and when important moments arise); at the end of the lesson; in the classroom; immediately before the lesson.

Ideally reflection will:

• raise the status of the children's contributions
• draw significance from the work
• help the children understand the meanings in their work, and how they have used dramatic forms to create those meanings
• move the drama forward – both in terms of the narrative and the quality of learning.

Reflection is often thought of as a backward looking process. There is certainly value in this but if the reflection also contains the seeds of future action then it is even more useful.

The reflective process often involves work in other curriculum areas, be it discussion, writing, artwork, computer programming. The most useful activities are those which stimulate children into thinking dynamically and constructively about what they have been doing.

Examples:

Consider the following:

• a painting of a giant
• a sailor's personal log
• a letter to a friend left behind after a move.

Each of these could be usefully used to reflect on what has occurred in the drama. But the reflection is likely to be more interesting and more challenging if the activity looks *forward* as well as over the shoulder, as it were.

1. The painting of the giant could become a picture which is going to be used to show a sceptical researcher (the teacher in role?) how big the giant really is – necessarily demanding that the child thinks about the concept of scale.
2. The sailor's personal log might not only record what has happened on the journey so far, it might also speculate about what the crew should do with the merman they've caught in their nets; it might contain thoughts about food and the way it is stored on board ship; it might suggest new ways of storing food.
3. The letter to a friend left behind after a move could contain thoughts about the way the family have been treated by immigration officials; the really interesting letter would not just recount memories, but also hint at the dreams and fears, the expectations and terrors of what lies ahead.

Discussion

The most obvious way for the teacher to initiate reflection with the whole class is to discuss the work. Such discussion should include thoughts about the *form* of the drama and its *content*.

If the children are going to develop skills in drama, time must be given to consider the way language and space have been used.

Examples

1. The teacher has been playing the Pied Piper, the children a group from Hamelin negotiating for the release of the children – 'How would you describe the way the Pied Piper spoke to you? Where was he looking? Did that make it easy for you to talk to him? I wonder how he would have responded if you hadn't been so angry/polite/upset by the loss of your children?'

Wondering is a very useful skill in drama.

2. The teacher, in role as a Roman Centurion, arrives in Nazareth to give the decree that everybody has to return to 'their own town'; the children as the citizens of Nazareth. The teacher steps out of role and asks the children a question:

Teacher: What is your private reaction to that? What are you thinking that you would not want anyone else in the town to hear?

Whatever the response, the teacher can add a further reflection, which could support or challenge the pupil, and in some cases move the drama on.

Pupil: I'm glad; Nazareth gets very dull.
Teacher: Nazareth is a small town, isn't it. And going back to somewhere you have not been since you were a baby could be very exciting. I wonder what you expect to find when you get there?

or

Pupil: I don't want to leave; my son died a year ago. I want to be able to go to his grave on the day of his death.
Teacher: And it's important to mark those anniversaries. I can see the journey may well be difficult for you. I wonder how the rest of us could help this woman?

It is in the nature of the work that we often ask children to make difficult decisions in drama; if the class are finding the process difficult it is well worth reflecting publicly on that: 'I can't imagine anyone would find a decision like this easy.' Sometimes it may be appropriate to support the child who appears to be being facetious: 'People often laugh when things are really difficult – maybe it would help us make the decision if we did something quite different for a little while.' Or: 'Making the decision does *seem* to be easy sometimes. We could just toss a coin. It's living with the consequences that's difficult.'

The teacher can help the children reflect by focusing the discussion or task in hand, or s/he can create opportunities for the children to consider their work for themselves.

Sometimes we need to reflect publicly, sometimes to provide space for a few moments of private reflection – this might mean the children sit quietly alone while the teacher asks questions which they respond to in their thoughts, or the reflection might take the form of a diary, or perhaps an 'emotional map' charting the highs and lows of a journey/adventure/exploration.

Showing or sharing work always contains possibilities for reflection. If a small group has shown its work, try to encourage discussion in terms of *meaning*, rather than by judging it. If, for example, a shy child has been very quiet in what is supposed to be a television interview, a positive way of dealing with it is to acknowledge it as something that has happened within the dramatic fiction: 'Most of us would get very nervous being interviewed for TV; I know I would. What can the TV crew do to make the situation less frightening?' Much better than booming out in an intimidating voice, 'We can't hear you!'

Still Image

The technique of creating *still images* (described in detail in Chapter 3) is very useful as a means of encouraging reflection. At the end of a drama session the children can be asked to consider the most important moments in the drama and create (say) three images or 'photographs' of those moments. The activity itself encourages reflection; the children are thinking back over what has happened and making important decisions in selecting the key moments.

If the drama continues from week to week it might be a good idea to adopt a similar strategy at the beginning of each session – a more active way of recapping 'the story so far' than through general discussion. Still image also allows you to slow the drama down and think about a situation from another's point of view. Look at the image which another group has created: what is each person thinking? And what might be the implications of those thoughts?

Children often play in role. One of the key differences between this type of play and educational drama is that the latter is specifically structured so as to create learning opportunities. Much of the learning that takes place in drama does so in periods of reflection when we are given time to consider our actions. That is why it is wholly inadequate to describe drama as 'learning through action' – in drama we learn through thinking in new ways about actions and about decisions we would not otherwise have the opportunity to take. And that is also why finding time for reflection is vital to good control. But the quality of the reflection is very dependent on the questioning skills of the teacher.

QUESTIONING SKILLS

By now it will hopefully have become evident that it is more important for the drama teacher to develop questioning skills than to have an armoury of clever ideas. It's the children's ideas we should be interested in, not our own. A skilful teacher uses questioning:

- to draw ideas from the class
- to introduce decision-making processes
- to provoke and encourage children in their use of language
- to draw reticent children into the drama
- to encourage reflection
- to enable feelings and thoughts to be articulated
- to develop skills of analysis and interpretation
- to consolidate learning
- to build tension
- to encourage research
- to create a focus for the drama.

A well-constructed drama session will also create opportunities for children to develop their own questioning skills.

The key organising question

A playwright once responded to someone who asked him about the message of his play that when he wanted to send messages he did so by telegram. It's far more useful to think about plays in terms of the questions they ask us than what they tell us. Macbeth, for example, asks us some very difficult questions about (amongst other things) the relationship between power and sexuality, about acquiescence in the face of evil and turning a blind eye to things we'd rather not know about. Different interpreters see these questions differently, which is why there can be so many different productions of the same play. But by formulating the central questions (sometimes subconsciously) the production is made coherent and given a focus.

Exactly the same is true of educational drama. Good theatre asks difficult questions; so too should our drama work. When a playwright embarks on a new play, the starting point is frequently 'What if?' The questions matter, more than the answers.

The concept of the 'key organising question', or the 'unanswered question', is very helpful both at the planning stage and during the project itself. It allows you flexibility while giving the work a strong sense of purpose and direction. Here are some examples of useful 'key organising questions':

- How can we persuade the Giant to leave us in peace? ('The Giant Awakes', Chapter 5.)
- At what point do group loyalties come into conflict with personal/family loyalties?
- How can we deal with bullying without resorting to violence ourselves?

Sometimes (as in the first example) we need to ask the question directly. There will be times (as in the second example) when it's more useful to keep the question at the back of your mind; asking it directly might be too intimidating.

Types of questions

There are many ways of categorising questions. As with most things in drama, there are many questions which slip between categories, but the attempt to define types of questions is useful if it helps us see more clearly what we are doing and what we could be doing.

Open and closed questions

This is perhaps the simplest classification – but beware the simplistic notion that links open with good and closed with bad.

Closed questions are sometimes perceived to be those which can only elicit a 'Yes' or 'No' response. The received wisdom is that they are not very productive in drama, where we're trying to open up possible responses. There are, however, times when closed questions are very useful. What is crucially important is that you, the teacher, should be aware of the type of question you're asking. The real problems come when you think you're asking an open questior which is in fact closed; and, worse, when you think you're asking an open question which is actually a 'Guess what's in teacher's head question?'

Branching questions 'Do we accept the coming of the railway, or do we resist?' – are closed questions. (Eventually the railway is either built or it's not.) Such questions are particularly useful when the social health of the group is poor, when the group is very unused to being given responsibility, when you want to draw individuals into the decision-making process, perhaps because they are mischievous or nervous. An open question, such as – 'How should we deal with this man who's come to do a survey for the railway company?' – can be very intimidating.

The better the social health of the group, the more open our questions can be. In the meantime, closed questions can start us on the path to fuller negotiation. When children have seen that their decisions, however small, affect the course of the drama their self-esteem rises enormously.

There are children so painfully shy that they find it difficult to voice publicly 'Yes' or 'No'. If you ask such a child 'How should we respond to the aliens' request for help?' s/he's not likely to respond very articulately. Narrow the possible terms of response by a branching question: 'I understand just how difficult this decision is, but you're the bio-chemist; I don't think any of us can make the decision. Should we allow the alien to come on board the ship?' The child is going to feel pressured, certainly, but it's my experience that after the decision has been made (maybe simply a nod or shake of the head) the child seems to grow almost visibly. Their decision has been crucial to the subsequent direction of the drama.

Questions for clarification

In many school situations teachers use questioning to check up on how much children have taken in. In drama there is rarely a single right answer, and it's often more appropriate to phrase questions so that it is the teacher who does not know, the children who do the clarification:

- Am I right in thinking . . .?
- Now, can I get this clear in my head . . .?

Questions that simultaneously convey information and demand a response

Consider what information is fed into the drama by each of the following:

- Without guns, how will we defend ourselves?
- Where can we find a map of the caves?
- What makes this particular tree so special?

Questions that suggest implications

Don't ask questions to which you don't want an answer! If you ask 'What should we do now that there's a reward been offered for our arrest?' you should be prepared to accept the response: 'Find whoever put up the poster and kill them.' You may ask further questions which suggest implications, but if you don't want to deal with the implications you shouldn't have asked the question in the first place.

Consider the implications of:

* Do we really want to know who put up the poster?
* Who'll do the killing, then?
* And will that put an end to the offer of a reward?

Questions that build tension

* Can I trust all of you to keep this secret?
* Is this bridge still strong enough to carry us all?
* What will happen if we fail?
* Just how dangerous is this giant?

Consider the other questions in this section and note how many of them also build tension.

Questions which seek information and/or stimulate research

Consider the wide variety of research opportunities (in role and out of role) which are created by the following:

* What do we have in our homes today that you think people didn't have a hundred and fifty years ago?
* How many people use the corner shop regularly?
* I wonder what really causes a plague of rats?
* What can we do about these bacteria then?
* What equipment should we take with us on our expedition?

Questions which encourage deductive reasoning

Consider what children might actually be required to do in response to each of the following:

* Why do you think the giant has come to our town?
* What evidence do we have that the alien means us no harm?
* What makes you think that the smugglers were never caught?
* What gives you the feeling that we'll be safe here?

Questions which lead to decision-making

* Sometimes these are closed, branching questions (as above): 'Should we leave the spaceship unguarded?'

- Sometimes they are much more open: 'What should we do about . . .?

Questions that are *too* open – 'Well, what do we do now?' – make considerable demands on the group socially as well as dramatically.

General skills related to questioning

- Be prepared to wait. If there is a silence don't jump in. Give the children time, a chance to respond.
- When you ask the whole group questions, give careful thought in advance to how you are going to deal with a flurry of waving hands and shouted answers.

Developing questioning skills for the teacher

The following activities are designed as skill-building and awareness-raising exercises to be used by groups of teachers:

- Play the 'Yes', 'No' game. One minute of questioning (in pairs, small groups or as a whole group) to try to make someone say 'Yes' or 'No'.
- Working with a partner, *A* asks *B* open questions, which B tries to answer as briefly as possible. How do you get them to open up? What sort of questions? How do you listen?
- *A* asks *B* closed questions, which B tries to answer as expansively as possible.
- Working initially in pairs and then in groups, pursue the question: 'What would you like to do a drama about?', seeking to find a *dramatic starting point* which stems from the interviewees' interests.
- Be curious! Develop the skill of wondering, of asking 'What if?'

The book *Teaching Drama*[1] has a good chapter on questioning that includes a number of useful skill-building exercises for teachers.

Developing questioning skills in children

There are particular roles that children can play which themselves encourage the use of questions:

- the detective
- the investigator
- the reporter (TV, radio, newspaper)

- the interviewer
- the researcher.

Use the strategy of teacher in role to create a character who is mysterious or enigmatic; then give groups the opportunity to question the role to find out more. In small groups they can decide in advance on the questions they want to ask. It's often productive to limit the number of questions allowed to each group. This encourages them to listen to the responses and to each other.

When sharing still image or small group work, instead of asking for comments about what's been seen, ask children to formulate questions about it. This is a very useful strategy in developing performance drama. The questions which are asked about a still image tell us a great deal about the narrative interest in that image. For example, an image is presented of one child threatening another. A comment about this might be – 'It's about bullying.' The responses to 'What questions do you want to ask here?' might range from 'What happens next?' through 'What has he done to deserve this?' and 'What can he do about it?' to 'They're both looking in this direction. What have they seen?'

NARRATIVE: DRAMATIC STRUCTURE AND DRAMATIC TENSION

Dramatic structure and tension

Throughout this chapter I have argued that the most productive way of maintaining good control is through the content of the drama itself. As in all teaching, if you can 'hook' the children, interesting them in the subject matter, you are less likely to encounter disruptive behaviour.

In drama we have a great advantage over other subjects in that non-verbal language and narrative are at the centre of our work. We can use the power of narrative to intrigue and draw children into the work at the same time as teaching them about narrative; teaching them how to manipulate it for themselves.

Ask a class to shut their eyes, play them a recording of footsteps and then ask what they have heard. Some children might say 'the sound of footsteps', but others will begin constructing a story – a prisoner being taken to his cell, perhaps, Mum or Dad coming upstairs to say goodnight or a murderer walking along the landing. We tend to want things explained, and stories (for the most part) create meanings for us. Play another sound effect – perhaps a door opening, keys jangling, a car moving off, a bomb exploding, or a dog barking – and it becomes difficult not to link the two sounds together and make them part of the same story.

However little 'plot' there might be in some of our dramas, there is always narrative of some kind; a series of events or incidents in which the sequence itself is meaningful. We should *use* narrative and dramatic tension to structure our work in such a way that it draws the children in, but we should also create opportunities to teach *about* narrative.

At whatever level we are working (be it with children in their first years in school, or with adults) the first engagement with the work comes through dramatic tension of some kind. The teacher should plan carefully first to create dramatic tension, and then to use it productively.

Let's first examine how we can generate and use dramatic tension, and then look at how we might teach narrative.

At its most basic level dramatic tension originates in the questions the participants are being encouraged to ask themselves:

- What's going on here?
- What's going to happen?
- We know something's going to happen, but *when*?
- How did things get to be like this?

Dramatic tension, and indeed drama itself, is frequently associated with confrontation. But it is not confrontation itself which creates the tension in dramatic terms. It creates the *possibility* of tension. The argument between two children which runs:

Tom: You stole my packet of crisps.
Jane: No I didn't.
Tom: Yes you did.
Jane: No I didn't

is certainly confrontational but it's of little interest dramatically. It becomes interesting when it seems that Jane might hit Tom, or when one of them stops for a moment and thinks. We don't know what's going to happen next – which is what makes it dramatic.

Confrontation only creates the possibility for drama when it raises the possibility of *change*. It is change, or at least the *potential* for change, which underpins any consideration of dramatic structure.

In most dramas we start (however briefly) with a *stable* situation:

- The prisoners of war in the prison camp.
- The smugglers who regularly bring their booty ashore.
- The islanders whose way of life has been unchallenged.
- The giant who has been buried under the ground for hundreds of years.

- The children who go to and from school every day.

That stable situation is then made unstable:

- Somebody proposes a breakout.
- The smugglers hear of a large reward for their capture.
- A terrible storm comes to the island and a whale beaches on the shore.
- The giant awakes.
- The children discover a great hole in the ground.

The instability of this new situation has to be acknowledged and built on. In other dramatic forms this is the job of the writer, director and actors. In educational drama it is up to the teacher to create and build the tension. To do so we make use of theatrical structures, which are built on contrasts; the contrasts between

- light and darkness
- sound and silence
- movement and stillness.

In this way we ensure that the pace of the drama lesson doesn't remain constant. There will be times when things are happening quickly, and times when everyone is hushed and expectant and everything hinges on a symbolic gesture.

We create suspense, mystery, an air of intrigue. One of the best ways of doing this is to take children into our confidence. We use the power of secrecy and confidentiality.

Above all *don't avoid the drama*. Don't be frightened of being dramatic. This doesn't mean putting on silly voices; but, rather, allowing those confrontations that are likely to create possibilities for change in the dramatic situation, that of themselves create difficult dilemmas.

We can create dramatic tension by building up expectations. The islanders who have heard on the radio (a pre-recorded tape cassette?) that a hurricane is heading their way. They know it is coming, but they don't know when. A similar device can be used by the teacher out of role: 'Something big is going to happen in the drama, I promise you, but I'm not going to tell you what it is until it happens.'

Tension is also created when we expect one thing, and something else, quite different, occurs.

Here, as elsewhere, we can learn by watching the way tension is raised in theatre, TV drama and films.

Teaching narrative

At its simplest we are looking at a sequence of events. When we change the order in which things happen, it changes the meaning of the story. This apparently simple concept of cause and effect will be at the root of much of our early work on narrative in drama. In drama children make decisions, and then they see the consequences of those decisions. This is another good reason for not pre-planning the outcome of decisions in drama; why it is good to work on the 'back story' but not to plan the outcome. If we set up tasks which ask children to plan what happens at the end of their plays, we not only eradicate the tension, but also lose considerable learning opportunities.

Example: Difficult decisions and their consequences

A year six class is working on a drama about undersea exploration. They have decided to go to Italy, where they have heard that there is the wreck of a Roman Galley. (Some useful Geography and History work in this.)

They prepare for the expedition, making lists of equipment and supplies, passports, negotiating to hire an appropriate boat (Maths as well – they'll have to calculate the costs involved – and Science). When they get to Italy the teacher decides it's all a bit cosy: there's a lot of good work going on in other curriculum areas, and the children are enjoying it, but where's the drama?! There's been nothing very dramatic since the secretive and highly confidential opening, when the teacher started with: 'I've been told about the wreck of a Roman Galley, which is buried in mud off the coast near Pompeii; and it's said that when it sank it was carrying great chests of treasure from Egypt.'

So the teacher decides to present a challenge. Taking on the role of an Italian customs officer, she comes on board ship and tells the children that the authorities know about their activities. They will be able to keep half of all the treasure they find (unrealistically generous, certainly) but it will all have to be declared.

The children are asked to decide what to do. Or are they? What if they say 'We'll kill the customs officer.' There's a strong temptation to tell them that they can't do that. But this is in a school where a high proportion of the children know people and have relatives who have been (or currently are) in prison.

Killing the customs officer is morally wrong, of course. But if we deny that as a possible choice to the children, we *tell* them it's wrong (which they are very used to) but we withhold from them a dramatic experience which, if handled carefully, would allow them to understand the morality of the situation. Allowing them to make such a decision does not sanction it – far from it. If they decide to kill the customs officer we'll take our time over it, we'll make it very difficult and very unglamorous. In the drama they will have to confront the isolation that comes from being outside the protection of the law. They may be asked to change role, and be a colleague of the officer informing her husband and family what has happened.

Don't avoid the drama. Seek it out. Drama gives us the safety to make bad decisions and time to think about them constructively.

A similar situation occurs in 'The Island' drama documented in Chapter 2, and in the Civil War drama 'The Deserter' documented in Chapter 5.

THE DRAMATIC FRAME

When planning and organising the narrative structure of our drama lessons we are essentially thinking about a sequencing of events. As we're doing this we should also consider the point of view from which those events are seen.

In real life we see the world through our own eyes. Much though we might sometimes like it to be otherwise, events unfold as they happen. Moments which we would like to savour disappear in a flash and moments which embarrass us seem interminable. But drama is not real life.

- In drama we act as if we were someone else, or as if we were ourselves in an *other* situation. In other words we see the world through another's eyes.
- In drama we can slow down time, we can stop and examine a particular moment, we can go backwards in time. If we are in a drama which moves forward at 'lifespeed' it is because we have chosen to do so.

These things are just as true of educational drama as they are of traditional theatre forms.

It is this manipulation of time and viewpoint which enables us to choose an appropriate *frame* through which to explore our dramatic situations. Thus we can examine any given sequence of events dramatically by seeing these events through different eyes, or we can look at the same events from a distance by framing our drama as an investigation or an enquiry: we, the participants in the drama, could be townspeople celebrating the history of our town, creating a pageant.

Example: Smuggling, various dramatic frames

Let's return to the smuggling example discussed in Chapter 2, 'Starting out'. Several examples of possible frames were suggested there. Here are some further examples. There is nothing absolute about the headings suggested. The court, the enquiry and the investigation are in many ways similar, and all will include elements of reconstruction. The intention in suggesting them is to stimulate further thought about other possible frames.

Continued

Example continued

First, look again at the Smuggling poster reproduced on p. 22, then consider the following possibilities:

The adventure story

Time – 1782
We are smugglers. One of us (the teacher in role?) has seen the reward poster . . .

Time – 1782
We are townspeople, knowing that smugglers use caves in the nearby cliffs. We want to stop the smuggling and claim the reward, but one of us (teacher?) is worried . . .

Time – the present
The teacher needs the children's help to find the smuggler's treasure which is rumoured to be hidden in a cave which is very difficult to reach. If we find the treasure, what is it? What should we do with it? To whom does it rightfully belong?

Time – the present
We are a group of divers undertaking an exploration of the Cornish coast, trying to find the wreck of the ship pictured in the Smuggling poster. What equipment do we need?

The reconstruction

Time – the present
The events of 1782 are reconstructed (and acted out in small groups) from letters, maps, pictures, posters, historical documents. This could be for a *television documentary* about the town or for a *town pageant*.

The Investigation or Enquiry

Time – 1787: (five years after the poster is displayed)
Three customs and excise officers have 'disappeared'; we are trying to find out what has happened to them.

The Court

Time – 1792: (ten years after the poster was first published)
Several villagers are in court, accused of aiding and abetting the smugglers. Is there a difference between the evidence given in court and what really happened?

Drama teachers have as much to learn from playwrights and screenwriters as they do from other drama teachers. Think of popular films such as *ET, Ghostbusters, Close Encounters of the Third Kind, Ghost*. There had been numerous movies about ghosts and aliens before these. *One* of the many things which made them successful was the particular dramatic *frame* they used. TV and film producers are notorious for asking 'What's the angle?' If it's true, as is often suggested, that there are no new stories, then one of the things that makes a piece of drama original is the angle – or the frame.

The chapters on *working with children in the early years* (Part Three), and on *planning* (in Part Five), give further suggestions about finding an appropriate frame. Chapter 7 also contains two alternative storyboards of the Pied Piper story, one from the point of view of the Piper one from a Hamelin family.

NON-VERBAL LANGUAGE: USE OF SPACE; SYMBOL

Non-verbal language – the use of space, gesture, facial expression, the understanding of symbol – is a vitally important part of drama to which we have to give careful attention if we are going to develop our work.

Use of space

In any drama session we need to consider:

1. how we're going to organise our use of space, and
2. how we are going to encourage the children to manipulate the dramatic form so that they, too, can use space intelligently and articulately.

We should try to see space itself as something which can be made as articulate as verbal language. We should try to make it a significant factor in the dramas we create. This is just as true of whole group dramas in which we might be working in role alongside the children as in small group work or performance based work.

Consider the different ways in which the organisation and use of *space* becomes part of the language of drama:

- How do we make the distance between people meaningful?
  How close? How far apart?
- Movement in space.
  Consider these contrasting types of body movement:
  fast   –   slow/static
  strong   –   weak
  heavy   –   light
  smooth   –   jagged
- Eye contact and eye movement.
  Who looks at whom?
  Who avoids eye contact, and why?
  How do people communicate across space without words?

- How do people relate to what is in the space around them?
  What does this tell us about them?
- Working at different levels.
  How do levels affect our perception of relationships?
- What can the 'audience' see?
  What are they prevented from seeing?
  What effect does this have on narrative?
  If something or someone is deliberately hidden from us what does this lead us to expect?
- How do we organise the space in which the drama takes place?
  How do we *represent* the zoo, ship, town, pet shop or mayor's office?

Once we start developing awareness of the use of space as part of the *language of drama* we are teaching theatre skills. It's worrying how many excellent drama teachers have been troubled by the idea that they might be teaching theatre skills as an integral part of their non-performance work. But we shouldn't be frightened of it. The language of educational drama and the language of theatre are the same. So it should come as no surprise that we can teach children to manipulate this theatrical language by the same *variety* of means as we can teach other aspects of drama; using the whole gamut of strategies (working in role or out of role, with small or large groups, using forum theatre, still images, games and exercises).

The organisation of space

Whether working in small or large groups, encourage the children to think what the space they are working in represents.

How do we translate our two-dimensional maps into three-dimensional drama space? We can use chalk, string, rope, cloth or benches to partition the space – so that different areas in the school hall represent different areas in the drama. Perhaps a long blue cloth laid down the middle of the hall represents a river – itself an important boundary. The representation of the river turns into an important symbol when crossing the river becomes highly significant – perhaps doing so will lead us into open conflict with the Abbey who are demanding an increase in tithes . . .

Organisation of space can be as simple as considering carefully how you place a single wooden table and chair – but it is always important.

Forum theatre

- Constructing a character. How do they move? What about their eyes? 'You say you want me to make him seem shifty. How should I do that?'

• Let's replay that scene. What happens if you stay standing up when you confront the Mayor? If you keep your distance?

If you, the teacher, take on the 'obstacle' role you can focus on their use of space/ body language/ eye contact in their attempts to get round the obstacle.

Working in role

• Always consider your own use of space when taking on a role. Think about the levels you're using, the body language, the use of eye contact and movement. When you come out of role to reflect on what's been going on your questions might include: 'What led you to believe the carpenter was nervous/hiding something from us?'
• When using those dramatic frames which require children to prepare and then share small group work (e.g. the investigation, the pageant, the making of a documentary) take the opportunity to question or comment on their use of space:

  • 'I wonder why the council official wouldn't look at the interviewer?'
  • 'The old man looked rather frightened by the TV crew. I wonder if that's why he didn't have much to say?'
  • 'Did you notice how they always kept their distance from each other?'

• When the class are getting ready to take action:
  'You say that you want to convince the Giant you're friendly. How close should we get to him?'

Discussing small group work out of role

When children discuss each other's work out of role it tends to be along the lines of 'The door opened different ways, Miss' or 'You just walked through the table.' Try to focus on the positive, on what a scene *did* achieve rather than what it didn't; give them a vocabulary for talking about the work. Ask the audience about the *effect* of specific aspects of the scene – eye contact, use of levels, distance between people etc.

Using *still images* makes it much easier to initiate discussion of the organisation and use of space: the constraints of the task allow us to focus on specifics; the stillness makes the work much more open to inspection.

The use of games to develop articulate use of space

Certain games can be used to raise spatial awareness – preferably not as an end in themselves, but to lead into some sort of drama work. Here are a couple of examples:

1.   Standing behind – or Watch your backs

Agree on a signal to indicate 'Freeze'.

'Everybody move around without touching anyone and not letting anyone else get near you. When you hear the signal, freeze. If anyone is less than a metre behind you, you lose a point; if you are less than a metre behind anyone else, you gain a point.'

2.   Hunting the space

Starts as a game of tag, initially in pairs *A* chasing *B*. When *B* is caught, reverse: *B* chases *A*. Then split class into the two groups, *A* and *B*.

Each child in Group *A* chooses someone in group *B*, *without saying who it is*. *A*s are to hunt down their 'prey', but not actually touch them, to get into a position so that when the teacher calls 'Time' (after say thirty seconds) the *A*s can strike. Discuss qualities needed to do it well – stealth, speed, pretending to look at someone other than your 'prey'.

A variation is for everybody to hunt an imaginary prey: 'Wait for a space to become empty, move into it quickly, wait, stalk the space . . .'

The spatial relationship between performers and audience is discussed in detail in Part Four.

Symbol

Symbol is part of the language of drama: 'The way in which the teacher draws attention to the symbol (gesture, word, object etc.) generates a collective meaning and also gives time and opportunity for the participant to endow that symbol with his or her individual meaning.'[2]

It is when actions and images begin to become symbolic, or at least contain symbolic resonance, that drama becomes really 'tingly' – both for teacher and children. And it's when the drama becomes 'tingly' that we know our organisation is working well; that we're beginning to get things right intuitively.

While it's not a good idea to overload a drama with symbolism, it's well worth keeping any eye open for possibilities, both in the planning stage and while the drama's underway.

Objects

Consider the different ways we can use a *key*:

- to open doors or containers or gates that have long been locked:
  'Are you sure you want to do this? We may find things that are best kept locked away.'
- to lock doors or a container:
  'Have we got all his things out of the house?'
- throwing the key away:
  'This really will mean no going back.'
- transferring ownership:
  'It's yours now. That's a great deal of responsibility.'

A *cloak* can be used:

- to conceal identity or diguise
- to give warmth and protection
- to assume or transfer power.

A *loaf or a crust of bread* can:

- be divided between everybody
- be snatched
- become part of a ceremony, or a ritual.

An *empty bowl* can:

- signify hunger and poverty
- be a gift from a skilled craftsperson.

A *rope* can:

- be what binds us all together as we make our journey through the secret caves
- be used to create a *Time Line*, whereby we create a visual representation of someone's life history on the floor of the school hall – perhaps with still images at various points, or carefully chosen objects to remind us of particularly significant moments in a person's life.

Actions

Delivering a letter can be both a very ordinary action and one which is rich in symbolic significance, providing the context is appropriate and the teacher draws out the meaning.

Example

An old man (the teacher in role) is refusing to sell his house to the railway company; everybody else in the town is keen for the railway to come through – and if he doesn't sell, the company will choose an alternative route. The Council (of children) has agreed to effect a compulsory purchase. (Chapter 5, 'Construction of a railway').

The class can simply tell him he has to go, but the moment of eviction is potentially highly charged and to let it slip by is to waste opportunities. If the council choose someone to act as bailiff, the act of serving the eviction order on the old man (in effect *delivering a letter*) becomes a highly charged dramatic moment. Because it carries deep symbolic resonance it will be memorable, dramatic and open up rich opportunities for discussion.

Consider how the following actions are both 'ordinary', and symbolic:

- Giving someone a mug of water.
  Suppose that person is a stranger and is very weak.
  Do they carry the plague?
- Tearing up a letter.
  Suppose we are US Cavalry and the letters contain orders to attack a Native American village.
  'It's easy to tear up the letter. It's what happens now that worries me.'
- Taking down a poster.
  Suppose it offers a large reward for someone's arrest.

Consider what *context* would give the following actions symbolic resonance:

- using a talking stick or talisman
- crossing a threshold
- turning off a radio
- knocking down a wooden post.

Think of at least two different contexts in which the use of each of the following might become symbolic:

- a book
- a goblet
- a photograph
- a necklace
- a fob watch
- a dried flower.

COLLABORATIVE TEACHING

Whether we're working on drama as a subject in its own right, developing a school play or using drama as a means of focusing and enhancing work in other curriculum areas, working with other adults is potentially very rewarding.

At a time when the school curriculum is becoming increasingly prescriptive, when there seems less flexibility than there used to be, it might seem difficult to set up collaborative teaching projects. But it is far from impossible. It's surprising how many people are keen to come and work with us, who are fascinated by what we do in drama. Providing we don't intimidate them, *collaborative teaching* can be a very productive way of convincing people of the value of drama.

The benefits

Collaborative teaching in drama:

- enables us to work from individual strengths, to develop skills, to learn from each other
- can give us more hall time, and/or more flexible use of spaces appropriate for teaching drama
- is a way of encouraging colleagues to start teaching drama
- makes it easier to develop inter-curricular projects because of increased flexibility
- is a way of demonstrating to parents both the methodology of drama and the value of it; it's a way of getting parents to argue for a greater emphasis on drama in the school.

The people

With whom do we collaborate?

In short, anybody! The most obvious people to approach are one's colleagues. But I have seen many examples of excellent practice involving collaboration between teacher(s) and student(s), teacher(s) and parent(s), teacher and auxiliary assistant(s), amongst others.

Working with experienced colleagues

If you're going to work with one or more colleagues who have some experience of drama, the experience can be very rewarding for both of you. The following become possible:

1. *A* in role, *B* out of role, focusing the children on aspects of the

role, constructing the role with the children. If one adult is in role and another remains out of role the roles adopted can be pushed farther; it is easier to take on very challenging Devil's Advocate roles. There's an additional safety net for children, in that they can see the function of the role more clearly through the responses of other adults.

2. *A* and *B* in role. If two adults are playing roles they can adopt quite a confrontational stance, challenging the children to act as mediators. This demands that one or both adults regularly move out of role in order to reflect on what is going on. *But* . . .

3. . . . if there are three adults working together, *A* and *B* can stay in role, *C* stays out of role, is able to focus the attention of the children, to reflect and summarise with them, and to give colleagues useful feedback both on the drama itself and on teaching techniques.

4. A greater variety of small group work becomes possible. A single small group can work on drama with one teacher whilst others get on with other (related) work. For example *A* can remove a small group and prepare them as journalists for interviewing other members of the class, who will in the meantime be making a detailed map of the area showing where the new relief road is going to go.

5. Splitting the class into two or more working groups – still united by a common fiction. When you're working on your own it is dangerous to allow the class to split when branching decisions have to be made: it creates considerable organisational problems and diffuses the drama because of the split focus. With two or more teachers working together this becomes much more productive. If (for example) the overall project begins in the potato famine in Ireland in the nineteenth Century, *A* can work with the group emigrating to America, while *B* works with those who choose to remain in Ireland.

6. *Forum theatre* with two teachers taking on roles and children in two groups as advisers. This might be a way of introducing teaching-in-role.

In an ideal world it would be wonderful to have two or three experienced teachers working together with one class. It's certainly possible to work with drama students in this way, although it's very important to be fair and clear about what you're asking them to do. But in most situations, when you'd be asking a colleague on the same staff to work with you, you'll need to find a way of working that is not going to cause massive disruption to the school timetable, that's not going to demand that the headteacher come and cover one of your classes while you're busy with your investigation into the disappearance of the crew of the *Marie Celeste*.

One solution to this problem is for two or more classes to collaborate on a project. Careful planning is necessary. The following are two ways for different classes to collaborate.

A collaborative teaching project culminating in two classes working together in the hall

The two classes work separately for (say) three weeks, and then come together in the hall in the fourth week. Each class needs to take a group identity. The planning will need to take account of the fact that the groups should come together at a later stage. It's also very useful to build in to the planning a mutual need – or else any conflicts which arise when the two groups do come together may be impossible to resolve.

Example:

A 'Space' drama in which each class takes on the roles of the inhabitants of different planets, each of which is in trouble. Perhaps the first (Caloria) is suffering from global warming and the second (Frigorix) is entering an ice age. Both groups need to leave and are intending to settle on a previously uninhabited planet. The two classes can send each other messages (in code if needs be, written, on audiotape or on video) and perhaps send small advance parties to the other world prior to meeting in the hall – which would signify the arrival of both groups on the 'New World'.

It would be advisable to build in at the planning stage something which would create a need for co-operation on the new planet. The following diagram should illustrate through a simplified example:

Inhabitants of Caloria	*Inhabitants of Frigorix*
Good at fishing	Grow crops
Reliant on fossil fuels	Use solar power for all machinery

When they get to the new planet, Terra Nova, they find that the fish are abundant, but the soil won't support crops; although the sun shines, there are no fossil fuels – so if the groups are going to survive they will need to share their technology and skills.

This type of collaboration can work well with different age groups. I have worked on a drama project in which Year Seven children were the Argonauts (without Jason!) and Year Three children developed a Greek island community. When the groups came together it was because in the fiction the Argonauts were landing and desperately needed food and shelter – which the younger children enormously enjoyed providing. In their turn they wanted the Argonauts to tell them stories of their journeys.

Although there can never be any guarantees, it is frequently the case that older children enjoy working with younger ones, enjoy the responsibility they are being given, and behave much better than they do when they are working on their own.

The performance project, 'The Donkeyman's Daughter', documented in Part Four, is another example of this kind of collaborative teaching in action.

Collaborative teaching in separate classrooms

Two, three, or more teachers jointly plan a project in which their classes work independently of each other, but produce material which another class can use in their own drama. They leave something behind, as it were, for the other class(es). The sort of material which might be produced, for example, could be:

1. *Documentation* • a census return, advertisements,
   • a page from a ship's log.
2. *Letters*   found in the attic of an old house.
3. *Maps*   of the journey in search of a dragon.
4. *Videotapes* • messages from spaceship to spaceship,
   • interviews with residents troubled by new building developments.
5. *Audio tapes* • weather forecasts (warning islanders or people on board ship of a storm).
6. *Information on a computer disc*
   • a database giving details of the crew of a spaceship,
   • or a message transmitted through space from the crew to settlers on a distant planet.

This sort of work frequently benefits from being set up to create a triangle, so that each group has some relationship with the other two, each group needs and services the other two. If the situation is basically stable, the drama then begins when something occurs which has the potential to destabilise it.

Here is a more down to earth example than the ones suggested above: the drama is set in contemporary Britain, in a small rural area by the coast.

• Class *A* are on an area of farmland. Some of the class are farmers. The land includes a caravan site and an inn.
• Class *B* live in a small town nearby. Some work in a hotel, some

make their living from the sea, maybe fishing, maybe making boats.

Thus far the situation is stable. Good drama could take place in each of the above groups independently of each other, and each group could interact with the other. But when the third group, Class *C*, is added the situation is destabilised and it becomes inherently dramatic.

Class *C* are a group of entrepreneurs who want to build a leisure park in the area. They are trying to find somewhere suitable or, alternatively, they are trying to make a documentary about the area, having heard that the inn is haunted. (The 'Smuggling' example in the section on 'Starting Points' could be adapted and work in this way.)

Each class working on the project develop their own strand of an interconnected narrative. The material (the letters, the maps, the inventories, etc.) which is produced becomes part of the dramatic fiction.

Collaborating with people who have not had any previous experience of drama

The methods described and examples outlined above demand a certain amount of expertise on the part of the collaborator. But it is possible to work with people who have had no previous experience of teaching or drama.

When working with inexperienced collaborators it is important to brief them carefully, and to use them in simple roles, and perhaps non-speaking roles, for example, as

- a lost child seeking his or her parent
- a friendly giant who cannot speak our language
  (but we have to explain to him/her how dangerous s/he is)
- the alien arrived on earth, not knowing anything about our way of life
- the refugee from a war zone, shocked and unable to explain what has happened

The collaborators can be used to play themselves in the drama. I have worked with a cook, a caretaker, a community policeman, a coach driver and an athletics coach – all of whom greatly enjoyed taking part in our drama and working with the children. Not surprisingly, the children also felt that day's drama to be very special.

Secondary School pupils, especially those studying drama, are often keen to help in Primary Schools. It's well worth approaching the Head of Drama to see if there's anybody interested in coming and doing their work experience with you.

Bibliography

General:

O'Neill, C. and Lambert, A. 1982. *Drama Structures*, Hutchinson.

Questioning

Morgan, N. and Saxton, J. 1987. *Teaching Drama*, Hutchinson. Chapter 4 – Questioning and answering.
O'Neill, C. and Lambert, A. op. cit., pp. 141–2, 157, 165.
Burgess, R. and Gaudry, P. 1986. *Time for Drama*, Open University Press, pp. 130–6.

Dramatic Tension/Structure

British Film Institute. 1988. *Picture Stories*, BFI Education.
O'Neill, C. and Lambert, A. op. cit., *Drama Structures*.

Use of Space

McCaslin, N. 1990. *Creative Drama in the Classroom* (5th edn), Longmans, New York.

Symbol

Morgan, N. and Saxton, J. 1987. *Teaching Drama*, Hutchinson Education, pp. 3–5.
Bolton, G. 1979. *Towards a Theory of Drama in Education*, Longman, pp 76–8.

Collaborative teaching

Fines, J. and Verrier, R. 1974. *The Drama of History*, New University Press.
Woolland, B. 1990. *Collaborative Teaching in Drama*, London *Drama Magazine*, July .

Notes

1. Morgan, N. and Saxton, J. 1987. *Teaching Drama*, Hutchinson pp. 70, 104, 5, contains a further selection of excellent skill building exercises for the teacher.
2. Morgan, N. and Saxton, J. op. cit. p. 5.

Drama and the whole curriculum

This chapter is concerned with using drama as a learning medium, to encourage and motivate learning in other curriculum areas. It contains a number of detailed examples of such work throughout the primary age range.

Examples:

- The Crashed Spaceship
- The Giant Awakes
- The Deserter
- The Iron Age Encampment

A detailed account of an extended cross-curricular drama-based project:

- Construction of a Railway

It is not difficult to see how role play and drama can be used to achieve many of the Attainment Targets for Speaking and Listening in the English National Curriculum documents. What is less obvious is that drama can have a central role in developing children's reading and writing skills, not only in English but also in most other curriculum areas.

Drama can be a powerful force for motivating and enhancing work in every curriculum area. While it takes ingenuity and careful thought it is possible and productive to use drama at the *centre* of the curriculum, rather than as an occasional extra. In this chapter we shall explore how drama can be used alongside other subjects; how it can be used to create and enhance learning opportunities, to stimulate research, and to give cross-curricular coherence. We'll examine in detail the specific possibilities created by writing in role; and then move on to examine specific examples of cross-curricular projects.

TOPIC WORK

All drama has to have content; it has to be *about* something. It is essentially cross-disciplinary. You can't have drama which doesn't refer to other curriculum areas. The fallacy that by using drama as a learning medium we necessarily dilute the drama is exposed by the fact that drama itself is usually greatly enhanced by the work that can accompany it in other curriculum areas. You can use drama without specifically teaching about dramatic forms (although in using drama as a learning medium, you cannot help but make use of dramatic forms), but you can't effectively teach anything about the nature of dramatic forms without some sort of content.

In the early years of schooling, for example, children's activities in the play area frequently include shopping. It would be wasteful not to make use of the children's interest in their dramatic play to do some work on counting.

If the only experience children have of drama is acting out stories that have been read to them, learning opportunities are being missed. In a similar way, simply asking children to draw a picture of what happened in their play is wasting an opportunity to move the drama forward and make the work purposeful: the picture could have an important part to play in the drama, in which case the quality of both the drama and the art work improves. The cross-fertilisation is in itself exciting and highly productive. The commitment to the drama becomes greater, and the work in other curriculum areas is tackled with real purpose.

Many teachers begin to find it difficult to contain their drama to occasional one-off sessions in the hall. Drama lends itself to becoming part of topic work because:

- it effectively gives you the *content* of your drama work
- it brings the topic work to life
- it facilitates continuity within a drama project
- it makes it easier to do drama in other spaces than the school hall.

By linking your drama and your topic work, you can take ten or fifteen minutes at various times during the day to work with small groups. If the whole class is involved in researching a topic – which might include using the computer, browsing through the library, watching a video programme – it becomes easier to supervise the work of one small group (that might, for example, be preparing an interview).

If the narrative of the drama continues from one day to the next, it makes sense to do at least some drama in the classroom most days. If you use *forum theatre*, or interrogate some *still image* presentations, you don't even need to push the desks back. It's possible to use classroom time for discussions and all the out of role preparatory work that greatly strengthens the children's commitment to drama.

The guiding principles in using drama alongside other curriculum areas are that it should:

* give greater purpose and meaning to work both in drama and in the associated curriculum areas
* create an appetite for research of all kinds
* create opportunities for the children to give their work authenticity
* create a context in which the relationship between the different curriculum areas is strengthened.

If the work is to do this it should be interactive, rather than tangential; it should have a clear purpose within the context of the drama. Some of this work will take place in the classroom, some of it during drama time. It can be done out of role – with the information gathered through research, for example, then used to inform the subsequent drama – or it can be undertaken in role.

WRITING IN ROLE

While it is perfectly valid for children to step back from what they have been doing in drama and write about it, the exciting alternative of writing (or drawing, or carrying out scientific experiments) within the context of the drama, as the characters they are playing, produces lively and highly motivated work.

Whenever we are looking at children's writing, it's a high priority to respond to the content, but this can sometimes be difficult; children themselves often become over-anxious about the surface features of their writing and frightened of making mistakes. By making written work (of all kinds – including Maths, Science and Artwork for example) a part of their drama we provide a sort of safety net, a 'No Penalty Zone' in which they can pretend to be someone other than themselves writing their letter, wording their advertisement or drawing up their menu . . . The motivation to write is heightened, and writing of great diversity can be encouraged – including, where appropriate, writing in the child's own language or dialect.

The drama itself also benefits from this approach: writing in role slows the drama down in a very productive fashion, encouraging children to look at a particular situation in much greater depth than they would otherwise.

Three specific projects described in detail exemplify the ways in which writing in role can be encouraged. In each of the following examples I used the technique of 'teacher in role' to challenge the children and focus their work.

Examples

The first two examples below are accounts of work undertaken with reception classes; one in a rural school, one in an inner city multi-racial school; the third is a brief account of a drama with Years Three and Four in a Liverpool school.

The Crashed Spaceship

We begin by talking about their daily routine of coming to school and returning home, which they enact individually and in pairs. I then tell them a story which they act out: one day the children all set off home only to find that a great big hole has opened up in the playground. I ask them to form a circle, as if standing around the hole, and close their eyes.

When I ask them to open their eyes, I am in the middle of the circle, at the bottom of the 'hole', wearing a pair of very dark goggles, clearly in role, but as what? A tense moment! We wait a little and then I step out of role, remove the goggles, and ask them what they think they have seen. The children decide that it is an alien creature. Two children climb down into the hole (having first borrowed a rope ladder!) and try to talk to the creature. I make this a little difficult, creating an opportunity to encourage a shy child to communicate with the alien. She discovers that the alien's space ship has crashed. 'Can you help me find all the pieces?' I ask.

They draw the pieces and label their drawings. Many of the children are not yet able to write in conventional form, but all tackle the task of labelling the bits and pieces of the space ship. The labelling matters; without it they cannot rebuild the alien's spaceship. I am able to respond to their *emergent writing* honestly and give it significance in the drama. 'I can't make this out,' I say (as myself, not the alien), to which several children respond: 'No, that's because it's written in the alien's language.' So the labels now need to be 'translated', and this becomes a collaborative process with children of different abilities working together. One child says his labels are in English, and they can't be read easily because they're in grown-up, joined-up writing!

The work is of a very high standard, with several children who have recently joined the school writing something for the first time.

The Giant Awakes

I begin by telling the children a story about a giant who was very unpopular with all the other giants because he wouldn't eat people or animals. I ask the children what his name might be; they decide on 'Herbert Thunder'. With each of them individually playing Herbert Thunder, they act out the first part of the story: Herbert finds a lonely spot for himself, and there he cries himself to sleep. His tears form rivers. Once he is asleep, he sleeps for a very long time – thousands of years in fact. While he is asleep leaves fall on him and turn into soil.

Continued

Example continued

It's not until 1992 that the giant wakes up and tries to dig his way to the surface. He looks for food. The children act out each of these actions individually. While looking for food they are careful not to eat animals or human beings. I ask them what he might like eating; some suggest eating car tyres and drinking oil. (Interesting echoes of *The Iron Man* here – any drama is likely to contain elements of other stories from home or school; it's good if they are given an opportunity to make these their own.) Herbert heads for a nearby town where, having gorged himself in a garage, he finds his way to an open space and falls asleep.

Up to this point the children have all been acting as the giant. I gather the class and ask if they can play grown-ups. They are keen to do so; and they become the townspeople. I take on the role of the mayor to ask – 'What on earth has been causing all this damage?' The townspeople say it is a giant; but the mayor doesn't believe them. He wants proof – in the form of pictures or photographs that show the size of the giant.

The children draw and paint their representations of the giant – several show the giant beside trees, some next to buildings, one remarkable painting has Herbert with his head in the clouds!

The mayor is convinced, and wonders what they should do next. The townspeople decide to write letters to the giant asking him to leave, reasoning that talking to him directly would be too dangerous. They set about this task with great enthusiasm. The mayor asks them to tell him what has been written because there are several which he cannot read. The children explain that these have been written in the Giant's own language. One child is particularly proud of his work: it contains many letters, large and boldly formed, and this was the first occasion that he had written anything since arriving in the school.

The Deserter

This is a history project, set during the English Revolution (1640–1660). The class takes on the role of a small rural community. After looking at various books and pictures of English rural life they decide what jobs they will have in this community – fishing, farming, milling, etc. In role they are asked to complete a census return: who are they, where do they live, what do they do for a living? This simple listing task is tackled with great gusto, and greatly deepens their commitment to their roles. When finished they copy their work onto 'parchments' (wallpaper stained with weak tea!).

Back in the drama, they are confronted by a stranger (a second teacher in role) who needs their help. It transpires that he is a deserter from one of the warring armies. They agree to hide him, providing he does his fair share of work – a great deal of negotiation going on here.

The teacher and the class agree that it would be exciting to have someone come looking for him. The first teacher becomes the King's envoy, seeking out the deserter. The class have to plead for mercy on his behalf, but the King's envoy will only accept written pleas.

The resulting letters were written with an extraordinary formality, but the content was deeply moving. In order to save the stranger's life the letters had to be good.

The brief list of writing-in-role activities below indicates some further avenues you might want to explore; many are suitable for children who have not yet learnt to read and write, providing that, as a teacher, you wish to encourage emergent writing.

Diaries

- journals
- ship's log
- starship log.

Letters

formal:
- pleas for forgiveness/mercy
- requests for planning permission
- requests that the selfish giant let people play in his garden
- from the Mayor of Hamelin to the Pied Piper
- petitions (for the release of the children of Hamelin).

informal:
- to Mum, Dad, grandparents, brothers, sisters,
- to friends, pen friend
- from Jack at the top of the beanstalk.

Messages

- telegrams
- memoranda
- messages in code
- reports from spaceship to Earth via computer
- messages in a bottle after a shipwreck.

Lists

- inventory of furniture in a Haunted House
- inventory of equipment to take on a journey/expedition
- menus for the King's celebratory banquet or
  a friend's birthday party
- shopping list for ingredients for a cake
- shopping list for Christmas presents
- census returns – who lives here, what do they do?

Advertisements

- classified to put in newspaper/magazine

- for sale/wanted
- who dares to stay overnight in the Haunted House?
- cards in shop window 'Lost – one dragon!'
- display advertisements/posters.

Scripts

- records of interviews for Radio, TV, newspapers

Newspaper reports

- by reporters who saw the children of Hamelin piped away

Headlines

- newspapers
- magazines
- TV/radio programmes.

Database

- details of the crew on the spaceship
- details of wild life survey by conservation workers.

Plans

- designs for a conservation area
- diagrams of how to put the alien's spaceship back together
- how do we foil a bank robbery?
- map of the giant's castle – showing how we might set Jack free
- town plan of Hamelin.

Much of this written work can be done alone, but some of it is best achieved in collaboration; it might be that the purpose of the drama is to work together to produce documents, for example:

- The letters written by the sailors on the Mary Rose as they left port (had they been able to write).
- The wording of a peace treaty, or an agreement between the people of Hamelin and the Pied Piper.
- The Rules of Space: how do we behave on our (or the alien's) space ship?

As elsewhere in the book these suggestions are not intended to be prescriptive but, rather, a stimulus for ideas. Here are some very brief ideas as to how the Pied Piper suggestions might work in practice:

- After the story has been read to the class, children might take on roles as the townspeople of Hamelin. The teacher as the Mayor asks for their help. Who saw the children being lured away? What did the newspapers/radio/TV say about it? What should the Mayor write to the Pied Piper? Can the townspeople help with the letter(s)? How do we deliver the resulting letter(s) to the Pied Piper?
- Or perhaps the teacher takes on the role of the Pied Piper and tells the class (still as townspeople) that they can write letters to their children (out of role the teacher could suggest these might be in code); the drama might focus on negotiations between the townspeople and the Pied Piper.
- It could be that the Pied Piper is never seen, but that all communication with him is by letter or petition – with the teacher writing replies but not actually appearing in the role.
- In any of these the life of the town could be built up through various activities including role-play, mime, map making, art work. Making a town plan can be done with young children by suggesting the children draw pictures of different parts of the town and sticking these onto a large piece of paper.

Many of the practical examples given in this book contain reference to work in other curriculum areas. The following brief notes are indications as to how one might use drama both to stimulate and support work in specific curriculum areas.

Maths

- *Map-making, co-ordinates, scale*
  The drama begins with the children being shown a treasure map. How do we read it? Can we plan a route?
  The children make their own maps or plans in role.
- *Calculation*
  How is food to be rationed – on the journey; expedition; during the siege?
  We're stuck in our spaceship. How do we calculate the volume of air left? And how long will this last us?
  Working out wages and bonuses.
- *Databases*
  Inventories of equipment.
  List of crew members (ship, submarine, spaceship) with country of origin, age, interests, training, previous experience, years' service.

- *Graphs*
  Bar graphs to record results of research into community prior to building of new leisure centre/road/railway station.
- *Codes*
  The spaceship and its crew are trapped on a distant planet; they need to understand the (coded) messages they are receiving from the alien inhabitants.

Science

- *Flight*
  We are in the mountains, on an expedition/fleeing a tyrant/trying to find somewhere safe to live after an earthquake has destroyed our town; we come to a ravine. We need to get a message to the people on the other side. A flying machine? A paper dart? What design will fly furthest and straightest?
- *Open-ended research*
  We (class and teacher-in-role) as space voyagers who have discovered a 'sister planet' to Earth. Or as time travellers returning to the present day from the future. Or as aliens planning a visit to Earth. In each of these cases their task is to find out what life on Earth in the present day is really like. This could be a way of introducing study of skeletons, use of a microscope to compare animal and human hair.[1]
- *Food preservation*
  A long voyage by sea in a sailing ship (as pirates, emigrants, smugglers, the Navy). How will we keep food from going off without the use of refrigerators? What food will be good to take with us?

Technology

- Teacher requests children's help, as experts, in designing a supermarket, pet shop – plans and model making.
- Lists of tools and equipment required for an expedition/rescue mission.
- Shipwrecked on an island with limited resources. We need to make a boat to get off. What could we make it out of? How do we make it?

Geography

- *Contour lines* on maps.
- *Research about population movements* – in drama about emigration.

- *Ecology and animal origins*
  The teacher (in role) has inherited a badly run circus or zoo. She requests the children's help and advice. What food and bedding should the animals have? How much space? What sort of environment would they enjoy in the wild? Should they be returned to the wild?

Art

- *Photography*
  Mug shots for identity cards or passports.
  Photographs taken of still image work.
  Photographs used as starting points for drama (see Chapter 2, 'Starting Out', and the section on 'using video in drama work' in the Appendix).
- *Three-dimensional*
  Making the artefacts and sculptures of a given community (as in 'The Island' in Chapter 2).

Music

- Making sound pictures using musical instruments and voices but not words – of (for example) a swamp, building site, storm at sea.
- Time/space travellers make audio tapes of the sounds and rhythms they have heard on the voyages. These are presented to the whole group as part of a debriefing session.
- Using recorded music to create atmosphere; or, better, ask one class to make an audio tape with the intention of creating atmosphere, then play it back to another class as a way of initiating the drama – 'When you hear this, where do you think we might be? Who might we be?'

Religious Education

Because plays and assemblies in the primary school so frequently have religious starting points, much of the practice described in *Part Four, Performance and Production* exemplifies the connection between drama and RE both in terms of religious and moral content.

History

One of the issues that faces teachers wanting to use drama in the teaching of history is the thorny problem of *facts and authenticity*. What do we do when we're engaged in a drama and the children come up with solutions to problems that are historically inaccurate? The following example illustrates the problem.

Example: The iron age encampment

A class of Year Five children are working on a project about Iron Age Britain. They have seen pictures of Iron Age encampments, but had done very little previous work on the topic before starting on the drama.

The drama starts with a brief discussion of how people might live without modern technology, and (using the model of the pictures they have seen), they build themselves a fortified encampment – a wonderful image this, with chairs organised into a large circle and then laid down so that the legs all face out.

They agree on a system of foraging and divide themselves into the groups they think important. These include: hunters, ironworkers, woodcutters, clayworkers, gatherers of fruits and . . . honey makers. The rules of the encampment are decided upon. We then move into a short period of dramatic play (or 'busy time' as it is sometimes called) in which each of the groups go about their business, which they greatly enjoy – until frustrations begin to creep in.

I stop the drama and talk out of role about the problem. I ask each group what they've been doing. When it comes to the turn of the honey makers I ask how they make honey. After a few moments of thought, a child replies, 'We collect it from bees.'

'That must be very difficult', say I, admiringly. 'How do you do that?' A rather longer silence this time, and then one of the group says hesitantly, 'We milk them.'

The rest of the group don't agree, but none of them are sure. They have reached a point in their drama when they need factual information, they want to get it right. So we stop work on the drama for a while and adjourn to the classroom and library, where there are several textbooks about the Iron Age and some encyclopaedias. For half an hour the children research into their own area of work. When they return each group enthusiastically reports their research findings back to the class.

I would wager heavily that years later those children still remember what they learnt that morning. The drama created a desire, a need for knowledge, which was useful to them – and when they later returned to their drama they were far more committed to it. At the same time they have successfully begun to develop research skills.

Children have voracious appetites for authenticity, but in drama we should never intimidate them with factual information. We should instead create opportunities which encourage them to seek that information. A child who actively seeks information is likely to make far better use of it than one who passively receives the same information as a chore and is constantly reminded how little s/he knows.

This is not to deny that accuracy is important. It does matter that children don't leave a drama lesson believing that Cromwell's army used bazookas and machine guns![2]

Maps

Many children are fascinated by maps. Maps are concrete representations of what is otherwise abstract; they can become an important part of the reflective process, making it easier for children to understand the meaning of their work. They are symbolic representations, but there's nothing absolute about the type of symbols we use on them. Consider the variety of symbolic representations in the following:

- electrical circuit diagrams
- map of the London Underground
- medieval picture maps.

When making maps you might start simply by asking the children to draw something on a sheet of paper that they want represented on the map – a house, a shop, the well, the woods . . . Initially we're using the activity as a way of *visualising spatial relationships* and of giving the children a concrete representation of what they have achieved in the drama. They can either draw their contribution directly onto the paper, or they can stick their drawings onto a large wall map.

As the drama develops we can make 'emotional maps', 'time lines': all ways of making the drama work more concrete, of deepening the work and broadening our perspectives on it. You'll find that the usefulness of the various kinds of map-making extends far beyond the obvious curriculum links with maths and geography.

The place of drama in a topic

In considering drama's place in topic work, we have to start by thinking how we might dramatise the topic; and that means seeking out human dilemmas, looking for the moments of change in a situation, or the moments when change might be possible; we're looking for those moments when people make choices.

In a topic on industrialisation one might look at the effect of industrialisation on a rural community without work. We should avoid easy moralising. There's a difference between moralising and opening up moral issues.

We know (and children know) that pollution is damaging; that children in Victorian schools were subject to rather repressive regimes; that the slave trade was a bad thing; that being an Ancient Briton after the Romans invaded wasn't nice. But we need to go beyond simplistic simulations. We can do so much more than simply acting as if we were all Victorians. Drama should explore the How and Why of situations.

We could ask, for example: what sort of personal sacrifices might people have to make in order to reduce pollution? The children might take on the roles of factory workers who stand to lose their jobs if the factory cleans up its act.

Continuity

Once you start linking drama and topic work you'll find that your drama projects can go on for weeks. You'll need to start thinking about structure and ideas in a slightly different way. While there's no need for each hall lesson to be self-contained, you still need to find strong, engaging starting points. The key to this lies in dramatic tension. Raise the tension, end sessions on a high point so that (rather like a TV serial) everybody wants to know 'What next?', sometimes described as 'The Flash Gordon syndrome'.[3]

Topic 'ideas'

The introduction and the section on 'small group work' in Chapter 3 shows how we set about planning the early stages of a drama lesson. The same approach holds good when planning to use drama as part of a topic. Think about *Who, What* and *Where* – and make sure that the *What* contains an issue or a problem of some kind. Always start by thinking about '*Who*?', thinking about people. We can't have drama without people. And if our drama is to be at all dramatic we'll need to put those people in a difficult situation, one which confronts them with choices.

Part Five, Planning and Assessment, contains detailed examples of how one might go about planning a topic based drama.

The remainder of this chapter is taken up with an account of an extended drama project which indicates how this interactive, cross-curricular approach works in practice. Although the work began life as a historical project, it involved work in most curriculum areas. The class involved is Year 6.

Example: The Construction of a Railway

For clarity – and in order to emphasise the amount of work in other curriculum areas – I have divided the account of this project into 'drama time' and 'class time'. In reality the divisions were not so distinct, and the 'class time' included researching in school libraries, homework, work out on the school field and visiting a local museum.

The techniques and strategies used in the drama work included:

- small group work – in and out of role
- forum theatre

Continued

Example continued

- still images
- simple mime
- writing in role
- whole group work.

Aims

1. To examine the effect that railway building might have had on a self-contained and isolated rural community.
2. To explore the conflicts of loyalty that might arise among people when faced with major changes in their way of life.
3. To stimulate interest in simple surveying and engineering, and to give the children opportunities to develop skills related to these areas.

Class time

The drama work is preceded by research into nineteenth-century life, including looking at maps of the local area prior to the coming of the railway.

Each child to name one item invented in the last 150 years. 'What do we use in our lives now which people didn't have a hundred years ago?'

Drama time

Mime work in pairs:

A mimes a simple activity, using gadgets from today;

B has to achieve the same end result by using materials available in the early nineteenth century, e.g.

A makes breakfast using fridge and electric cooker

B milks cow, draws water from well, chops firewood, lights fire, takes eggs from chicken, etc.!

A small imaginary town (Seatown) is established. Children agree on roles within small groups (farmers, miners, shopkeepers, mill workers, etc.), create still images of these people at work. Teacher comments.

The commitment to the roles strengthened through improvisation work in small groups, each with a small problem which must be solved, e.g. broken cart, insufficient labour at farm or mill; then trading in the market-place. The teacher takes on a role as a member of the local council who has been away on business. He returns with the news that he has been asked to ensure that the Parish Registers are all up to date. In the meantime he has to go back to the town on further business, but first his horse needs shoeing, his cart needs repairing and he needs food and shelter. The difficulties of the journey on bad roads made evident.

The role chosen by the teacher here is as neutral as possible, to avoid confrontation, effectively a messenger. The shoeing of the horse and repair of the cart are simply ways of intervening in small group work, using the role to value and focus it.

Continued

Example continued

Class time

The children examine original documents loaned from the local library, showing what a parish register from this period would have looked like. They then create their own 'Parish Register' – a way of confirming the roles they've adopted.

Further research is carried out into rural lifestyles in the 1840s.

Drama time

The teacher returns in role to collect the new Register – and comment on its usefulness. He also enthuses about the extraordinary steam trains he has recently seen for himself, reading from a journal which he has been writing while away. (This description is taken from a contemporary source. Wherever possible use authentic contemporary material. Children are excited by it; it helps reinforce the children's understanding of and commitment to the time shift, and in this case introduces the idea of a journal as part of the fiction, thereby leading into writing-in-role activities.)

He brings a large, but incomplete, map of the village and surrounding area, saying that he's been approached by one of the railway companies who are interested in building a railway line to Seatown, and that they have asked him to have the map updated. The map shows the village is close to the sea, has a natural harbour, but is cut off from nearby large towns by hills and a large marsh.

Class time

Map work includes map symbols, contour lines, co-ordinates and introduces some simple surveying tasks. The children work on completing the map provided.

A growing body of material is provided to create opportunities for possible research – books, photographs, maps, documentation, letters describing reactions to the railway, old newspapers, prints.

Drama time

After recapping through still images, the teacher explains that he will now be taking on a different role. A meeting is held which the teacher attends in role as a railway engineer. He is carrying the map the class have made, which his 'friend' has delivered; he thanks them for the excellent job they have done.

'I am an engineer, not a surveyor. Surveying is clearly something that many of you are very good at. We want to build a line which will connect Seatown with the big cities. And we need your help with the survey.'

As the meeting progresses it becomes clear that the railway link will be very expensive, involving tunnelling through the hills and viaducts across the marsh. In order to cut costs elsewhere the company want to build the line right through the middle of the town and across much of the farmland

---

Continued

Example continued

which the children have established (in role) as belonging to them. Most of the children want the railway and are prepared to help with the survey, but a few want things to remain as they are, and they want to organise resistance to the coming of the railway.

There are *organisational problems* in allowing the group to split into two such distinct factions. There is not only a danger of the drama becoming very confrontational; the focus can split, resulting in confusion and loss of control. This is less of a problem if *team-teaching* is a possibility. If you're working alone one way of dealing with it is for the class to look at each side in turn: they can *all* play the townspeople who want to join the survey team, and then *all* play those who don't want the railway to come through the town. The potential confrontation does, however, create opportunities for practising and developing skills of negotiating, persuading, listening, and compromising.

Class time

Discussion and research about railway lines, straightness and gradients. Historical research into survey methods. Discussion about industrialisation and possible effects of *not* letting the railway be built. We do not yet, however, discuss what might happen in our drama.

Drama time

The children start by working in small groups, continuing to improvise their daily routine, but with the added task that while they are working they should be discussing the issue of the railway route. The teacher moves from group to group, occasionally spotlighting one of them, saying 'Let's see what's happening in different parts of the town' and then reflecting on what's been heard and seen: 'Feelings are running high. Whatever happens it seems the town will never be quite the same again.'

Still images of the conflicting feelings. A short scene played out between four farmers and the railway engineer (teacher in role), who tries to persuade them to sell their land to the railway company. The teacher uses this opportunity to introduce the idea that the railway will open up new markets; and the children are persuaded.

The real drama appears to be over! It seems that the children have been too easily persuaded to sell their land and houses, for what matters in a drama like this is *not* that the children should act out what actually happened in real life, but that it should open up and help them understand the *dilemmas* of industrialisation. In this case it seems that the structure of the drama has made it too easy for the children – perhaps because of the non-confrontational role adopted by the teacher as messenger early on, when he was excited and enthusiastic about the railway and its effect on another town.

But all is not lost! One of the advantages of using drama in this way (when the narrative continues over a period of several weeks) is that both the teacher and the children can change roles, enabling us to look at any given topic from different points of view.

Continued

Example continued

> The drama session ends with the railway engineer offering contracts of employment to those townspeople who want to work for the railway on the construction of the line.
>
> ### Class time
>
> The map is marked up with the lots that have been sold. Research begins on the materials needed for railway construction, with some children producing a broadsheet (on computer) reporting what has been happening in the town – which they 'sell' in the next drama session. Others write letters (in role) to relatives and friends in other parts of the country telling them what has happened, and (for the most part) excitedly proclaiming how easy it will be to visit once the line is built. Work also begins on planning the construction of a bridge. How will the line cross the marshes? Model-making, drawing, scientific testing of materials and further historical research.
>
> ### Drama time
>
> At the next opportunity – in class time – the teacher relates the 'story' of the drama so far, taking care to include reference to all the groups of children, but concluding:
>
> 'So the railway engineer's job appeared to be complete. He was about to go back to the company when he realised that in the middle of the town was a house where an old man lived, exactly where the company were planning to build their new station; and the old man was refusing to sell.'
>
> The teacher asks the children what they know about the old man. Together they 'construct' the role, which the teacher then takes on. Using the techniques of *forum theatre*, the class try to persuade the old man to sell his house and land.
>
> A letter arrives from the railway company, stating that if they can't purchase all the necessary land for the agreed route, they'll pull out.
>
> ### Class time
>
> We look at maps of Britain in 1840, 1890 and today. Did any towns thrive which were *not* connected to the railway system?
>
> ### Drama time
>
> The pressure is on. How will they persuade the old man to leave his house? Should they? There's no easy moralising here. It's tough and difficult. Through their research the class know that no railway will mean rapid decline. They decide to threaten the old man with violence.
>
> It's tempting to stop the drama at such morally dubious moments, but it is precisely here that we find the greatest learning opportunities. If we are to examine the consequences of actions, we must allow the choice.
>
> Having threatened the old man (the teacher has continued in this role

Continued

Example continued

---

whenever necessary), he agrees to leave his house. The railway will come through. They appear to have triumphed. They're asked to make *two* still images showing what the townspeople might be feeling at this moment – first, about their success in getting the railway to the town, and secondly, about what they have done to the old man, who is now homeless.

Each member of the class is asked to think quietly: 'Listen to your own thoughts for a moment or two' then 'If there is something you want to say to him, go to him and say it now.'

The project finishes there, with the children expressing considerable remorse for getting the old man out of his home. But they have learned far more about morality this way than they would have done if they had been stopped from making their threats.

Although this project was not taken any further, it is not necessarily 'the end'. What happens to the old man? What happens during the construction of the railway? What happens to people ten years later who leave their small town and go to the big city to find work? We could easily move on to a project exploring other aspects of Victorian England.

There is a key 'branching' decision being made in the drama described above – when the children decide to accept the coming of the railway, or turn it away. The drama comes not from discussing what each decision *would* mean, but in making the decision and working through the consequences.

In a drama based on a similar starting point another group of children vehemently refused to let the engineer carry out the survey – and the focus of the drama shifted: how do people cope with rural decline, losing markets and jobs? In this instance they decided to emigrate! And the drama continues – reaching out, as ever, into exciting areas of exploration in history, geography and science, etc.

Bibliography

Bolton, G. 1984. *Drama as Education*, Longman. (Contains an argument for placing drama at the centre of the curriculum.)

Coleman, T. 1965. *The Railway Navvies*, Hutchinson.

Hoskins, W. G. 1955. *The Making of the English Landscape*, Hodder and Stoughton. (Chapter 8 is on railways.)

Parsons, B., Schaffner, M., Little, G. and Felton, H. 1984. *Drama, Language and Learning*, NADIE, Tasmania.

Siviter, R. 1984. *The Settle to Carlisle, a Tribute*, The Baton Press.

Wagner, B-J. 1976. *Dorothy Heathcote: Drama as a Learning Medium*, National Education Association, Washington DC

Notes

1.   This idea of making the world with which we are familiar seem strange to us, and thereby increasing our curiosity about it, is one which theatre practitioners will be familiar with through the work of Berthold Brecht.

David Shepherd's excellent article in *London Drama Magazine*, 'The Appliance of Science', gives a detailed account of a drama in which the class are aliens planning a visit to earth. The class study magazines, television programmes and old films to find out what life on earth will be like. The Media Studies work takes place in the context of a dramatic fiction. David Shepherd *London Drama Magazine*, Vol. 7 No. 2.

2. In the television programme *Three Looms Waiting* Dorothy Heathcote discusses this with reference to a child who suggests that Coventry is in London. She argues that while the child should not go home believing this to be true, it is important to find the right moment to correct him. There is also an entertaining and very intelligent discussion of the issue in Fines, J. and Verrier, R. 1974. *The Drama of History*, New University Education. The issue informs the whole book, but the discussion in Chapter 8 (pp. 79–91) focuses on it.

3. Davies, G. 1983. *Practical Primary Drama*, Heinemann.

4. Jonathan Cape used to publish a series called Jackdaws. These are no longer in print, but many libraries (particularly in colleges and universities) still hold some in stock. See Appendix.

PART THREE

Early Years

Drama with children in Key Stage One

Although working with young children in their first years in school sometimes seems very different to working with older children, many of the principles and approaches that we use in drama are similar.

Much of the theory and practice suggested in Part Two of this book, 'Drama in Practice', holds good when working with very young children. Indeed, many of the suggestions for practical work are specifically intended for use with children in Key Stage One and several of the drama projects documented there are accounts of work with children in their first years at school – notably 'The Crashed Spaceship' and 'The Giant Awakes' (in Chapter 5).

PLAY

Although there are several different theories about play, there is certainly a consensus about its importance in human development.[1] From a very early age we use various forms of play to make sense of the world.

Young children play with language, trying out sounds before they start experimenting with words. I was intrigued recently to read an interview with Roman Polanski, the film director, in which he claimed that he learns languages not by learning tracts of vocabulary, but by playing at the sounds of a new language, first speaking a 'gibberish' version of it, finding out what it feels like to be making those sounds and those speech patterns. As he claims to be able to speak seventeen languages, it would seem to work.

Adults learning to use computers are frequently taught very basic principles (like how to switch on the machine and 'boot' a disc) and then encouraged to simply play with it for a while. The word processor package which I'm using to write this book has a couple of games built into it – partly for light relief, no doubt, but also to give newcomers the opportunity to play with the system, to get confident in using the tools.

Children's own free play is not in itself drama, although it's a close relation. They use role, they develop stories, they give symbolic significance to the spaces in which they play – a bed becoming a pirate ship, the arm of an armchair becoming the back of a horse. And they use this role play to explore their interests and their concerns; in similar ways and for similar purposes to the way we use drama – to explore and develop their understanding of the world.

Drama with children in Key Stage One – what's the difference?

Drama with children in their first years of school differs from drama with older children only in content and organisation, not in basic approaches to the subject. In fact what young children demand of us is not that we dilute the work, but that we make it more exciting, more tightly focused. Whereas with older children we can sometimes talk our way out of a sloppy beginning, with young children we have to grab their interest from the outset.

Five, six and seven year olds are perfectly capable of working on drama for an hour and a half or more at a time, but they need very clear tasks, strong images and narratives which are intriguing and above all dramatic. Script writers are often urged to 'Take your characters closer to the centre of the action.' It's very useful advice for drama teachers, especially when working with young children. If a giant has come to town the children will allow you to have your council meeting to discuss what the townspeople should do about it, but what they really want to do and what they will learn most from is dealing with the giant.

In terms of organisation, working with this age group we can go in several directions:

1. We can provide a small group with a stimulus in the play area and let them get on with their own play, occasionally intervening (as described below).
2. We can take part in their small group work.

3. We can organise them and lead them through highly prescriptive sessions in which they act out the teacher's scenario.
4. We can work together as a whole group in which there is a clear focus and a clear task.

There are times when each of these strategies is appropriate, although I am reluctant to use the third unless it serves a very clear purpose. When I do use it, it tends to be as a way into a narrative for which the children themselves will take increasing responsibility. 'The Giant Awakes' (Chapter 5) is a good example of a highly prescriptive opening which is then used to stimulate much more open-ended work.

MAKING A START

Whatever the age group we're working with (be it five year olds or fifty year olds) the basic elements of drama remain the same:

- narrative
- role play
- verbal and non-verbal language (for example, gesture, body language, facial expression, the space between people).

We should never underestimate the vast range of vernacular knowledge that children bring to school with them when they first arrive. Their knowledge and experience of drama will be far more wide-ranging than is commonly acknowledged. Consider the following:

- their own play (which is likely to have involved role play – though this is certainly not always the case)
- stories – telling and being told
- film and television
- puppets, pantomimes, theatres.

In some of these the child is an active participant, is making drama of a kind, in others s/he is responding to what others have made.

All the basic elements of drama are present to an extent in children's own play. But while many children enter the school having already enjoyed many hours of 'pretend' play; there are some whose experience of such play is very limited, who find it very difficult to differentiate between being in and out of role. We need to take account of this range of experience when we plan drama with young children. What we can, however, be reasonably certain of is that they will have at least some common experiences of television dramas; these can themselves provide us with useful starting points.

While an experienced teacher might start by working with the whole class, drawing the more reluctant children into the drama through the excitement of the drama itself, full of dramatic tension, rich in imagery, there's much to be said for working in the classroom with small groups. The best practice combines these two approaches – with the whole class working in the hall (or drama room) on a regular basis and small groups working for much shorter periods in the classroom.

WORKING IN THE CLASSROOM

Intervention in the children's own dramatic play; structuring play corner activities

The simplest way of starting is by intervening (sometimes very briefly) in play corner activities, taking on a role yourself in the children's own play. This intervention can be very simple:

*   buying items from a shopping list and needing change
*   having a cup of tea and asking questions about the neighbours – 'Is the old man next door still poorly? He really appreciated it when you got his shopping for him last week.'

Even at its simplest your intervention –

*   supports the children in their role-play
*   introduces the idea that you, the teacher, can play a role yourself
*   creates the possibility of formalising their language
*   creates the possibility of introducing some simple work in other curriculum areas (e.g. counting)
*   encourages them to think beyond the immediate, maybe introducing simple notions of cause and effect narrative
*   gives you the opportunity to introduce simple signals indicating when you are in and out of role, thereby accustoming them to this strategy for when you use it later in a whole group drama.

To the children who find any sort of role play difficult (perhaps because it has been discouraged at home, or because they are very shy) it communicates to them that you approve of such play.

As the children get used to your interventions, you can make them more challenging. Perhaps instead of asking questions about the neighbours, you can yourself be the old person who lives next door:

I know you're very busy [acknowledging and supporting what they're already doing] but I wonder if you could help me? I've been very poorly and I can't get out to the shops. Can you help me make a shopping list?

When intervening in this way with a small group working on their own in the play corner you'll need to think through how much time you can afford to give them. How long can you leave the rest of the class to get on with their own work? You'll need to be clear about the purpose of your intervention. Is it

* to challenge?
* to support?
* to focus?
* to stimulate?

It is often a combination of these. If the children are already working well, perhaps all you need to do is to enter very briefly and present them with a stimulus: 'I'm trying to arrange a birthday party for my nieces and nephews; could you help me organise it.'

A stimulus to imaginative play

With very young children, a very effective way of getting imaginative play started is to put 'something magic' into the play area: 'Here's a magic box. I wonder if you can find out how it works, what it does?' The magic box could equally well be a key, a trinket, a crystal – or even a saucepan. This approach is particularly useful when their play has become 'stuck', when they continue to enact the same situation in the same way.

I once said to a small group of Reception children working in the play area: 'I've heard that this bracelet has some strange magic powers. Could you find out what they are? It doesn't seem to work for me.' I let them get on with it, and returned ten minutes later to find them 'space-walking'. The bracelet not only made them fly, but had taken them to the moon.

You might also try: 'This magic chair seems to make people who sit in it very grumpy. It's not supposed to do that at all. Can you help me put it right?' Note that the basic approach, with very young children, is in many ways similar to that which we use with other age groups: I, the teacher, do *not* know. Can you help me?

Using an item of costume can be a powerful stimulus to initiate dramatic play. *A well stocked dressing-up box* is a very useful resource. Make sure it contains plenty of different fabrics and textiles as well as props and items of clothing. Hats, caps and headgear of various kinds are useful because they are so easy to use quickly and without fuss. I most often use it as a resource which the children can go to during their own dramatic play. Although it can become distracting if the children always want to use it when you're working as a whole group, there may be times when you want everybody to take a piece of cloth and make themselves something with it – a headband or a belt in a particular colour, for example to identify them as belonging to a particular group. In this way they're not only using the clothes in the box but also using textiles and fabrics creatively.

If there is a school play try to appropriate as many costumes as possible at the end of it. Young children get a lot of pleasure from using the costumes and re-enacting (and adapting) in their own play what they have seen older children doing.

You'll need to spend longer with children who find role-play itself difficult, or who will work alone but not with others. Simply entering and offering a stimulus could provoke argument, disagreement and even tears. Taking on a role yourself and making that role the focus of the dramatic play enables you to support contributions as they're made. When you have some children who find it very difficult to work with others, one solution might be to work with much smaller groups, maybe even just a couple of them at a time for five minutes or so. You can then set up a number of pair group 'plays' which can perhaps later be merged into small groups of fours or sixes.

WHOLE GROUP WORK

So far I've described what might be called a 'gently, gently' approach. It not only gives the inexperienced teacher an opportunity to build up confidence, it also gets children used to role play being taken seriously. The problem with using small group work with young children is that it's inevitably rather disparate: they will happily play for long periods, but find it difficult to share each other's work unless there is a powerful dramatic context, as is provided by whole group work, which gives us the chance to really focus the drama. We can work with the class to create a story in which they all have a stake, slowing it down at particular moments, thereby creating strong dramatic tension, deepening understanding and also enabling us to value publicly the contribution of particular children.

The two ways of working (in small groups and in a whole class group) should never be seen as mutually exclusive. As discussed in Chapters 3 and 5, whole group work rarely means the whole class doing the same thing at the same time. It's more useful to think of it as a way of giving coherence and focus to the work of small groups. The whole group work can be used as the stimulus for small group tasks, or can itself spring from work which the children have originated in separate small groups.

Example: The Magician who Lost his Magic

The Magician who Lost his Magic by David McKee[2] is a story which is popular with young children; it tells the story of how Melric the Magician, woke up one day to find he no longer had any magic. Everyone in the castle where he lives had become totally reliant on him to do everything for them, so the loss of the magic is somewhat disastrous. In the story Melric goes off on a quest to various fellow magicians to seek help. In our drama we can change the frame (see Chapter 4) and look at the story from the point of view of the people in the castle.

- What's happening in the Castle Kitchens?
- How does everyone manage?

We can break into small groups and look at what's happening throughout the castle. The pictures in the book are a useful stimulus because they hint at the disasters and yet allow the children to flesh out the world of the carpenters, the gardeners, the cooks, the soldiers, the furniture makers (perhaps using small pieces of fabric to indicate who they are). Children love acting out 'disasters'. From here we could go on to explore how the people in the castle manage without Melric. Frequently, young children use 'magic' as a way of solving problems, and thereby avoiding the drama. This story itself offers a useful control device in that you're asking them how they manage without magic.

Here are some brief alternative suggestions:

1. Class as nearby townspeople who have never had the dubious benefit of Melric's magic. Teacher (in role) goes to them to seek advice: 'Melric, our magician, has lost all his magic; and we don't know how to do anything. We don't even know how to get water from the well. Could I stay with you for a few days and learn how you manage without magic?'
2. My name is Mertel; I'm Melric's sister. I've heard that my brother has been wasting his magic. If we're to help him get his magic back I'm going to need to know just what he's been up to.

The dramatic frame

This example illustrates how we can use different dramatic frames to develop drama from story with this age group. As with older children we use the story as the possible starting point, but shift the point of view, so that they are not simply acting out what they have heard but rather they are making decisions which affect the drama.

Although the king in *The Magician who lost his Magic* is not named in the story, he seems to be King Rollo, a character who has featured in an animated television series based on a series of David McKee's books. Shifting the dramatic frame enables us to use the dramatic fictions that are shown on children's television as starting points for drama. When I use a well-known television series as a starting point I start by talking to the children about what we're going to do and the way we're going to work: 'We're going to make up a play together. It's going to have King Rollo in it, but it'll be our play.'

Example: The Circus

When I first started teaching drama the stock infant lesson was 'making a circus'! Times have changed, as have circuses and public attitudes towards them. Not many children are likely to have been to a circus; but although they're not as glamorous or as attractive as they once were, they still hold a fascination for children.

If we're going to use The Circus as the theme for our drama we need to consider another dramatic frame than simply putting together all the different acts, for example:

• Teacher in role produces a large document. 'Uncle Chippersmart's(!) Last Will and Testament.' 'My dear old Uncle Billy died recently and I've inherited his circus. I've got to run it and I don't know anything about circuses. What's worse is that before he died all the people who looked after the animals had left and got jobs with other circuses. All the animals are in their cages, but they don't seem to have very much space, and some of them haven't been fed properly for a long time. I really need your help and advice.' The drama's about how to look after the animals, finding out what they eat, where they come from, maybe whether we can release them back into the wild.

Organisation

One of the problems often associated with working with young children is their apparently short concentration span. What this tells us is not that we should not attempt serious drama work with them, but that we need to give particularly careful thought in our planning to the appropriateness of the material. Exactly the same principles apply as with any age group. We need to catch and hold their attention. We'll best do that with good strong images; by intriguing them, by creating tense dramatic moments. To this end teacher in role work with young children is especially effective.

PRETEND AND REALITY

It still surprises me sometimes how difficult some children find it to distinguish between the drama world of pretend and the real world. There is a danger in letting the drama become too real for young children; we don't want the dragons and giants of the drama to follow them home and give them nightmares. We need to remind children that what we're doing in drama is pretending. This is another reason that I deliberately choose to move frequently in and out of role in drama with young children, and why I often use the strategy of asking them to help me create (or construct) the character that I play.

Discussion

However dramatic and intriguing you make the work, however visual, there will nevertheless come times when you need to sit down with them and talk things through. These periods of reflection and decision-making are important, but we must not let them get out of hand. Discussion is only of interest to those participating in it, and many young children find it extremely difficult to articulate their ideas verbally – especially before they've actually done what you're talking about.

I tackle the problem by trying to act on suggestions as soon as they're made. Any discussion occurs after the action.

We have a problem. We need to discuss it. Draw the children to you; take them into your confidence. You'll have to use more than words to convince them just how special they are in this process. You clarify the problem as visually as possible; and then you get ten different solutions shouted out. What do you do? You act on one of them at a time, and then decide which, if any, is going to be most productive.

Example: The Giant's Toothache

In advance of the drama session I've made several large sweet papers. When they come into the Hall they see these giant wrappers leading to the corner of the room. We talk about why they might be there; who they might belong to. They're all pretty certain that they belong to a giant.

I ask them: 'Do you want to meet the giant?' They do. 'What will he be like?' We construct the character of the giant; a child makes a suggestion, and we all have a go at enacting it, seeing what it would look like. How does he walk? They show me. I pick up on one idea at a time, and we try each of these as a group. I try it myself, to see if I've got the right idea. How does he talk? How does he eat? They want a frightening giant, big and loud and angry.

I then ask if they're ready to meet the giant. They are; and he's pretty much the way they'd constructed him, except that he's in the corner, bent over and moaning. They gather round, tentatively asking what's wrong. I point to my mouth and my tummy.

I come out of role and ask them about what they've seen. What do they know about the giant? They tell me he's got toothache and tummy ache from eating too many sweets. They want to help him, and I have to remind them that he might be frightening (that was the way they had wanted him to be) so we'll need to approach him very carefully. (This adds to the dramatic tension.) So the issue becomes: How do we help a giant who is poorly, but who might get very angry with us if we annoy him?

Continued

Example continued

> As you'd expect with this age group, there is an immediate barrage of responses. 'Clean his teeth for him,' says one child. With older children we might spend some time discussing this (perhaps wondering if the giant would ever let us get near enough to open his mouth and clean his teeth for him); with this age group, however, I immediately enthuse about the idea: 'Right, that's really good. But aren't we going to need a very large toothbrush. We'll have to make that ourselves. Go to the shops and buy anything you think would be useful to make a giant's toothbrush.' And then, when we've bought all the materials and made the giant's toothbrush (which could itself be a Technology task), that's when I go back into role as the giant and refuse to let them come anywhere near me with their (mimed) toothbrush.
>
> I come out of role again and ask them what we should do. One child suggests we give him a bath. You can see how firmly grounded the drama is in their own reality. So we have to make the bath tub and then fill it with water. It needs to be hot water, so we have to be careful. And the drama continues in this way: a stimulus to excite and intrigue; a problem, action, and then thought about the action. Action and then reflection. People frequently get into difficulties with this age group by trying to think through the consequences of suggestions before trying them out, which requires an inappropriately sophisticated level of thought on the part of the children.

MAGIC

Several of these examples refer to 'magic' in some way. In drama magic is both blessing and a curse; a blessing because it creates a wonderful control device, and because it can be very stimulating to the imagination; a curse because children can – and often do – use it as a way of saying 'This is not a problem', using magic to get them out of seeking a solution.

Magic as a control device

When working with young children it is sometimes a good idea to invoke magic: 'When we go into the hall we are going through a magic door', as if it were a door to a magic wardrobe. You can say that if they don't keep to the agreed rules of the drama, then the magic will start to fail; if they climb up the wall-bars when you have asked them not to, you can say that the magic only works when their feet are touching the ground, thus using the fiction of the drama to limit the space they work in and remind them through a dramatic device of those rules which you will have agreed before the lesson begins (see also the section on 'Control' in Chapter 4).

The hall, the drama itself, becomes magic. Anything can happen, as long as the rules of the magic are adhered to. Using the device of the 'magic door' also allows you to contain the world of pretend within the hall if, for example, there are children in the class for whom the drama frequently becomes too real.

The curse of magic

Anybody who has taught drama with primary school children will have come across many examples of magic being used as a 'Get out'.

For example: We're stuck in a cave. There's been a rock fall. There seems to be no way out. At which point a child says, 'It's alright, I've brought a magic spade with me. It can dig us out in ten seconds'. You could, of course, reply, 'Nonsense, there are no such things as magic spades' (and I've been tempted often enough); but that wouldn't be very supportive, and there's a good chance that the child who offers the spade is doing so in good faith. Instead, try: 'Thank goodness you've brought that. How marvellous,' and then start asking questions about the magic:

*   'How long does the magic last?'
*   'What are the dangers of using it?'
*   'Where did you get it? It's not stolen, is it?'

Enter into the world of the magic, accept the idea, but challenge it. In other words, use the magic, but create limitations for it. Establish the parameters. What does the magic spade do exactly? When does it, and when does it not work?

By giving the magic limitations, asking in which particular circumstances it works, the drama is actually enhanced. The children have to make a decision about using the magic, they have to think when would be a good time to use it and when would be harmful.

In this respect the following is a technique which I have found particularly useful:

We're stuck (again)! It doesn't matter where. The problem is how to get away from the encroaching flood water. A child says she has brought a magic carpet.

'How wonderful. Can I look at it? Oh it's magnificent isn't it . . . A bit small, but beautifully coloured. Oh, what's this? A label?' And then I 'read' aloud: ' "Magic carpet. Danger. Do not use except . . ." Oh dear. the rest of the label's been torn.'

We're exploring the world of exciting new technology. It's magic, of course, and it brings great benefit to us but it could also have terrible dangers in store for us – just like magic carpets!

The focus of the drama shifts to discovering the dangers, and weighing up pros and cons of using the magic carpet.

Avoiding the problem

There are times, of course, when one simply feels it is inappropriate to be dealing with magic; and 'magic' can take many forms, including laser guns which appear from nowhere.

It is important to establish at the beginning of a drama lesson/ project whether magic is to be allowed or not. If it is agreed that there is to be *no* magic, the teacher and the children must stick by their decision.

Before any sort of an expedition – be it to South America, or a distant star – I often ask the children to make a list of all the things they will be taking with them. This becomes an important task in itself, and can be done either in the hall or in the classroom (perhaps in role). With older children it could be that each child makes his/her own list on a piece of paper; with younger children maybe we do it as a class, and the teacher writes everything on the blackboard; or perhaps nothing is written down by individuals, with each giving what they will need to the teacher who's a 'quartermaster'. The lists could be written or sketched. Maybe some of the items have to be purchased.

What matters is that a limitation has been set; and *now* if a child brings out a gun, a knife, a rope ladder or even a box of matches you can check with the list and then either stay in role and say 'You may have meant to bring that rope ladder, but it's not here', *or* come out of role and discuss the agreed rules of the drama, one of which is perhaps that in *this* drama there is no recourse to magic. The lists have been agreed, and anything not on the list cannot simply 'appear' from nowhere.

Most of the ideas, techniques and strategies described in Part Two hold good for working with young children, but it is worth devoting time to a specific discussion of how one might adapt the work on still image and forum theatre for use with this age group, as they are sometimes thought to be strategies that can only be successfully used with older children.

STILL IMAGE AND FORUM THEATRE

Still image

Reception children are used to stories told in the form of consecutive images through comic strips; they're also familiar with 'freeze frame' on video. A simple way of introducing still image work with this age group is to have them walk or run round the hall and then stop and freeze at a given signal. You say you'll try to lift up the child who is stillest. We can then look at one or two of the still images as if they were statues or models in a theme park. Perhaps we then go on and create a drama about a theme park. Maybe the class are model makers; they could make still images of their favourite cartoon characters.

Consider two images:

1.   children taking apples from a tree
2.   a farmer shouting at the children.

In this order it's a story of crime and punishment. If we reverse the order we get a story of revenge, the children getting their own back. Working with the images develops the concept of cause and effect in narrative – a very important early stage in teaching about narrative. We can do the work by using photographs or drawings initially, but it's often more exciting for the children to make the images themselves, perhaps later drawing what they have done in comic strip form, making their own comic based on the story that's been created in the drama. (See also 'storyboarding' on pps. 156–9.)

Forum theatre

'The Giant's Toothache' (earlier in this chapter) exemplifies how we might use forum theatre[3] to construct a character. This method is very useful with all ages. By giving young children the opportunity to create the more 'dangerous' characters themselves, they are made safe; the elements of pretend are made clearer. They like their drama to be exciting, but not too frightening.

The technique is one which is wonderfully adaptable. Suppose we need a dragon in a drama. If we're going to stick by the principle outlined above of keeping close to the centre of the action, we'll need to meet the dragon in the drama, to find out what it's really like, maybe to persuade it to come and melt an iceberg for drinking water.

How do we create a dragon? Ask the children. 'If you like, I'll pretend to be the dragon, but you'll have to help me. How can I do it? Have you seen the dragon? Can you show me what it looks like? My arms aren't big enough to be wings; what can I use for wings? Is there anything in the dressing-up box that looks like dragon skin? And what about its face?'

Having gone through this process, and perhaps used various bits of PE apparatus to create the dragon's lair, maybe ask the children to shut their eyes and imagine the dragon in its lair, talking them through the suggestions they've made, helping them to visualise their creation, before taking on the role. And when you take on the role always hold something in reserve, so it's what they've created, but here's something unexpected about it. Maybe the dragon's lost its old fire, maybe it's an endangered species, maybe it's rather timid. Be careful with your questioning. Don't ask questions to which you don't want answers. If you want a fireless dragon, don't ask them if the dragon breathes fire.

Fantasy and the power of story

There are several schools of thought about whether young children get more from working on what they know – dramas about shopping, going to school, their daily routines – or fantasy. My own feeling is that we at least need to start where the children feel most comfortable, and then to introduce elements which are better described as mythic rather than fantastic; that is, to dramatise or create stories which contain imagery and symbolism which are likely to excite the children, and yet which they can relate to their own lives. I'm sure that young children like stories about giants so much because that's what adults seem like to them. Dealing with dragons (or aliens) in drama is an enjoyable and safe way of dealing with our fears. And in all these dramas the children's responses are very much about their own world – as exemplified in 'The Giant's Toothache' earlier in this chapter.

The Appendix contains a brief selection of stories and picture books which I have used as the basis for drama with children in Key Stage One and can personally recommend.

Chapter 5 contains two examples of drama projects undertaken with Reception children – 'The Giant Awakes' and 'The Crashed Spaceship'. The section on 'Drama and Story' (in Chapter 2) contains a number of brief practical examples which are well suited to use with children in Key Stage One.

Bibliography

McCaslin, N. 1990. *Creative Drama in the Classroom* (5th edn) Longman, New York. (In particular chapter 3, Play; chapter 4, Movement and Rhythms; chapter 7, Puppetry and Mask-making.)

Lambert, A., Linnell, R., O'Neill, C. and Warr-Wood, J. 1976. *Drama Guidelines*, London Drama, Heinemann.

Davies, G. 1983. *Practical Primary Drama*, Heinemann Educational Books.

Smilansky, S. and Shefatya, L. 1990. *Facilitating Play*, Psychosocial and Educational Publications, Gaithersburg USA.

Notes

1.   'Being a social activity, drama is inextricably linked with the origins of

society itself. The full range of dramatic play (from play to theatre) is observed in each civilised society . . . In one sense, the origins of society are the origins of drama because it is by impersonation and identification that man, in all history, has related himself to others.' Courtney, R. (1968) *Play Drama and Thought*, Cassell, p. 125. For further reading about the relationship between play and drama see: Bruner, J. (ed.) 1976. *Play: Its Role and Development and Evolution*, Penguin. The chapter by Vygotsky. L. S. – 'The role of play in the mental development of the child' – is particularly useful. Also see: Smilansky, S. and Shefatya, L. 1990. *Facilitating Play*, Psychosocial and Educational Publications, Gaithersburg, USA.

2. David McKee. 1970. *The Magician who Lost his Magic*, Abelard Schuman.

3. Forum theatre is described in detail in Chapter 3 – 'Working methods'. See also Boal, A. 1979. *Theatre of the Oppressed*, Pluto Press and Boal, A. 1992. *Games for Actors and Non-Actors*, Routledge.

PART FOUR

Performance and Production

Developing the work towards presentation

The introductory rationale to this chapter and the section on the School Play were written in collaboration with Lib Taylor.

Plays, productions and presentations – a rationale
The school play
Theatre skills and skill-building exercises
Masks, costume and lighting
Audience/performer relationships
Scripts and spontaneity
Example: Sharing spontaneous drama work

'Drama is a social art where people are and do, and other people may see them doing and being.'[1]

The intention in this part of the book is to show how it is possible to use the techniques discussed earlier to develop work for an audience. Throughout this part of the book I shall use the term 'classroom drama' to describe the drama which takes place as part of the day-to-day timetabled school activities – in the classroom, the hall or elsewhere.

PLAYS, PRODUCTIONS AND PRESENTATIONS – A RATIONALE

For a long time views about educational drama seemed to polarise into two camps: in one camp were those who saw it as something which inevitably led to presentation of material; in the other, those who saw such presentation as an unrelated activity, even at odds with the 'essence' of 'Good Drama'. A terminology began to grow up in which 'drama' was seen to be different from 'theatre'.

As a result of this sometimes uneasy relationship between educational drama and performance work, teachers have often become confused, perplexed and uncertain. It is therefore worth examining the terms 'educational drama' and 'performance'.

Educational drama is usually seen to be that drama activity

1.   which occurs as part of and in support of the school curriculum

2.   which takes place in a convenient space, be it the hall or the classroom
3.   which actively involves all members of the class continuously;

Performance is often seen as something

1.   which is presented to an audience who have no previous knowledge of the material
2.   which involves a selected group of children
3.   which disrupts, or runs contrary to the school curriculum.

While the former is generally supposed to be educationally worthwhile, the latter is often viewed (with a certain amount of trepidation) at best as fun and at worst as a waste of time. I believe it is much more useful to think of the two areas of work as part of a continuum. Even the most private of educational drama work shares with 'performance' the use of dramatic forms and conventions. The key to the problem lies in this relationship between form and content.

Small groups who present their work to their peers in the classroom are working in the same spectrum of dramatic activity as children involved in a major school play, performed to a large audience of parents, relatives, governors and friends; and yet it is sometimes claimed that there's a fundamental difference between classroom drama work and presentation work of any kind.

The argument goes like this: educational drama work is concerned with *process*, not *product*; a presentation of any kind is essentially a 'product'. Educational drama is for the benefit of the participants, rather than for an audience. Even if a presentation is at least in part for the benefit of the participants (as most people would claim a school play should be) it is also concerned with an audience in a way that educational drama is not.

I agree that there are times when the dramatic work that children do in the classroom is intensely private, and it would be inappropriate to share it with a larger audience. And there are aspects of producing a school play which involve a certain amount of 'marshalling of the troops' – neither an appropriate nor useful classroom activity.

Participants and spectators

I would argue, however, that any drama (or theatre) work necessarily involves an audience at some stage; in intimate classroom work the children are working as both participants and audience. This does not necessarily mean 'performing' in the sense of one group showing another group what they have prepared. It might be that a whole group is participating in a drama, all of them involved simultaneously, all of them 'in role', when the teacher stops the activity and asks the children to reflect on what has been happening; she asks the children in effect to act as an audience to their own work. The children are asked to engage in the drama as participants, and then to step back from what they have been doing and consider the meanings of their actions and the implications of the decisions they have made. They are performers at one moment, and then spectators to their own work. The section on *Reflection* in Chapter 4 gives examples of this strategy in action.

THE SCHOOL PLAY

The school play is both a 'presentation' and a 'production': it's a product, coming at the end of a lengthy process; the building blocks which go to make it up are, effectively, a series of presentations. Seen in this way, producing the School Play need not seem so daunting a task. It requires careful organisation and co-ordination, but it can and should be an activity which originates in classroom drama, which encourages good practice, and which furthers the curriculum work of the school.

It is also worth bearing in mind that even if the school play is mainly a PR exercise, we surely want the PR to be about what we actually *do*.

If presentations, productions and plays are seen as a continuum, a spectrum of dramatic activity, then one end of that spectrum might be the private dramatic play which occurs in the play corner of the lower primary classroom, and the other end of that spectrum would be the full-blown production involving the whole school. It is worth considering how this spectrum might look.

A schematic spectrum of presentational work in schools

What follows is an attempt to set out in schematic form a 'spectrum' of those dramatic activities which directly involve presentation.

It is by no means an exhaustive list, but rather an indicator of the *range* of different types of presentations which might be possible. You could try to categorise and pigeon-hole each, but better at this stage to simply get some sense of the richness and diversity which is possible.

Types of performance and presentation

1. *An individual observed*
2. *Small group to small group*
3. *Small group to class*

Variations: spontaneous work (such as the child working in role in the play corner, observed by the teacher) or prepared and polished; improvisation based or scripted; presented as self-contained entities in their own right or in a wider context (such as part of a whole group drama).

4. *Class-to-class presentations* One class presenting their work to another. This could be self-contained, the summary of work so far, or (as in the project described in Part Five) presented in a wider context, placing the audience, for example, in a specific role.

5. *Assemblies* A small group or a class presenting material to the whole school. This might be primarily theatrical, or might simply include theatrical elements. It might include sharing with the school part of a piece of drama which has been developed by a group or class as part of their curriculum work. As in the previous examples, the work might be spontaneous or rehearsed. An example of an assembly involving unrehearsed performance is given at the end of this chapter.

6. *The Drama Club Play* A piece of theatre performed by a group of children who have chosen to work in extra-curricular time and could therefore be seen to be self-selecting; you would expect them to be highly motivated with strong interest in and commitment to the project.

7. *Performances outside school* Performances to a specific group within the community, perhaps in a retirement home or a hospital.

8. *The school play* A major, fully realised theatrical event in which as many children could be involved as possible.

Possible audiences

- the teacher
- a small group of children
- the rest of the class
- friends
- another class
- members of staff
- another class from another school
- the rest of the school
- another school
- younger children
- old people in sheltered housing
- hospital patients
- a variety of people from the local community
- parents, relatives, governors, invited guests, press.

Purposes and aims

Consider also the different functions that these presentations might serve. Some of these aims might be more appropriate for more informal, small group work; some more appropriate for more formal work on a larger scale. It is again worth stressing the idea of the continuum; that the large scale, formal work *originates* in the small group work that might go on in the classroom.

The possible aims of presentations

Content

- to share ideas
- to motivate further development of ideas
- to raise questions
- to present dilemmas which could lead to further discussion
- to demonstrate the solution to a problem
- to set up a dialogue within a class
- to encourage positive reflection.

Dramatic form

- to contribute to the narrative development of a drama
- to develop theatre skills
- to develop a theatrical vocabulary
- to encourage participation in the editing and shaping process involved in creating a text
- to try out a script in a practical way
- to encourage positive critical analysis
- to experiment with theatrical forms
- to experiment with audience/performer relationships
- to give a group the opportunity of performing in an unfamiliar space
- to develop an understanding of the way in which theatre communicates.

Social

- to make a contribution to the life of the local community
- to celebrate the life and/or history of the school and/or the local community
- to entertain
- to promote public relations.

Theatre forms

Presentation seems to become anathema to people when they see it as separate from the process which leads up to it. But a large-scale production should involve very similar work to that which we undertake regularly in educational drama. The production itself can become a way of sharing that work. Consider the variety of forms which presentations might take. Consider first the different strategies we already use in our classroom drama. Many of them will be as suited to inclusion in a large-scale production as to the classroom:

1. spontaneous improvisations 'spotlighted'
2. polished, prepared improvisations
3. forum theatre
4. still images – either alone or sequenced, with or without captions
5. a short sequence of scenes
6. an episodic narrative devised in sections by different groups, then put together – possibly with a linking narrative
7. a dramatic presentation of classwork from other curriculum areas (e.g. Maths, History, Science, RE)
8. a condensed, edited version of a whole group drama.

Once we start thinking how we might formalise our classroom work in order to share it with a wider audience (be it another class, the rest of the school or parents) we should consider the variety of theatre forms available to us. Plays can, and should, take many forms:

*   documentary – contemporary or historical
*   melodrama
*   a musical
*   a pageant
*   a pantomime.

Each of these can be organised either with

1. A simple linear narrative with a central character and a single through story line; or
2. As a multiple narrative (in which a number of different narrative lines are woven together – as in Shakespeare's plays and television 'soaps').

Any of these might involve scripted work to a greater or lesser extent. They might also involve:

*   dance drama
*   mask work

- mime work
- puppets (glove, string and shadow).

Putting on a school play

As I have already shown, presentational work can take many different forms in primary schools; but of all these the school play is the one which is most worrying to many teachers.

Most people have some memory of dramatic performance in their school days and it is usually an experience they remember vividly, occasionally as something painful but, more frequently, as something pleasurable and fun. But is it all worth it – the disruption, the stress, the upheaval and the time commitment?

My view is that the production of a school play is most likely to be a rewarding, stimulating and enjoyable experience for all when it is a collaborative venture, involving consultation, consensus and sound organisation. Nevertheless, before embarking on a school play of any kind many teachers are beset by doubts and anxieties, so I'll start by addressing these and asking a very important question.

Why do a performance at all?

Some answers might be:
- *Educational* – it will be a valuable educational experience for all those taking part (both staff and children).
- *Public relations* – a sound way of encouraging parents and governors into the school.
- *Tradition* – we always put on a play at Christmas.
- *Prestige* – attracting the attention of the press, the local community, prospective parents.
- *Finance* – the school funds need the valuable boost a successful school play brings.
- *Staff development* – a teacher is interested in developing an extra-curricular drama class.
- *Social* – it will bring together children, parents and staff in a positive working environment.
- *Pleasure* – the children enjoy it.

In different ways each of these responses are valid but are they sufficient justification for the mayhem which can sometimes ensue? We need to be able to answer two further, quite fundamental questions before embarking on a project of this scale; your response to these questions should help you to focus specifically upon your objectives.

What are the most positive functions of the school play? and what are the problems involved in putting it on?

Let's first deal with the positive; looking at what can be achieved:

The possible benefits of a school play

- We should never lose sight of the real potential a school production has as *theatre*. As such it can be educative in itself. Good theatre has a moral purpose. Just as we would hope that the children working on a school production would themselves gain and offer real insights into the 'story' they are working on, so the audience too might find themselves with their perceptions altered. We want them to be moved and excited by what they have seen, to have learnt from it.
- It can provide opportunities for celebrating the work and culture of the school.
- It can enhance the self-esteem of the pupils.
- It should give artistic satisfaction to the participants (pupils, staff and parents): there is the sheer joy of creating and sharing one's work in a supportive and interested environment.
- If a school play is something which originates in the work of the school and develops out of curriculum drama, it demonstrates to parents the educational value of drama.
- The production of a school play can strengthen the bond between the school and the wider community it inhabits, making the school a more integral part of that community.
- It can encourage a better understanding of theatrical form, fostering the development of appropriate skills and a growing critical awareness.

Now let's look at the second point: the *problems* that can arise. Only if we are aware of them can we deal with them; and only if these can be overcome, or at least diminished, is the project likely to be of real value.

The problems and dangers associated with a school play

- It can, and often does, severely disrupt the normal timetable and routine of the school.
- It can detract from the National Curriculum.
- It can produce considerable stress both for the member of staff with overall responsibility and within the school as a whole.
- Because of this disruption and stress the production can set staff member against staff member; it can create considerable liaison problems.
- A large-scale production can make considerable demands on time and energy, stretching the already over-packed school day for both teachers and pupils.

- Some children, taking what they perceive to be leading roles, might begin to think of themselves as 'stars', undoing the benefits of the collaborative approach used elsewhere in educational drama.
- Contrary to the popular wisdom that being on stage in itself gives children confidence, it can traumatise some children; it can damage a child's self-confidence. It's important to remember that simply taking part in the school play is not in itself necessarily a 'good thing'.
- One of the characteristics of educational drama is frequently its spontaneity. A school production can compromise good quality work, and can create an attitude among the children that the play is the real drama and what happens elsewhere is less important.

In short, far from being the positive, celebratory force that brings the school and the community together, it can damage morale and create an atmosphere of resentment, jealousy and exhaustion.

No doubt each reader can add other reasons, derived from personal experience, for *not* doing a school play. My concern is to offer an approach which is both idealistic and realistic, which takes account of the very real problems teachers face in trying to do this type of work; but which clearly recognises the enormously rich and exciting potential there is in it.

Negotiating the priorities

The first thing to do in tackling these problems is to draw up a list of *priorities*. These should be clarified and negotiated before embarking on the production of a school play; I believe that many of the problems listed above arise when there is no consensus among the staff of a school as to what the priorities should be.

Any teacher who is asked to take on overall responsibility for a school play should *insist* on discussion and agreement of these priorities with the whole staff *before* embarking on the project. Asking for an agenda item at a staff meeting with two weeks to go is too late.

What are the basic priorities?

- having a large cast?
- parental involvement?
- fund raising?
- the content of the play?

Who is most important in the production?

- the children participating?

- the staff involved?
- the headteacher?
- the parents?
- the governors?
- the local education office?

What is the scale of the production to be; who will be taking part?

- small scale
  – a selected group, perhaps a class or drama club?
- medium scale
  – involving every child who wants to take part?
- large scale
  – involving every child in the school?

What about the content?

- should it develop out of work already going on in the school?
- should the play itself be used as a way of initiating work throughout the curriculum?
- should it be unrelated to other school work?

Who should decide that content?

- the staff, by consensus?
- the staff in consultation with the children?
- the headteacher?
- the member of staff who will take overall responsibility?

I believe that many of the *problems* described above originate with the notion that the school play is somehow separate from the rest of the school curriculum. What I'm proposing in this book is that such a large-scale production can, and should, have its origins in day-to-day educational drama work.

THEATRE SKILLS AND SKILL-BUILDING EXERCISES

It might seem inappropriate to be teaching what might be termed 'theatre skills' in the primary school. But if drama and theatre are essentially the same thing and there are excellent reasons for teaching drama as a subject in its own right, we should think about what we might mean by the term 'theatre skills'. What skills might children acquire as they learn about the subject of drama and learn to manipulate dramatic form?

In developing a production, theatre practitioners go through a process which is very similar to the one we ask of children in educational drama. I believe it is by analysing this process that we find the crucial skills.

What do actors, playwrights, directors actually do? What are their skills? They observe carefully, they select from all the material they have gathered, they structure that material in such a way that it begins to become meaningful, and they present it so that its meanings are made apparent to an audience.

Let's consider the basic processes that the actor goes through in building a character:

1. *Observing*: People's physical and verbal mannerisms, their external behaviour characteristics, how they behave in different situations. These observations will not only be from 'real life'; we learn a great deal from other sources – biographies, documentaries, plays, films and television. An actor may look further afield and in greater depth, but the source material is essentially the same as the child's.

2. *Understanding*: Attempting to understand the people observed, by relating other people's experiences to their own.

3. *Selecting*: Having made these observations (and, of course, the process is a continuous one) the actor then *selects* carefully from the material that has been gathered. Not all of it can be represented, or shown. Choices are made. We can never see all of a character, nor would we want to. And the choice of what to use, the *selection*, is guided by a director with the intention of keeping an audience focused.

The process of gathering material, selecting from it, editing it and focusing it is more evident when we look at narrative. Strong narrative is as much about withholding information as giving it. We choose particular moments to dramatise, and leave out others. Just as in a good story even the apparent red-herrings are pertinent, so too in theatre.

The writer, the director, the designer, everybody involved in putting on a piece of theatre – they are all involved in a similar process.

So I would maintain that the key theatre skills are:

- observation
- selection
- editing
- structuring and sequencing
- shaping and focusing
- visualising – making images (written, verbal, non-verbal)

These different skills, and a combination of them, are then used to develop:

- character and/or role
- narrative
- non-verbal sign systems (movement, costumes, set, lighting, etc.)

We'll now look at each of these areas in turn, suggesting appropriate ways of building up skills in each of them. Many of the 'skill building exercises' overlap with much of the work we're already doing when we use drama as a learning medium.

Character and role

In the primary school we neither want nor expect children to develop full blown, in-depth characterisations. We use role play for different purposes. But if we expect children to get better at adopting roles, if there is to be improvement in their work, we have to be able to say what it is they're getting better at.

I would suggest that a child is good at role play when they make an *appropriate* selection. Many teachers will have come across a child who puts on a very convincing American accent – in a drama about a medieval village. It might be entertaining for their friends, but it's very distracting. In classroom drama we are asking children to think about problems from a variety of different points of view; in classroom drama the skill of role-play is crucially about adopting and understanding attitudes. When we then ask our class to move onto a stage and present their work to the next door class (or to the whole school in an assembly) we are asking them to share that understanding with others. If this were to get in the way of the initial exploration it could be counter-productive; but we can use the presentation itself as a way of deepening understanding. Presenting work often consolidates learning.

Skill building exercises – character and role

Forum Theatre

In the sections on 'Forum theatre' and 'Teaching in role' (Chapter 3 'Working Methods') and in Chapter 6 on working with children in the early years there are several examples of the children helping the teacher to construct a character through a series of simple questions: 'If you'd like me to play the Pied Piper how should I do it?' The strategy of constructing a character exemplifies the way in which it is possible to highlight the selection of characteristics as a crucial skill in building children's understanding not only of character, but also of dramatic structure. If we're working on creating a play which is to be performed to an audience, the strategy can be developed: we can ask children to go through the same process for each other.

Acceptance exercises[2]

The exercises referred to in the section on 'Teaching in role' (Chapter 3) are useful. Sometimes called *acceptance exercises*, they involve one person starting an improvisation and using the first few moments to give sufficient information to the other through the role to enable the other person to join in. Once the children are familiar with it, they can use it for themselves. The exercise builds listening skills and encourages spontaneity. Much of the spontaneous work we do in educational drama, especially in whole group work, is constantly developing skills of acceptance and endowment (whereby we endow someone else with certain expertise.

Still images

We can use the strategy of making still images as a way of building character, asking either participants or spectators:

- 'Who are these people?'
- 'What does each of them want?'
- 'Tell me something about them that's surprising.'

Costume

There's a theatrical anecdote that it's not until an actor knows what sort of shoes someone wears that they can really begin to build the character. The point is that while you can build a character from inside – through understanding of the emotional life – it's also very helpful to adopt external appearances. Wearing the shoes works as a kind of mask; it makes it easy to start the thought process. I'm not suggesting that you should necessarily ask children to think about a character's shoes, but you might ask them to decide on one item of clothing that a character might wear. Why do people wear different clothes? Function, status, group identity? This sort of work becomes easier if we're going to present our drama to another group because the children need to think about communicating these ideas to others.

Narrative

Work on narrative will inevitably include aspects of story telling. But at a more basic level we are thinking about how the sequencing of events and incidents itself creates meaning. Put a series of pictures in one order and they tell a very different story to the one they tell in another sequence.

We should also be thinking about dramatic structure, about creating moments of dramatic tension, giving the children the opportunity to manipulate dramatic structures for themselves. 'How can we make this more exciting?'

The section on *dramatic tension* in Chapter 4 gives practical examples of how the teacher can use dramatic tension in structuring her drama lessons; and the children will learn a great deal from taking part in well-structured drama lessons that are dramatic. They begin to understand that drama's much more exciting when they don't have it all planned out, when they don't know what's going to happen, and when the solutions to their problems are not easy. But we should also be giving them a chance to explore dramatic tension, to create and play with structures for themselves.

Conflict and change

It is often said that drama's about conflict. That's not only a dangerous over-simplification, it's also very misguided. Conflict frequently creates the possibility for change; and it's change, or the possibility of change, which is always at the heart of drama. So we also want to give children the possibility of exploring and creating moments of change (and possible change) within their work.

Skill-building exercises – narrative

Storyboarding

Having watched a group present their work (be it a spontaneous or a prepared improvisation, or at the end of a session involving the whole group), we can ask them to create a storyboard. The concept is borrowed from film makers who always translate a written script into a visual storyboard before embarking on filming. Many theatre designers do the same thing in the preliminary stages of working on a design. Children are familiar with the idea through comic strips, which are effectively a form of storyboard. You don't need to be a good artist for the exercise to be highly effective; and it's a useful link with Media Studies.

- Choose the five or six key moments in the drama. Draw them in comic strip style.

The exercise is about selecting the key moments and expressing these visually. It's worth keeping the drawings because we can use them again as part of the process of creating a script. It's something we can come back to again and again, reminding ourselves of the most important visual images in a drama; using it as a way of thinking about scenes or about the whole play. The diagrams of the story of the Pied Piper of Hamelin (reproduced on pages 158 and 159) illustrate how a story can be told through storyboard – and also how the same story can become quite different when told from different points of view – in this case from the Piper's point of view and from a Hamelin family's.

Creating dramatic tension

As part of the continuing process of reflection it's always worth asking questions such as 'What was the most exciting moment in the drama?' and 'I wonder what would have happened if . . .' Always remember how powerful silence can be dramatically.

- As an improvisation exercise in its own right, as part of small group work, set the task of acting out a scene in which there is at least ten seconds of silence, at the end of which one of the characters makes an important decision. This exercise is also useful when children are reworking and polishing scenes.
- In the context of a whole group drama, perhaps some of the class are reporters who have to interview members of the local community about the building of a new railway line: during the interviews we can comment positively on the silence of those interviewees who found it difficult to respond.
- Using forum theatre you can take on the role of somebody from whom they need vital information; but you are rather taciturn. They have to try to get you to talk.

How can we make this more exciting?

Still images

The strategy has numerous uses, of course. In this context encourage the children making the images to do so in such a way that the image poses a question. Then ask the audience

- What do we want to know?
- What questions do we want to ask them?
- Look, for example, at drawing number five in the Pied Piper story from the family's point of view:

Why are the family being given a handout by the Mayor?

A game

The game of Keeper of the Keys is described in Chapter 3. Play it normally, and then discuss why it's so exciting to watch – because we

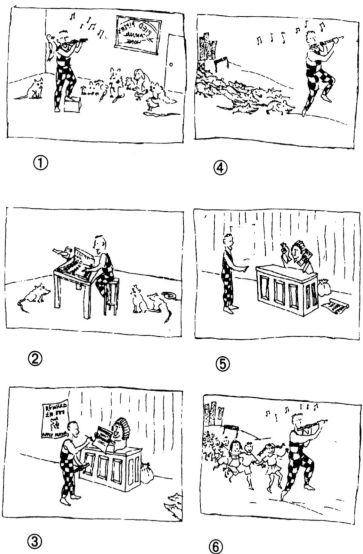

The Pied Piper from the Piper's perspective

Fig. 7.1

The Pied Piper from a family's perspective

don't know what's going to happen; because the two participants come very close, but don't quite touch; because there are a number of near misses. It's less interesting, less enjoyable to watch when it's all over very quickly, when there's not time for the tension to build up.

- Try playing the game with your eyes open, but pretending you've got them shut. Make it as tense as you can.
- Try representing the moments of tension and release of tension on a graph; then play out a short scene with the same dramatic structure – perhaps a bank robbery or an escape attempt.

Non-verbal sign systems

Throughout their regular classroom drama, children will have been using non-verbal sign systems; they will have been reading body language; thinking about the way the space between people becomes important. In presentation work, the manipulation of this should be something they begin to do more consciously, but you're only asking them to think more formally about something which should have been an integral part of their work from the beginning. They should be familiar with the rich significance and power of symbols.

Skill-building exercises – non-verbal sign systems

1. Set up *forum theatre* work in which *eye contact* and the *use of space* become highly significant. For example:

   (a) tackling the obstinate old man who refuses to move from his house ('The Construction of a Railway', Chapter 5)
   (b) persuading the giant to move away from the centre of town ('The Giant Awakes', Chapter 5). How do we position our-selves? Do we want to look him in the eye?
   (c) first contact with an alien. How do you think the alien reads our facial expressions?

2. Examine still images as if they were photographs, picking up on the moments and avoidance of eye contact, thinking carefully about the way the space between people itself becomes significant.

3. If you have the use of a video camera use it as part of the drama: in non-performance based work; in rehearsal; and even as part of the performance. Perhaps an interview on video could be part of the performance – with a TV monitor showing in close up the details of facial expression which most people in the audience would otherwise have missed. (See also Appendix.)

'Stage sets'

As with costume and props we should be thinking how we can effectively create a sense of place with the minimum of fuss. Reception children who create a dragon's cave by using the gymnastics horse covered in cloth are making a set.

In Chapter 5 there is a specific example ('The Iron Age Encampment') of children building a set as part of a drama project. It is this spirit of experimentation that we want to encourage. Children do it all the time in their own play. Encourage it formally:

How many different ways can you use a chair? Can you use it as if it were:

- a television
- a motor bike
- a bob sleigh
- a lawn mower
- a push chair
- a cooker
- a cauldron
- a door
- the bars of a cage
- the railings in a park
- the controls of an aeroplane
- a periscope
- a hat.

We can then encourage this same sort of experimentation with other objects – a piece of string, a rope, a garden cane, an easel, a waste paper bin, lengths of coloured fabric.

It's not only far more educational to involve children in the process at every stage (from deciding what the school play is going to be about to designing and making the set); it also makes your life easier. If they genuinely have a responsibility as great as yours the quality of work will be greatly enhanced, and the opportunities for learning will be greatly expanded.

Designing the play can become part of an Art and/or CDT project.

Look at the sets toured by theatre-in-education companies. They are usually both visually and financially economical, creating strong visual images which enhance the play, engage the audience's interest before the play has even started and focus the audience's attention.

MASKS, COSTUME AND LIGHTING

We will now look in a bit more detail at how these different aspects work together, and at what are sometimes considered the more technical aspects of theatre. It is worth bearing in mind, however, that working with masks, lighting and costume can be useful not only in terms of the production of a school play, but can really enhance your day-to-day classroom drama.

Masks

Masks are useful both in performance and as part of the process of drama. Consider the way masks are used in other than theatrical and dramatic contexts:

- to protect
- to identify
- to disguise
- to conceal
- to serve as symbols (in rituals).

In 'real life' and in dramatic fictions the different functions frequently work together: Batman's mask both identifies him to us as Batman, and conceals his true identity; a welder's goggles (or knight's helmet) are a form of mask; they protect, certainly, but they also identify and conceal. The *protective* function is less interesting to us in drama than the other functions, although as with all generalisations there will certainly be some fascinating exceptions to this – such as when someone enters wearing a protective mask which conceals the face. But even here it is the concealment that creates the dramatic tension.

Masks can cover either part or all of the face and head. Half masks – covering the eyes, but leaving the mouth unimpeded – are particularly useful because they allow the user to vocalise clearly, if that's required.

Children are familiar with plastic Halloween-style masks but these are probably the least useful to us as drama teachers because they are so specific, and because using them wastes an opportunity for children to create their own masks (which can be an exciting way of encouraging children who enjoy art but are nervous of drama).

The benefits of using masks

1. Using masks encourages the development of non-verbal communication skills; the spoken word is much less important than non-verbal language, so masks can be very useful when working with children for whom English is not their first language. Because masks force the wearer to communicate through simple movements, their use can be liberating and enabling. Shy

children (and adults for that matter) find that they are able to 'hide' behind the mask; their movements become larger, more definitive, more meaningful; they frequently feel released from inhibitions and familiar behaviour patterns, they no longer behave as they think they are expected to.

2. 'Children project their feelings and ideas through a mask, while they, themselves, remain hidden.'[3] In this respect they are very like puppets. Both masks and puppets enable children to play with language and use it more freely than they would otherwise.

3. Masks enable us to make cultural explorations. They have been, and still are, an important part of many cultures; they can be used in specific cultural contexts – such as enactments and explorations of the Rama and Sita story, or in a celebration of Chinese New Year.

We can use masks in a ritual that we construct as part of a drama, so we will be making our own masks and deciding on appropriate uses for them as part of a drama, which could either remain in the classroom, or become part of a shared performance.

Making masks

The essence of good mask work is simplicity. You can buy masks commercially, but they are never as interesting as the ones you and the children make for yourselves. The simpler the mask the more effective it is. Really good masks can be made from:

*   paper bags
*   paper plates
*   sheets of card
*   photographs stuck onto sheets of card.

Using masks

Some people like to put their mask on in front of a mirror and get to know it like that; but while working in front of a mirror tells you what the mask looks like, it doesn't tell you about people's reactions to it. I prefer working with masks collaboratively from the beginning.

The following exercises should either be done with a partner (one wearing a mask, the other responding as audience) or with individuals working in front of the class. Perhaps you, the teacher, can lead the way by trying on a mask and asking the class for their responses.

Put the mask on. What does your audience think the mask is expressing when you:

*   tilt the head forward?

- tilt the head to one side?
- turn your head to one side?
- turn and tilt at the same time?

What sort of movements seem to suit the mask:

- heavy and ponderous or light and airy?
- quick or slow?
- confident, wholehearted movements or short, hesitant ones?

Try to find ways of showing how the mask expresses:

- happiness
- excitement
- anger, aggression,
- the desire to be friendly
- curiosity, inquisitiveness
- fear
- shyness, nervousness.

It's unlikely that any one mask can express all of those. Experiment and find out what yours can express. How does it surprise you? Often a mask which looks angry can express remarkable tenderness, can unexpectedly appear timid.

Having experimented with the head movements, try taking them into the whole body. Give the mask a name. How does this person, or creature:

- walk?
- sit down?
- stand up?
- go into a shop and ask for a bag of sweets?
- respond when being ticked off?
- respond to a strange object?

In performance work, remember that most masks work best when facing the audience. A performance involving mask work is usually best staged 'end on' (see p. 169).

Costume

Simple use of costume can greatly enhance any drama, be it exploratory and spontaneous or carefully prepared and presented to a large audience. The basic function of costume (in a theatrical sense) is to signify and to symbolise:

- character
- power and status
- group identity.

Over elaborate, fussy costuming is distracting and unproductive.

Children of all ages enjoy dressing up. As adults we talk about 'dressing up' to go out; putting on special clothes makes us feel different, it helps us feel we're changing roles, moving out of the humdrum.

Teachers who use the strategy of working in role often use an item of clothing to signify that they're moving in and out of role. It's helpful to you and to the children. In this sense we could think of a briefcase as an item of costume – 'When I am carrying it, I'm in role as the managing director; when I put it down I'm your teacher again.'

In a similar way it sometimes helps for children to take on one simple item of clothing to indicate that they are in role. It's by no means always necessary; but it's a useful way of signifying visually a commitment to the role. The item might be as simple as a piece of coloured cloth draped over the shoulders like a cape.

When we're working on presenting work to an audience we can ask the children for suggestions. How do we make sure the audience will know who we are?

It's well worth arranging for space somewhere in the school to store various simple costumes which might prove useful.

Fabrics and textiles as costume

It's also worth collecting together a range of fabrics and textiles – not just to turn into costumes, but to use *as* costumes. The Appendix of this book includes a section suggesting how you might get hold of such items.

If you're working with a school drama club, where you're less pressured for time, you can work with the children on creating costumes from various lengths of cloth, fabrics and textiles. You might start by laying out a long piece of blue fabric down the centre of the hall. 'This is the river. How can we use what we've got here to show where the forest is?' 'Who lives in the forest? Find something and wear it in a way that tells us something about this person.' So fabrics are used as belts, leggings, shawls, scarves, capes – and we begin to get a sense of colour and texture becoming meaningful.

Costume for the school play

Always keep costume as simple as possible. Frequently parents are asked to help with costumes on school plays. Make sure that everybody knows what's required as far in advance as possible.

Parents are often much more competitive than children. Be sure that the costume-maker volunteers know the purpose of the costumes; while the parent who makes the spectacularly bright and colourful costume might feel proud, the child who has to wear it (knowing full well how inappropriate it looks) is likely to be exceedingly embarrassed.

If you've decided that it's worth trying to make a large number of simple unifying costumes (coloured tabards, for example) it's well worth making one yourself – or working closely with a colleague or parent and using this to create templates.

Your presentation may take the form of a ritual, in which case the act of putting on and taking off costume can become highly significant.

If you're working in a school with a multi-cultural intake, make use of the rich variety of costumes that the children themselves know about. Try at least to create opportunities to indicate the way that costume is used in other cultures.

Lighting

The following brief notes are offered as a simple guide to using lighting effectively. Buying, or even hiring, lights can be an expensive business.

Using lighting

Lighting has four main functions:

* to illuminate
* to delineate space
* to focus attention
* to create 'atmosphere' and alter our perception of the way we 'read' a theatrical event.

All these functions can be brought into operation both in performances for an audience and in drama sessions not intended for an outside audience.

Light can be manipulated in three ways:

* by the positioning of the light sources
* by varying the intensity or brightness of the different light sources
* by colouring the light.

One of the easiest ways to understand how lighting works is to begin by experimenting with powerful torches in a darkened room; the great advantage of this is that children can be involved actively in all stages of an experiment, which could also become part of a science scheme.

- The *positioning* of the light source changes the effect that it has. Lighting from below, for example, creates a grotesque, eerie effect because we are so used to human faces being lit by 'natural' light, which comes from above. Asking *why* someone looks so strange when their face is lit in this way could open up a number of fascinating discussions.
- The *intensity* of torch light can be changed by putting different thicknesses of white cloth in front of the torch lens; the colour of the light can be changed by putting a coloured 'gel' in front of the torch. Experiment with minimal colour. 'Straw' (very pale orange) or 'steel' (very light blue) gels are remarkably effective because they subtly change the atmosphere.

Stage lighting

In the theatre lights are known as *lanterns*, and the bulbs that go in them are referred to as *lamps*. This is useful to know if you're hiring or borrowing; and I'll stick to the terminology here.

There are four basic types of lantern:

1. *Fresnel* spotlight – is the most versatile and most widely used. It has a frosted glass lens and creates a soft edged beam of light which can be focused and made wider or smaller. If the school wants some lanterns of its own buy a few of these.
2. *Profile* spotlight – a much more expensive and technically sophisticated lantern. It has at least one clear glass lens which focuses the light into a hard-edged beam. (The follow-spots which play on the front curtains in pantomimes are a kind of profile spot.) They have very little general use; even in the professional theatre their usage is limited and specialised. Because of this, however, secondary schools frequently have some which are surplus to requirements.
3. *Floodlights* provide a big, rather weak, wide beam. They have no lens, simply a mirror behind a lightbulb. They cannot be focused. They are certainly cheap, but are extremely difficult to use effectively and are only little used in the theatre. If a local secondary school was giving some away it might be worth accepting them.
4. *Parcans* – a comparatively recent development. Much loved by pop and rock groups, these are extremely powerful and very robust lanterns which are cheap to buy. The catch is that the lamps

which power them are very expensive! The lanterns are effectively car headlight units in a metal can and provide an intense beam of nearly parallel light. As with floodlights, no adjustments and no focusing are possible. Wonderful for special effects (one pointing straight down from the ceiling would be a perfect teleporter in a science fiction drama). *Pinspots* are a variation of 'Parcans'. They are very similar in that they cannot be focused, and project a powerful beam of nearly parallel light – the difference, as you might expect, is that the beam of light is very narrow.

All the above lanterns have slots or catches in which gel holders can be placed to alter the colour of the projected light.

Technology is catching up with stage lighting and there are other types of lantern – most of them very expensive. The above, however, are likely to remain the *basic* types for many years to come.

Safety and other important considerations

1. *Lamps for stage lanterns are very expensive*   (In the case of a 'Parcan' they are more expensive than the lantern itself.) Modern lights are tungsten halogen and made of quartz glass. If you have to change a bulb never handle it directly. Always use the plastic glove provided, and read the instructions.

2. *Always use a lighting board*   If you are hiring or borrowing lanterns, always obtain a portable lighting board at the same time. There are several varieties of lighting stands now available which are supplied complete with simple lighting board control. It is dangerous and foolish to plug a lantern directly into the mains. At the very least plugging directly into the mains drastically shortens the life of the bulbs – and replacing one bulb could cost you more than the hire charge for a simple lighting board.

3. *Never move a lantern until it has cooled down*   Stage lanterns get extremely hot when they have been in use for even a few minutes. When they are still hot the bulbs are extremely fragile. If you try to move one not only will you burn yourself, you will almost certainly damage the bulb.

4. *Always attach a safety chain* immediately after fixing lanterns.

5. *Always hang lanterns the right way up,* that is with the flex at the base. If they are inverted the light can easily be damaged and might explode – which, at the least, is rather distracting.

There are several companies who specialise in stage lighting and sound equipment, etc.; many of them offer a hire service. Most will send a representative to the school to offer advice if required. Contact the drama officer of your local Regional Arts Board (see Appendix) for addresses and telephone numbers. If you want to borrow lighting it's also worth contacting your local secondary school, Teachers' Centre or Drama/Arts Centre. Even if they cannot loan you the equipment you want, you should be able to make contact with someone who can offer useful advice.

AUDIENCE/PERFORMER RELATIONSHIPS

Whenever children show their work – be it to other members of the class or to a large audience – we should ask them to consider their relationship to that audience. This might simply mean asking 'Where do you want them to be?' or it might involve quite complex decisions about staging. All too frequently high quality work does not realise its full potential simply because the audience and the performers are at opposite ends of the hall.

The discussion of staging which follows relates specifically to assemblies and school plays, but the principle of seeking out the most appropriate form of audience/performer relationship applies to all types of presentational work.

'End on' staging

The commonest form of staging any kind of presentation is known as 'end on', with the performers at one end of the hall and the audience in the body of the hall, as in proscenium arch theatres. Sometimes the performers are raised on a stage, sometimes the audience are raised in tiers to be able to see better. But although this is probably the most familiar form of staging, it's not necessarily the most effective. One of the big problems with it (especially where the audience cannot be tiered) is that those members of the audience sitting near the back can neither see nor hear clearly.

It's probably more productive, and certainly encourages greater flexibility, if instead of thinking in terms of a 'stage' we think about *performance space* or *acting areas*. This certainly makes it easier to see the relevance of the discussion to classroom drama work.

Consider the basic requirements:

- The audience need to see and hear what's going on.
- We need to be able to get people on and off the acting area easily.
- We will want to be able to focus the audience's attention.
- The audience should be clear about what is and is not part of the play.
- We may want props and simple scenery in the acting area.
- We may want to light the acting area.

Various staging possibilities

Diagrams illustrating each of the following appear in the Appendix (pps. 240–1).

* We can set our audience at one end with the performance space at the other ('end on' style, as described above). (Diagram 1)
* We can make our acting area the centre of the hall, with our audience down each side (as described in the example at the end of this Chapter). (Diagram 2)
* We can seat our audience on three sides of the performance space. (Diagram 3)
* We can have two or three different acting areas, with each representing different places in the narrative of the play and ask our audience to promenade, moving between different acting areas. (Diagram 4)
* We can perform Arena style with our audience all round – making sure the performers can get to the acting area. (Diagram 5)
* There are other possibilities, such as having an acting area which traverses the Hall in both directions. (Diagram 6).

Each of these has advantages and disadvantages. Different types of presentation are suited to different types of staging. Do give serious thought to some of the alternatives suggested. It's well worth experimenting in classwork and assemblies before risking all in a major school play.

SCRIPTS AND SPONTANEITY

There is an understandable wariness about using scripts in primary schools because it is sometimes feared that they can intimidate children and inhibit the children's own creative work.

Children's artwork often suffers when they are shown the 'right way' to represent things. But I don't believe that any child's artwork has been inhibited by looking at the work of artists per se. It all depends on the context. If we use the work of the artist as a way of showing what is possible, rather than as a model for imitation, looking at an artist's work can be an experience which stretches, liberates and encourages.

If we use scripts as restrictive models ('the right way') they will certainly inhibit children's own creative drama work; but they can be used as creatively as any other stimulus.

We can create our own scripts or we can work with existing texts. Both activities are useful and mutually enhancing.

Creating scripts

The form

'Scripts' can take many different forms; the one we're most familiar with being the published playtext, with stage directions to suggest moves and lines of dialogue attributed to specific characters. But scripts can take other, simpler forms. Children's first attempts at creating scripts could take one of these forms.

- A storyboard is itself a form of script – as is a comic strip.
- A summary of scenes, indicating their running order, but not prescribing dialogue – using words and/or pictures. This is particularly well suited to the type of play which includes much improvised dialogue.

Developing a script

- We can use forum theatre to develop a script, trying out different lines of dialogue and different ways of playing a scene (aggressive, frightened, hesitant, conciliatory, ready to compromise, defensive – whatever, in all sorts of different combinations) running back over a scene until it feels right, or has the effect that we want.
- Interviews can be scripted (possibly in the context of a whole group drama, where the interview needs to be recorded on video or audio tape).
- Stories can be turned into scripted form (using the written word and/or pictures).
- The skill of editing can be put into practice: working with a published 'script' of perhaps ten lines. Cut it down to six.
- The same exercise, but in a dramatic context: record an interview for TV or radio. Transcribe it. Now cut it down in length because the producer says we can only have twenty seconds 'On Air'.
- Scripts can be written for puppets as well as for human actors.

When thinking about a script, or when working with children to create one, the following very simple questions can often get you out of the sticky, unproductive mess we all find ourselves in from time to time. In our play -

1. What do these people want?
2. What is stopping them from getting what they want?
3. Where do they start? What's normal for them at the beginning of the play?
4. What happens to change this, to threaten our characters?

5.   What sort of struggle do they have? What sort of a mess do they get themselves in?
6.   And how do they get out of it?!

The problem of trying to recapture spontaneity

It is very common for work which originates in improvisation to become dull, flat and lifeless when it's repeated. It's one of the reasons people are wary of presentation work. We want people to share in our excitement, and it's terribly disappointing when what we know was exciting is parroted nervously.

There are no simple solutions to the problem, although one way is to allow people to share in the spontaneous work itself (there's an account of this type of work at the end of this chapter). By following the guidelines suggested in this book (seeing exploratory, spontaneous drama as part of the same continuum, the same spectrum of dramatic activity, as large-scale productions) the problem should be minimised. But there are some specific things you can do to alleviate the problem:

*   Encourage children to create their own dialogue. Discuss it with them. Give them the responsibility. The dialogue can be created in any of the ways already suggested.
*   When rehearsing always try to give clear tasks; make sure each child knows what the character they are playing wants at any particular moment. Use rehearsals to explore, to find out.[4]
*   It's much easier to remember images than lines. Give children clear visual paths through the play – moving from one image to another.
*   Don't over-rehearse. Each rehearsal should have a clear purpose.
*   Make sure that if children do have to learn lines they understand not only what they're saying, but why they're saying it. There's a story (and I don't think it's apocryphal) about the little boy playing the innkeeper in the Nativity play who answers the door to Mary and Joseph; and in response to Joseph's 'Is there any room at the Inn?', he replies warmly 'Oh, yes. Come in.' No doubt he was trying to please.

Working with published scripts

Scripts in a wider dramatic context

If we're going to study written plays, we need to do so in ways which are exciting and non-threatening. Remember that many adults find plays difficult to read. We need to begin by familiarising children with scripts as a particular written form.

Consider the following – all of which are forms of script – and the ways we might use them within a larger dramatic context:

- A short transcription of an interview – which then becomes vital evidence as part of an enquiry.
- A stowaway's journal is found – in which there is a transcription of an incriminating conversation overheard.
- A spaceship computer displays on its screen a written account of the dialogue between itself and an alien life form.

Storyboarding

Using a short scene from a play, ask the children to create a still image from it. Develop a short sequence of images. Add a couple of lines of dialogue from the original script. Storyboard them. Before reading the whole play encourage the children to speculate about it. Don't read it all at one sitting. Start working on it in manageable sections. Having looked at several scenes, create another storyboard and put the images together in different sequences, always trying to stimulate curiosity about the play. What you want is that they should be impatiently nagging you to find out more.

Concealing dialogue

Give children two lines of dialogue extracted from a suitable play. Ask them to conceal this dialogue by working out (either through improvisation or as a written exercise) what might come before it; what might follow. They should start by considering Who, What and Where (essentially the same process as is outlined in the section on small group work in Chapter 3). The rest of the class then tries to guess which lines were written and which were improvised.

The exercise is enjoyable in itself, but you will have to be careful that it doesn't become too competitive by discussing what you need to do to hide the dialogue effectively. The exercise involves children in quite sophisticated textual analysis and synthesis. To be successful they have to consider speech rhythms, style and tone as well as content. And then they have to construct dialogue which matches the rhythm, style, tone and content of the original. It's quite remarkable how good children are at the exercise once they're grasped it.

Here are some sample texts to work with:

A   No, I don't want any. Where are you going anyway?
B   You can come with me tomorrow, if you like.

A   What's the matter?
B   Nothing. I've come to see Grandpa.

A What's the machine going to do?
B You think Grandpa's crazy don't you.

The extracts (with references to specific characters removed) are all from *Perpetual Motion*, a play for seven to twelve year olds.[5]

In each case the first line is itself clearly a response to something; it's better to choose a piece of dialogue which implies action of some kind.

There are regrettably few scripts specifically written for the Primary age range, although a number of excellent plays originally written for theatre in education companies have now been published.

Chapter 8 – 'The Donkeyman's Daughter' – gives a detailed account of how a school play might be developed out of classroom work.

Chapter 10 – 'Planning a Project' – explores how one might plan and teach a project which culminates in presentation work.

Both these examples involve preparing work before showing it to an audience. It is worth considering ways of sharing spontaneous drama work with an audience, as the following example demonstrates.

Example: Sharing spontaneous drama work

I recently arranged to work with a class of Year Five children for an afternoon, only to discover that at the end of the afternoon they were supposed to be performing 'something' for an Assembly. But the 'something', whatever it might have been, was in their teacher's head – not theirs and not mine – and the teacher was not in school. So, what to do? Cancel the Assembly? Spend the whole afternoon polishing up something specially (in which case most of the children would have been sitting around for most of the time)? Or have a good long drama session in the hope that we'd find something really interesting and want to share it with the rest of the school?

I put it to the children – it was going to be a risk for them as much as for me – and they were very keen to have a go.

We did a drama about the people of Nazareth asked to leave home for the Roman census. We set up the community; I entered in-role as a Roman Centurion. (The example has already been referred to in the sections on 'Teaching in Role' and 'Reflection' in Chapters 3 and 4.)

The children were very engaged in the drama and all of us forgot the time. With fifteen minutes to go we realised we had no Assembly prepared. We discussed what had happened, and agreed that we should try and share our afternoon's work. I asked the children if there was anybody who didn't want to take an active role in what we were going to do. In the context it was especially important to negotiate this. In this instance everybody said they wanted to take part; exciting for all of us, but pretty scary as well.

When the rest of the school came in they were asked to sit down the

---

Continued

Example continued

two long sides of the hall. Like this there would be a much larger acting area for the class; and everybody in the audience would be able to see the work.

In order for the presentation to work I had to function as a sort of MC, linking the work and occasionally narrating. They set up still images of life in Nazareth prior to the arrival of the centurion – with each image given a spoken caption by one of the group – and then brought them to life. One person from each group then said something about the nature of their work.

I then entered in role, as before, and read the decree aloud – this time stopping the drama immediately afterwards, asking the children to get into family groups and show, through their attitudes to their work, a response to the decree. The children worked briefly on this, the audience able to see only those children nearest to them. So we stopped and spotlighted several groups, eavesdropping on the conversations.

It was at this point that I asked the children to think about their private reactions: 'What are you thinking that you would not want anyone else to hear?' Volunteers shared their thoughts with the audience (see 'Reflection', Chapter 4).

We played out a farewell scene – small group spontaneous improvisations, one group at a time. This was followed by still images conveying the hardships of their journeys.

Using an extract from the Bible as a narrative link we moved the drama to Bethlehem, although no children had been specifically playing Mary and Joseph – and then used similar techniques to explore the problems facing the people working in King Herod's court, focusing particularly on the moment when they heard of his decree to have the firstborn sons slaughtered.

We had feared that we'd have barely enough material for ten minutes; but the assembly lasted nearly half an hour. The children were proud of themselves; the audience (other children, teachers and parents) had been enthralled – the work had been highly dramatic!

I would certainly accept that in that type of forum the shy and nervous children were unlikely to volunteer; if that was the only experience of drama they were getting it would be woefully inadequate. But while there has to be space for very private work, the excitement of occasionally working in the public arena complements it very positively.

Sharing the sort of drama that is usually private had been its own best advertisement; parents who'd seen it were very enthusiastic. If we're going to hope to develop drama in schools we have to convince parents of its value. What better way than allowing them to share in the excitement of what we actually do?

Bibliography

Alkema, C. J. 1981. *Mask Making*, Sterling, New York.

Bari, R. 1977. *Behind the Mask*, Personabooks, Oakland, California, USA.

Johnstone, K. 1981. *Impro*, Methuen.

Lacey, S. and Woolland, B. 1989 'Drama in Education – A Radical Theatre Form', *2D*, Vol. 8, No. 2, Summer, pp. 4–15. The article argues that drama in education 'is itself a particular form of theatre practice', both innovative and radical.

Lacey, S. and Woolland, B. 1992. 'Educational drama and radical theatre Practice', *New Theatre Quarterly*, Vol. VIII, No. 29, February. (With reference to a specific drama project, the article develops further the notion that drama in education and theatre are inextricably linked.)

McCaslin, N. 1990. *Creative Drama in the Classroom (5th edn)*, Longman, New York. (Contains some excellent chapters on Mime (pp. 70–98), Movement (pp. 50–69), Mask (pp. 145–52) and Puppets (pp. 122–45).)

Morgan, N. and Saxton, J. 1987. *Teaching Drama*, Hutchinson Education, pp. 109–17.

O'Neill, C. 1989. 'Ways of seeing: audience function in theatre', *2D*, Vol. 8, No. 2, Summer, pp. 16–29. Cecily O'Neill's article 'traces the growing awareness in recent years of the audience or spectator dimension in classroom drama'.

Redington, C. (ed.) 1987. *Six T.I.E. Programmes*, Methuen.

Spolin, V. 1963. *Improvisation for the Theatre*, Hutchinson.

Spolin, V. 1987. *Theatre Games for the Classroom*, Northwestern University Press, Evanston, Illinois, USA.

Notes:

1. Johnson, L. and O'Neill, C. (ed.) 1984. *Dorothy Heathcote – Collected Writings on Education and Drama*, Hutchinson.
2. Johnstone, K. 1981. *Impro*, Methuen. (Contains a great many excellent acceptance exercises. The book is for adult drama students, but some of the ideas can easily be adapted.)
3. McCaslin, N. 1990. *Creative Drama in the Classroom* (5th edn), Longman, New York. p. 147.
4. Spolin, V. 1963. *Improvisation for the Theatre*, Pitman Publishing. Contains numerous excellent short exercises to improve concentration which work by focusing the players on a specific task, distracting them from worrying about how they're doing in the eyes of their peers. The philosophy can be summarised as 'Get on with the task and everything else will fall into place!' If this sounds rather simplistic, remember it's the teacher's job to find an appropriate task – and while that's never an easy task, Viola Spolin's book is very clear.
5. Woolland, B. *Perpetual Motion* commissioned by Hampshire Theatre in Education Company, first performed 1991.

CHAPTER 8

The Donkeyman's Daughter

.

Introduction

This detailed example is given to indicate how a play involving every child in a primary school might be developed from a New Testament Christian story. The example is deliberately chosen because it seems in some ways to be similar to the 'traditional' school play, both in its subject matter and in that it could be performed to a large audience of parents, friends, relatives and governors. This is, however, conceived as a project in which the performance arises out of day-to-day classroom work and educational drama, complementing it rather than forcing it to be put on the 'back burner'.

Many schools perform a Nativity play of some kind at Christmas. This example offers a play on an Easter theme involving research and celebration of the Jewish Feast of Passover (Pesach); but the methods and principles described could be very easily adapted to a Nativity or to a play which celebrates any religious festival.

The example presumes that the school has six classes, about 170 children in all, with an age range from five to eleven year olds.

Spaces used in preparation/rehearsal:

Classrooms, music room, school hall.

Performance space

School hall.

AIMS AND OBJECTIVES

The overall aims of the project:

1. *To develop*:
    - knowledge and understanding of the New Testament story of Christ's last days on earth;

- an understanding of what people's lives were like in Palestine two thousand years ago;
- theatrical skills of presentation;
- an appreciation of the value of the work of others.

2. *To explore and examine*:
   - the responses of groups of 'ordinary' people (who are mentioned only in passing in the Christian gospels) to Christ's arrival in Jerusalem and His subsequent crucifixion;
   - the meanings of trust and forgiveness;
   - how we can stand up as individuals for what we believe is right when there is great pressure from our peers to do otherwise; how we decide whom we can trust.

   (These might be seen as the *key organising questions*.)

3. *To integrate*:
   - the teaching of Drama, History, Geography and Religious Education in such a way that they complement each other;
   - the work of different classes so that children can learn from each other.

Objectives

In a project of this size, the *aims* of the project should be agreed by the whole staff (and perhaps those parents who had volunteered to be actively involved) at a preliminary meeting, but it is reasonable to assume that many of the objectives would be set by the individual class teachers; those appropriate for the top junior class would hardly be workable with reception infants.

I would want to include the following as objectives:

1. to enrich language development (including skills of listening, reporting, describing, negotiating)
2. to develop an understanding of cause and effect narrative
3. to motivate extensive research in related curriculum areas – particularly History, Geography and Religious Education
4. to enrich and develop art work associated with or related to the project
5. to initiate and encourage research into stories in other world religions.

PRELIMINARY PLANNING

One of the dangers of a project like this is that it can get out of hand and can even have a demoralising effect on many of the staff participating in it. It's clearly important to have an initial planning meeting and regular meetings thereafter, but they do need a very clear agenda. If well organised they can be short and energising.

I would suggest that the agenda for the opening planning meeting might be as follows:

1. Agreeing dates and deadlines. (See notes on rehearsal schedules in Appendix.)
2. Agreeing the scale and form of the project
    *   whether to include music
    *   audience, whom to invite
    *   intended length of performance
    *   budget available
    *   performance space(s)
    *   resources and equipment availability.
3. Agreeing the content of the play
    *   Brainstorming ideas to agree on the groups of people involved in the story (see below).
    *   Which classes will do what.
4. Agreeing class and teacher responsibilities
    *   Will individual teachers take specific responsibilities, or will these be shared – costuming, lighting, etc.
    *   How detailed should the costuming be, how will it be lit, etc.

Any production of this size will inevitably involve some timetable disruption, but it should be kept to a minimum, and the project should be organised in such a way that the individual classroom teachers can make their own contribution, drawing on their own strengths.

It may be appropriate if one teacher, who is confident about teaching drama, deals with all the initial drama development work and hands over to the other teachers once the children have the ideas up and running, as it were. It will certainly need one teacher to be prepared to co-ordinate the work; but this does not have to mean that person taking on a role as a 'Director'.

Let us presume that as a result of the initial planning meeting, the staffroom brainstorming has resulted in the following:

Groups of people affected by Christ's entry into Jerusalem

Romans

*   Roman Soldiers – those in the garrison
                           those on crucifixion duty
*   Pilate's guard
*   the families (in Rome) of the soldiers posted to Palestine as an occupying army
*   Pilate's family

Pontius Pilate's Palace

*   those working in the kitchens
*   those working as servants elsewhere in the palace

Roman and Jewish Tax collectors

The Jews

*   the Moneychangers in the Temple
*   those visiting the Temple to worship
*   the Jewish Sanhedrin
*   the inhabitants of villages near Jerusalem, through which Jesus passes on his way
*   those who patronise or work in an inn on the edge of Jerusalem
*   the cross makers
*   those who watch the procession to Calvary
*   the owner of the room where the Last Supper takes place
*   the thieves in prison awaiting crucifixion
*   Zealots
*   Pharisees

IMPLEMENTATION AND DEVELOPMENT

At this point some might want to create a simple story line; but I would suggest that, although the final play definitely does need its own internal narrative structure, the Bible story itself gives sufficient coherence to the project to enable one to leave the precise narrative of the play to develop out of the work of the children with their individual class teachers.

There are many different ways of proceeding from this point:

*   Each class has a separate responsibility, the overall narrative arising out of the different incidents occurring in the different locations.
*   The work starts with Year Six children who develop a number of different points of view – village people, Pharisees, Zealots, Romans – and then take on these different roles as they go in small groups to work with other classes.
*   The work starts with a drama club, a group of twenty to thirty children who volunteer to take on the major roles in the play. The other children become involved at a later stage in the project, taking on the roles of specific groups.

I will assume that we've chosen the first of these, in which case each teacher chooses one of the groups mentioned above and works with their own class to develop a simple drama involving that group. Assuming that the class number corresponds to their age (i.e. Class 1 comprises Reception and Year 1 children) we might organise the project thus:

Class 1	Those working in Pontius Pilate's Palace.
Classes 2 and 3	The inhabitants of villages near Jerusalem.
Class 4	Those who live in Jerusalem and watch the procession to Calvary.
Class 5	The Jewish Sanhedrin and those visiting the Temple to worship.
Class 6	Romans – soldiers and families.

In addition I would want, at this early stage, to allocate responsibilities (among staff and parents) in the following areas:

• publicity
• front of house

and possibly (if and as required)

• props
• set construction
• lighting
• sound
• costume
• music.

If there were Jewish children in the school I would ask them to explain about the feast of Passover to other children. It might be that we would ask parents to work with their children in this, talking not only about Passover, but also the wider cultural context.[1] Our play would be as much about the experience of living in Palestine at the time of Christ as it is about the Christian Easter story as such.

Preparations for all

With each of the classes we would start by working on what they already knew about, maybe how they imagined day-to-day living and working in pre-industrial rural communities, maybe cooking unleavened bread. This could lead to a variety of inter-curricular work which could be tackled in varying degrees of depth. It might include research into:

- Jewish names and festivals, particularly Pesach
- clothes
- houses and homes
- work – farming, shepherding, fishing, crafts
- climate, geography
- history – organisation of the Roman Empire. How long were troops stationed abroad?

There follow some brief suggestions about the drama work that might be undertaken with each of the classes at this stage. Each of the suggestions demands a working knowledge of the working practices described in Part Two. If the teacher wanted to work in role at this stage it could be very productive, either asking a child to take on the role at a later stage, or adopting roles which will be 'offstage' in the final presentation.

We would probably not involve the younger classes at the beginning of the project. I don't think it would be fair to expect them to sustain a single project for so long. But they could take part in the project and enjoy doing so. It would be up to the individual teachers to decide at what point they joined in.

It is important to establish early on with every class that girls can take on the roles of men, and boys can play women.

Class 1

Those working in Pontius Pilate's palace –

- What is their work?
- What do they think it would be like working in a palace?
- Preparing food in the palace kitchens.
- Buying the necessary food and drink in the market place.
- Making the market place – both in drama and in art work.

Possible dramatic starting points:
1. Teacher working in role as Pontius Pilate – 'I'd like to come and inspect the kitchens.'
2. Teacher working in role as a newcomer to the palace, someone arrived from a nearby village: 'What's he like, this Pontius Pilate. I've heard he makes you work very hard. Can you help me, show me what I need to do.'
3. A small group of older children spend some time with us as newcomers to the palace, where they are seeking work. Our Class 1 children would by now be ready to be the experts, acting as teachers to the older children, showing them the Palace and all the work that needs to be done.

Classes 2 and 3

The inhabitants of villages near Jerusalem –

*   What is their work?
*   What is their attitude to their work? How can they show this visually?
*   Researching and then preparing for the Feast of Passover.
*   What have they heard about Jesus?
*   Who believes that he is the King of the Jews?
*   Who is frightened of Him?
*   Has anyone gone to hear Jesus teaching?
*   What do you think about Him coming this way?

Possible dramatic starting points:
1.   Teacher in role as a member of the village who returns having been travelling; wants to know whether there's any truth in the stories about Jesus.
2.   Older children come to the village as Romans wanting to know about the 'King of the Jews', perhaps threatening the village.

Class 4

Those who live in Jerusalem and watch the procession to Calvary

*   The same as for classes 3 and 4.
*   Preparing for the influx of people into Jerusalem expected at the time of Passover.
*   Seeking work in Pontius Pilate's Palace (i.e. working with Class 1).
*   What do they know of Barabbas?
*   Looking after the old and the sick.

Possible dramatic starting points:
1.   Again, as for classes 3 and 4
2.   Teacher in role as a Zealot seeking sanctuary
3.   Stories told about Jesus's miracles

Class 5

Zealots. Pharisees and their families.

*   As for classes 3 and 4.
*   How do we communicate with our brothers and sisters who have been imprisoned?
*   Why have they been imprisoned? – enacting the incidents which led up to their capture.

- Is the only way to get rid of the Romans by force?
- Scribes teaching and children learning the Ten Commandments (and possibly other aspects of Jewish Law).

Possible dramatic starting points:
1. Teacher in role (Devil's Advocate?) urging an uprising against the Romans, planning it.
2. Teacher in role as a messenger from Pilate seeking advice from Pharisees about Jesus and Barabbas.
3. Teacher in role as a Roman officer seeking to bribe informers.
4. Pharisees meeting to decide on what they should do if Jesus tries to ride into Jerusalem.

Class 6

Roman soldiers:

- What is their daily routine?
- What are their duties?
- What are conditions like in their barracks?
- How do they feel about being in an Army of occupation?
- What is the worst about their job?
- What do they hope for?
- How is Palestine different from Rome?
- If they could send a letter back to their families in Rome, what would they write? (This might become the basis for the subsequent narration.)
- Sending delegations to other classes to observe what they are doing.
- Seeking out dissidents – planning operations.
- Preparations on the night before the crucifixion.
- Stories told of the journey to Palestine from Rome; shared moments of great stress.

Possible dramatic starting points:
1. How do they decide who will undertake crucifixion duty?
2. Teacher in role as Pontius Pilate asking them for reports on the activities of the Zealots.
3. One of the officers has been killed by a Zealot. How should we respond?

After the initial work I would hope that, as part of the drama work, small groups occasionally move from one class to another – either presenting short scenes, or taking written work. For example, class 3 might send a delegation to class 1, asking them if they can get work in the kitchens, or asking for their help because they want to speak to

Pontius Pilate, to persuade him to release Jesus. Class 1 might write letters pleading for Jesus's release.

Second major planning meeting

Where do we go from here?

1. *Sharing work so far* This can be reported on in the staff meeting or classes could send messengers and envoys to each other as part of the drama.
2. *Developing a story line* The purpose of drawing out a story line from the work is partly for the benefit of the audience, but also as a way of drawing groups together so groups of classes can rehearse together; to ensure that no class is going off at too much of a tangent.
3. We also need to start thinking about *narrative shape and structure.* In this instance the journey through the outlying villages to Jerusalem could either be a fairly straightforward linear, chronological narrative or it might be interspersed with scenes showing what's going on at the same time in Jerusalem, in the temple, in the Roman garrison, in Pilate's palace and possibly even in Rome.

One possible story line which might evolve is illustrated in the diagram 'The Donkeyman's Daughter' below, which illustrates one possible way of pulling the work together and giving it narrative shape. This might be all the 'script' that is needed if children are not going to have all their lines written out for them.

The diagram also shows the four possible locations within which the narrative would take place – i.e. the village, the temple and streets of Jerusalem, Pontius Pilate's palace and the Roman garrison. These could be in four different parts of the school hall.

It's a complex multiple narrative; it would, of course, be possible to stage it much more simply – with the four locations appearing in a chronological order. The *type* of narrative affects the staging. If you have four or five scenes it's quite possible to stage this 'end on'. The more complex multiple narrative suggested here would be better served by representing each location in a particular area in the hall. (See staging diagrams in Appendix.)

Note that our play is about the decisions made by the people who come into contact with the life of Jesus, not a dramatisation of the last days of Jesus himself. I would always try to avoid asking a child to play Jesus. That's why in this instance the play's central character is not even the man who loans the donkey to Jesus for him to ride into Jerusalem, but his daughter.

*The Donkeyman's Daughter – a **possible** narrative structure*

A village outside Jerusalem	Jerusalem – the temple and later the streets	The Roman garrison and prison	Pilate's palace
The donkeyman's daughter leaves the village to go and seek work in Pilate's Palace.			
			She seeks work in the palace and is taught what is needed.
	Children in the temple are taught the Ten Commandments.		
		The Romans tell stories and enact for each other the hardships of life as an occupying army.	
	A thief goes to the temple to buy doves for Passover.		
The daughter returns to her village to hear stories of Jesus, and that her father has lent him his donkey to ride on into Jerusalem.			
	The thief steals the dove and gets away with it because everybody is so shocked by Jesus's action in overturning the moneychangers' tables.		
		The thief is arrested and sent for trial.	
	The Pharisees decide what to do about Jesus. Pilate has called for them.		
			The thief is tried.

A village outside Jerusalem	Jerusalem – the temple and later the streets	The Roman garrison and prison	Pilate's palace
		In the garrison Roman soldiers are drawing straws to see who will have to undertake crucifixion duty.	
In the village there is an argument between those who do and don't believe that Jesus is the Messiah.			
	The Pharisees meet with Judas (or some-one who knows Judas).		
		The Romans hear that Jesus has to be arrested. They are worried about popular unrest.	
			As work proceeds in Pilate's kitchens they hear that Jesus has been brought to the Palace.
		In prison with Zealots and other common criminals, the thief tells of having met Jesus and Barabbas.	
The villagers are preparing for Passover, whilst some of them are determined to follow Jesus into Jerusalem, to take their sick for healing.			
			In the kitchens there's a request from upstairs for a bowl of water. Pilate wants to wash his hands.
	Villagers, Pharisees, Zealots and Romans line the route to Calvary.		

A village outside Jerusalem	Jerusalem – the temple and later the streets	The Roman garrison and prison	Pilate's palace
		The Roman centurion who bathed His wounds is mystified and awed by his encounter with the dying Christ.	
The donkeyman's daughter returns to her village telling of an empty tomb.			

The principle is exactly the same as outlined in Chapter 2, where we take a well-known story and look at it through unfamiliar eyes.

It may be that by the time it comes to performance, some of the children might still have difficulty with dialogue, whether improvised or scripted. In which case it might be necessary to have a narrator. If so we would try to involve as many children as possible in the process of writing the narrative. The task could be shared amongst several children.

The Appendix contains a brief section on the organisation of rehearsal schedules.

Bibliography

Paths to Understanding, Religious Understanding in Hampshire Schools. 1978. Hampshire Education Authority, Globe Macmillan.

Note

1.   For further information about the Jewish Feast of Passover write to: Jewish Education Bureau, 8 Westcombe Avenue, LEEDS, LS8 2BS.

PART FIVE

Planning and Assessment

CHAPTER 9

Planning and assessment

ASSESSING RELEVANT FACTORS WHICH AFFECT PLANNING

In planning any drama work – whether it is a single lesson or an extended inter-curricular project – we have to start by considering the factors we should take into account. What should affect our planning?

These factors can be summarised as follows:

- the children
- the teacher
- the curriculum
- other circumstances.

This order is deliberate and significant. However prescribed a curriculum might be 'it is the children who are the learners . . ., and this gives them the key position . . . The children must be allowed to do their own learning.'[1]

The children

- What are their interests?
- What are their strengths?
- What do you perceive their needs to be?
- How do they function as a group?
- What experience do the children have of drama, and of the lesson subject matter?

In drama we need to work with the interests of the children. That doesn't mean that if a large number of boys in the class are interested in motor bikes, and our topic is Roman Britain we should put the legion in crash helmets. But we do need to observe the children we are working with closely and perceptively. What is likely to hold their interest in this project? Divided loyalties? Conquest? Betrayal? Bullying? A drama project about Roman Britain could deal with any of those.

And what do they need? Maybe they are a group with no experience of compromise. Then in your planning you might focus on the need for negotiation and making concessions. Maybe they are a group with poor command of spoken English, maybe some of the children desperately need to develop confidence in their writing skills. Then we bear this in mind and we try to structure the drama to meet some of those needs.

Our knowledge of the group will inform and colour all our subsequent thinking. The more we know about the specific children we're working with, the more finely tuned we can make our starting point.

The teacher

At the centre of all teaching is the teacher–pupil relationship. It's misguided to ignore half of the equation. We should stand back and assess ourselves. How can we make the most of our strengths, develop our own skills? As a teacher you have to know your own comfort level. While it's good to take risks, they should be measured. We need to extend ourselves, but not always be working at the limits of our ability. If you feel uncomfortable working in role, for example, structure the lesson and scheme of work to give yourself the opportunity to try it out, to develop your skills, but don't lumber yourself with leading the whole session through role until you feel confident about it as a strategy.

If you can see the potential of using the whole group strategy, but are worried that it seems very complicated, set about your planning to lead up to a short period of whole group work. Organise it so that the work in the whole group comes at the end of the session – to give yourself plenty of time to prepare for the next one.

The curriculum

We have to deliver a curriculum. We owe it to our children to do so. But we should never lose sight of the fact that the real 'consumers' in education are the children; the curriculum is for the benefit of the children, not the other way round.

- Which aspects of the curriculum are best delivered through drama? While it's crazy trying to do everything through drama, there are many topics which will be greatly enhanced through drama work.
- How can we prepare for our drama through work in other curriculum areas?

Other circumstances

And lastly we should think about all those other circumstances which are likely to affect the work. These range from very down-to-earth practical considerations to important long term educational goals.

- Where is the drama to be taught?
- How long do you have in the space?
- To what extent can you support the drama work with research and related work in other curriculum areas?
- Can you collaborate with any other teachers?
- Can you involve any other adults in the work?
- What is expected of drama in the school?

The key to planning good drama is not having a million and one ideas, but in finding dramatic situations which are likely to engage the children and develop their thinking; situations which contain the seeds of difficult dilemmas; situations which the children can relate to; which encourage them to think about the world they live in; which empower them as human beings.

When writing a scheme of work or a one-off lesson plan I preface it with a short section headed 'Pre-conditions and rationale', in which these factors and the rationale for the scheme are summarised.

AIMS, OBJECTIVES AND INTENTIONS

There are several different ways of looking at aims and objectives. Perhaps the simplest is to think of aims as being long term and guiding. They should point us in a particular direction and they should allow for flexibility. It will not always be possible to measure the extent to which one has achieved one's aims in *quantifiable* terms.

The achievement of an *Objective*, however, can be measured. In our objectives we can state that 'By the end of the lesson or project, the children will have done x, y and z.' And in some cases we'll have achieved it, in others not. The fact that sometimes we don't achieve all our objectives (perhaps because other more immediate learning opportunities have presented themselves) does not mean we're bad teachers. We need aims and objectives, but we also need to be flexible. Good planning caters for that flexibility.

Consider the analogy of going down to the shops. I'm going to the shops because I want to get a newspaper to find out the football results. My aim is to find out the results, my objective is to buy a newspaper. If, on the way I meet someone who already knows the results I don't need to buy a paper! My objective is a way of achieving my aim, and my objectives can and will change during the course of a scheme of work.

Redundant aims and objectives

Aims and objectives such as

- to encourage co-operation
- to develop language
- to develop sensitivity

may well be worthy enough, but there is no point including them in a specific scheme of work because we can assume that they guide and underpin *all* the drama that we do in the school. Worthwhile aims are not easy to formulate, but it is worth making the effort; they should always be specific.

Enjoyment and good fun

Another type of aim that frequently appears in schemes of work for drama:

- 'The children should enjoy the drama;' or that
- 'First and foremost the drama should be fun.'

Of course learning should be enjoyable; but the worrying implication of the 'drama for enjoyment' type of aim is that other subject areas aren't. A good teacher should always make the subject interesting. Children who enjoy school are much more likely to learn from it than those who don't. But the hard fact is that drama is *not* always going to be enjoyable; it should not always be fun; there are times when it should be difficult.

I was once working with a group who had wanted to set their drama in a prisoner of war camp. It wasn't long before they were escaping. They were confronted by a guard. What to do? 'Kill the guard'. I let them kill the guard, but I certainly didn't allow them to have fun killing the guard. This action became the central focus of the drama. It was a difficult session – for them and for me. Learning which really shifts your perceptions is not easy. Think about the plays and films and TV dramas you've seen which have really affected you. Some are 'fun', certainly, but not all. Presuming that all children want from life is 'good fun' is patronising, insulting and dangerous.

When constructing your aims, try always to be as specific as possible. Any drama scheme should include aims which fall into the following categories:

1. *Content* Those aims which relate to the content of the work. What is the project going to be about? What is it going to be exploring?

2. *Dramatic form*   Those aims which relate to drama as an art form. What are the children going to learn about the art form of *drama*? What do you hope to *teach* them about drama itself?
3. *Social*   Those aims which relate to the children's social health – as, for example, getting boys and girls to work collaboratively in small groups.

The scheme of work in the next chapter and the lesson plan outlined below both offer examples.

Good planning should not be prescriptive and limiting; it should help you think the work through so that it is appropriate and beneficial for the particular children you're working with; good planning should also make you feel more secure as a teacher and give you greater flexibility.

OPENING UP A TOPIC

So . . . if that's the framework, how do you set about the business of filling it in? As a simple principle, start by trying to open up your thinking about any given topic, try to think laterally, to give yourself breadth so that you can then start focusing in on the specific. Having assessed the preconditions, having decided what the children want to do and assessed what you feel they need to do, you're ready to start looking for an appropriate dramatic starting point; that is the point where the drama itself really gets going.

Dramatic starting points

The dramatic starting point may not be where the first lesson of a scheme begins, we may need to do some preliminary work to prepare the children (and possibly ourselves) for the 'meat' of the drama. In whole group drama the dramatic starting point will frequently be the moment when the teacher enters in role. Here, for example are what we might term the dramatic starting points of some of the projects documented in Chapter 5:

1. 'The Construction of a Railway' – teacher as surveyor (not the first role adopted) asking for labourers to help in drawing up a route map. This poses a threat to the community; it will have to cope with change.
2. 'The Deserter' – the stranger asks for help.
3. 'The Giant Awakes' – the mayor calls a meeting of the townspeople to assess what they should do about the damage.

In each of the examples the children were engaged in work which led up to the dramatic starting point – both in drama and in the classroom: research, role play, writing, exercises. I sometimes jump in at the deep end, as it were, and start with the dramatic starting point. Wherever you use it, however, it should be strong and engaging, containing at least the seeds of a dilemma.

In order to find an appropriate starting point, it's often useful to go through a series of simple tasks which are designed to avoid the problem of sitting and waiting for inspiration.

Brainstorming

Setting down as visually as possible any and every idea that comes into your head on the topic. It's important not to censor yourself as you do this. You may well find yourself going off at a tangent; you may well find that you come up with ideas that are totally inappropriate for the age group. Follow them through – almost like doing a word association game, but set it down visually. The process is itself liberating and opens up new possibilities.[2]

Groups of people

Then ask yourself about the people involved. Simply list all the groups of people referred to or implicated in some way.

Possible dramatic frames

While you're still trying to think broadly about the topic, begin to consider the various dramatic frames. Is the drama set in the here and now, moving forwards as a simple linear narrative? Are we in the future, looking backwards at the present? From whose point of view do we see the events of the drama? Could it work as an investigation or an enquiry?

Finding a dramatic starting point

You should now have a variety of ways of looking at the topic. This is the point at which you need to start focusing these ideas down, seeking out a dramatic situation involving one of the groups of people you've listed; preferably a situation which contains a dilemma of some kind.

The unanswered question or key organising question

One of our aims should be formulated as a question. What are we trying to find out through the drama? This should be a question to which the teacher does not know the answer. Just as many playwrights see their work as an exploration, so too with educational drama (be it a private exploration or one which culminates in a presentation). A well chosen *key organising question* makes it much easier to keep the drama well focused, and will itself sometimes lead you to appropriate activities. Even if we can't answer the question, the drama will at least help us to respond to it.

Structure and organisation

How do we introduce the dramatic starting point?

- using the teacher in role strategy?
- giving instructions on pieces of card?
- through related work in other curriculum areas?

The organisation of the lesson will include noting all those preliminary activities which are sometimes needed to prepare the children for the work ahead. It's not advisable to spend too long on this. We can sometimes spend much more time preparing children for the work than actually doing it. The preparation time should not be used as a way of avoiding the drama; that's where the real learning takes place.

Under this heading of organisation we also need to include resources. What do we need to prepare by way of materials? How is the space we're working in to be organised?

LESSON PLANS AND SCHEMES OF WORK

The next chapter contains a detailed account of the planning that might go into a large inter-curricular drama project. It shows how the above tasks might be used in practice. It also serves as a model for a comprehensive scheme of work. A *lesson plan* for drama might look as follows:

Topic – Time

Pre-conditions
Date: ....
Class: .... Years Four and Five

Space and Time available:
- School hall 1.30–2.30 pm
- Classroom then available for immediate follow up work 2.30 to 3.15.
- Desks moved back for small group work or forum theatre if deemed necessary.

Other relevant factors affecting planning decisions

The school is an inner-city multi-racial school in the middle of Reading. Approximately half the children are white, the other half contains a mix of races, including Chinese, Asian and Afro-Carribean. Although this is a one-off lesson, the children have some previous experience of drama with last year's teacher. There is an even mix of boys and girls in the class. The class have been studying the Iron Age in history. This lesson is likely to be the first in a project lasting about three weeks. Two further drama sessions are available at the same time.

Rationale

Many of the children (both boys and girls) enjoy various forms of science fiction on television, the cinema and in the books they choose to read. They are familiar with the concept of time travelling (through films such as *Back to the Future*). The school topic for the term is Time.

Aims

Content
1. To explore the passing of time, and thereby familiarise the children with preliminary notions of history.
2. To explore the meaning of personal responsibility.
3. To develop skills of deductive reasoning.

Formal
1. To introduce the concept of 'still images' as a narrative device in drama.
2. To develop the sense of an appropriate vocal register.
3. To encourage the children who have English as a second language to use their own first language within the fiction of the drama.
4. To develop the children's questioning skills.

Social
To encourage the boys and girls to work together in small groups.

Objectives

The children will:

1. Question the teacher and use powers of deductive reasoning to decide on courses of action.
2. Use their knowledge of history to inform the drama.

3. Work together in small groups collaboratively, creating still images and then interpreting the work of others in a dramatic context.
4. Opportunities will be created for members of the class for whom English is a second language to use their own first language in role as part of the drama.

Introductory activities

1. Control exercises:
   (a) listening to the fading sound of Indian bells
   (b) using Indian bells as a signal to 'freeze' movement
2. Looking at individual children in 'frozen' positions. Suggesting titles or captions for these, as if they were still photographs.
3. Small group work: making still images as if they were photographs taken on a holiday.
4. Small group work: making still images of life in the Iron Age.

(Note that the planning for this lesson would have started with the teacher finding an appropriate dramatic starting point, and then working backwards, asking what would be useful lead in activities for this.)

Dramatic starting point

Teacher in role as a historian. Children in role as experienced time travellers. The historian wants to travel back in time to the Iron Age to find out how they used to make simple tools. He starts by interrogating the still images as if they were hologram pictures taken by the time travellers. He is very keen to travel back in time, but knows it is very dangerous.

Likely activities from here on

- Time travellers (the children) teaching the historian the rules of time travel. What are the dangers? What precautions do we need to take to minimise the dangers?
- Time travellers questioning the historian to see if he is fit to travel in time. What qualities are they looking for? How can we be certain he is sufficiently responsible?
- Making a representation of the time machine.
- Having travelled back in time to the Iron Age the teacher (as historian) could act as Devil's Advocate, breaking the rules of time travel. What is to be done?

- In subsequent lessons the focus may change to the problems and dilemmas of an Iron Age community. If necessary the teacher or children could change roles.

Strategies likely to be used after the dramatic starting point has been reached:

- still image making
- teacher in role
- writing in role
- unrehearsed small group work, leading to forum theatre and spotlighting
- small group improvisations prepared and presented to the class in the context of video evidence
- meetings.

Resources

1. Sugar paper, felt tip pens, Blu-Tack, children's notebooks, pencils, chairs, PE mats
2. Other items which will be useful if available:
   - large poster of a cave painting
   - cassette recorders
   - pre-recorded and blank audio tapes
   - video recorder and monitor
   - VHS extracts from *2001* (opening) and/or *Quest for Fire*.

Possible future developments

- A chart of missions back in time.
- Further back in time – to the Stone Age. Why did the Stone Age people paint on cave walls?
- A dangerous mission to rescue a colleague lost in time.
- A time travel mission to find the makers of the first clocks.

Work in other curriculum areas (follow-up activities)

English: Extracts read to the class from H.G. Wells, *The Time Machine*.

History: Research into early clocks and clockwork.
              Research into Stone/Iron Age.

Science and Technology:
              Plans and drawings of the time machine.
              Measuring time.
              Making candle clocks, water clocks, etc.

Note that in practice you would also need to consider carefully the amount of time you intended to spend on each of the introductory activities. It is also vitally important to build into the work periods of reflection. In this instance that could well take place back in the classroom immediately after the lesson; but there are occasions when it needs to happen in the hall.

Never skimp on reflection. It's when children are given opportunities to think about what they've been doing that the real learning takes place.

ASSESSMENT AND EVALUATION

In any form of assessment, evaluation or appraisal, we need to consider both our own performance as teachers, and to evaluate the work of the children. [3]

In terms of the children's work we need to consider them as individuals and as a class. Keeping records of individual children in drama is not easy and is certainly not always appropriate. At secondary level, where children are taking an examination in drama or theatre studies, sophisticated check lists have been devised. At primary level the records can be much simpler, indicating the development of drama skills (such as readiness to take on roles, ability to sustain a role, ability to construct and interpret still images) and associated social skills.

The Appendix contains a suggestion for *drama policy* guidelines for primary schools. This is offered in the same spirit as the rest of this book – not as a finalised prescriptive curriculum document, but as the basis for discussion. In these guidelines I've deliberately not attempted to offer any sort of prescriptive attainment targets, but the document may be adapted for use as a basis for evaluating progression in drama – for a school, a class and for individuals.

The Arts Council *Drama in Schools* document[4] offers useful advice when it categorises three different types of drama activity in schools:

- making drama
- performing drama, and
- responding to drama.

We should be monitoring the children's work to ensure that they are given opportunities for work in each of these areas.

When evaluating work always start by considering what has been achieved. Be critical in a positive sense. Try to pick out the strengths in the children's work, and in your own. The children can only get better at what they are doing if they know what they are doing well. This underlines the need for periods of reflection when you can help them discover the meanings and significance of their work and encourage them to be self-evaluative.

When writing an evaluation of a drama lesson be as specific as possible. Always try to use the evaluation not just to look back at what you have done, but also to look forward. Where next?

Occasionally try to record and evaluate a drama lesson in detail. The exercise will enhance your own skills of evaluation. One simple, but very effective way of recording the lesson is to lay out the documentation thus, with a straightforward account of what happened on the left-hand side of the page, and detailed comment on the right. Where there is no need for a comment, don't make one. The following brief example is based on the lesson plan earlier in the chapter.

Content and timing	Comment
1.30 The children enter the hall noisily. Three minutes to settle.	Better to have started with a concentration exercise in the classroom, and quietened them down before moving to the hall.
1.33 Indian bells concentration exercise.	Effective – possibly because it calms me as much as it calms them.
1.37 Indian bells as a control device for making still images.	Good transition. Children initially very responsive. But the activity carried on too long; allowed certain children to dominate.
1.50 Still images in small groups. 'Holiday snaps'.	It's taken too long to get here. I'm rushing now, and that results in unclear instructions. Perhaps it would have been useful to have asked them to bring holiday snaps with them and represent these. Once they understand the task, however, most groups tackle it with wit and clarity. The domestic scenes include . . .

Content and timing	Comment
2.00 Viewing the scenes.	Good to see all the groups at the same time. The feedback to the whole group is helpful at this stage – particularly the reference to eye contact.
2.05 Making still images of life in the Iron Age.	Instructions very clear this time. The activity seems appropriate for the group. The small groups co-operating well together. Only group X and Y have any problem integrating boys and girls. But most groups' depictions betray worryingly sexist attitudes. Need to tackle these through the drama.

Evaluating and appraising your own practice as a drama teacher

The guidelines in the Appendix are very much to do with evaluating children's work. The model suggested above allows you to record both the children's work and your own (or another teacher's if you are able to observe a colleague at work). The following list is a suggestion of areas to look at. The questions can be used both to interrogate one's own practice and also when observing others at work.

Planning

1. What were the initial interests of the children?
2. To what extent did the teacher use these interests in planning the session?
3. How was the drama presented to the children?
4. If an image of some kind was used, how effective, engaging and appropriate was it?
5. Did the planning give the teacher sufficient security in the opening stages?
6. Did the planning allow for contributions by the children to affect and change the direction and content of the lesson?
7. Were suitable materials available for use by the children?

Teacher/pupil relationship

1. How important were the children?
2. Did the teacher genuinely value their contributions?
3. How flexible was the teacher in accepting unexpected ideas from the children?
4. • What was the relationship between 'teacher talk' and 'pupil talk'?
   • How much time did the teacher spend talking?
   • How much time did the children spend talking?
   • How much time did the teacher spend listening to the children talking?
   • How much opportunity was there for the children to listen to each other talking?
5. To what extent did the teacher perceive that the needs of the children changed during the course of the lesson?
6. How did the teacher use language?
   • Was it formalised?
   • Was the vocabulary selection appropriate?

Strategies

1. What teaching strategies were employed by the teacher?
2. What proportion of the lessson was spent in:
   • Dramatic play? Exercises? Games?
   • Practicing or preparing to 'show'?
   • Showing or sharing work in a theatrical way?
   • Active discussion in role?
   • Activities in role?
   • Reflection on what had happened.

Content

1. What was the overt content of the lesson? (e.g. 'It was about a village in which the villagers had to decide whether or not to care for a stranger who had developed a mysterious sickness.')
2. What learning opportunities were created within the lesson?
3. Were these opportunities made full use of?
4. What did the children learn?
5. What opportunities were created for further learning – in drama, and in other subject areas?
6. When were the children given time to reflect on their activities and decisions, and learn from them?
7. Did the teacher learn anything from the children – both in role, and as teacher?
8. Did the teacher use role? Was it effective and useful?

9. Try to categorise the type of role used.
10. What opportunities were created (and utilised) for language development?

Control and organisation

1. What methods (in and out of role) did the teacher employ to control the class?
2. Were the 'stragglers', the quiet shy children, the mischievous ones engaged in the drama? If so, how? If not, was the teacher aware of the problem?
3. Did the lesson have a clear focus? Did this change?
4. If the teacher used role, how did s/he indicate that s/he was moving in and out of role? Was this sufficiently clear?
5. When were the children given clear opportunities to make decisions?
6. How was the decision-making process organised?
7. Did the drama allow for the children to examine the consequences of any decisions they made?

Questioning

1. When the teacher asked questions were they: open or closed? How often were 'checking up' questions asked?
2. How often did the teacher genuinely ask questions to find out information?
3. Did the teacher ask any questions to which answers were not required?
4. Were the children encouraged to ask questions themselves – of each other, and of the teacher?

Follow-up

1. Does the drama demand follow-up in other curriculum areas?
2. Will it be possible to do this work?

Notes

1. Fines, J. and Verrier, R. 1974. *The Drama of History*, New University Education, pp. 17, 18.
2. See also Morgan, N. and Saxton, J. 1987. *Teaching Drama*, Hutchinson Education. Chapter 6 contains a detailed section entitled 'Dramathink – or how to take the source apart', which gives further task-based exercises enabling you to find appropriate and challenging starting points.

3. Chapter 7 of Morgan, N. and Saxton, J. (op. cit.) offers a detailed breakdown of evaluation and assessment for children and teachers.
4. Arts Council of Great Britain. 1992. *Drama in Schools – Arts Council Guidance on Drama Education*, ACGB.

CHAPTER 10

Opening up and planning a topic-based drama project
(written in collaboration with Lib Taylor)

When people look at a drama project, or read an account of one that has gone well it can either appear ever so simple, or frighteningly creative, in that it looks full of interesting ideas, although in a well-taught drama lesson most of these frighteningly good ideas will have come from the children.

This chapter is an attempt:

1. To illustrate the thinking that precedes the development of a scheme of work.
2. To show that the 'creative' thinking that goes into planning a project like this can be tackled in simple stages; that it involves setting oneself a series of realistic tasks which are not unreasonably time-consuming nor demanding.
3. To offer a detailed example of how one might develop a topic-based drama project, involving inter-curricular work which culminates in a presentation to a parallel class. In this instance the presentation itself is given a fictional context.

The intention in this first part of the chapter is to open up the thinking behind the project and the pre-planning.

What should be apparent from this is that the 'ideas' which are central to the final project don't just come out of nowhere, they are generated as part of a process, in response to a specific sequence of tasks.

While it might be tempting to lift this project 'off-the-shelf', as it were, its real usefulness should be as an example of the suggested planning process.

THE PRELIMINARY STAGES

Brainstorming

The topic – Environment and Pollution – has been decided by the school. We begin by opening up possibilities.

At this stage I'm trying to avoid any form of self-censorship, trying to get myself thinking as widely as possible, *not* worrying about whether or not any of these ideas are suitable for the age group I'll be teaching. So here's my initial brainstorm:

- destruction of rainforest/ozone layer, etc.
- pollution – rivers, etc.
- factory farming – pesticides, fertilisers, etc.
- waste disposal
- nuclear power
- renewable resources
- recycling
- new building
- urban renewal
- public/private transport
- Third World exploitation
- sharing resources
- famine
- natural disasters – drought, earthquakes
- colonialism
- arms trade.

Related social issues

- housing shortages
- unemployment
- scapegoating
- road building
- relationship of local community to technological 'development'
- public/private health care
- caring for the old

There are two things here which particularly interest me. The arms trade and waste disposal: the arms trade because many of the boys in the class are fascinated by war, and I would like to challenge the attitudes to violence which make it appear an easy option; waste disposal because most children in the school are involved in paper, bottle and can collections, because they are familiar with exhortations to keep the playground tidy.

Although I will certainly abandon one of these, at this stage I want to keep my options open. If I can open up my own thinking, I'm much more likely to be receptive to unexpected ideas that come from the children. So I continue my brainstorming, focusing first on the arms trade:

The Arms Trade

- trying to fight an enemy with inadequate weapons
- employment implications in country of origin
- distribution of power and wealth
- priorities in spending – who decides medical, agriculture, educational budgets?
- pressure selling, arms fairs
- dependency chains
- covert colonisation
- technological overkill
- destruction of the environment
- misuse of resources
- militarism
- top heavy police and armed forces – privileges to armed forces
- propaganda
- security implications of not having advanced weapons
- weapons testing
- secrecy
- violence as a solution to problems
- historical context
- appeasement – 'peace in our time'.

Looking at what I come up with I think, 'This is my project. I'm going to find it difficult to get away from my own concerns.'
    Now I turn to the next topic.

Waste Disposal

- *Recycling*: metals; chemicals; plastics; paper; glass; wood; nuclear fuel; handling, treating and reprocessing dangerous materials.
- *Non fossil-fuel power sources*: tidal, wave, wind, water, solar, geothermal, nuclear, disposal of nuclear waste – long/short-term solutions.
- *Using up raw materials*: food, water, fuel, building supplies.
- *Ownership*: of raw materials; of the sea; of places sacred to indigenous groups.
- *Farming and feeding*: fertilisers, stubble burning, water pollution, use of pesticides, herbicides and fungicides; factory farming, fish farming; intensification – dustbowl phenomenon; rain forest destruction for ranching.
- *Transport*: public, private; road, rail; sea, air; freight, passenger.
- *Ecosystems*: threats to the environment: chemical, atmospheric, heavy metals in water supply, treating dangerous materials, ozone layer destruction, greenhouse effect – flooding.

- *Priorities*: financial, profit, who pays?, employment, capital; one world – exploitation/colonisation; sharing – benefits and problems.

Note that I'm still trying not to censor myself. It might well be inappropriate to deal with many of the above with a class of 9 and 10 year olds. Having opened up the topic, I'll certainly need to focus it down; and that is the stage at which I think carefully about the age, experience and interests of the group with which I'll be working.

But this aspect of the topic is looking more promising. I'm beginning to see various possible dilemmas. So I decide this is the general area we'll be working in. I move on to the next stage of the process, posing the question 'Who might we be?'

Groups of people involved

Those who are:
- inventors
- working for a company involved in waste disposal
- campaigning against dumping dangerous waste at sea
- workers in a factory which is polluting the environment
- trying to initiate investigation into serious chemical leaks
- campaigners
- keeping incriminating information from the public
- investigators
- organisers of recycling programmes
- farmers
- fishermen
- factory workers
- sailors
- lorry drivers
- explorers
- property developers
- financiers
- families of any of the above
- living in a non-technological society.

Possible frames and dramatic starting points

Working in the here and now

- Isolated community discover a valuable mineral on their land.
- Yanomami Indians under threat from gold prospectors.
- Class as children on school trip discover sinister canisters.

- Small coastal town seriously affected by chemical drums washed up on the beach. Children as townspeople.
- Company wants to buy up land on remote island to build a factory to recycle dangerous waste.
- Teacher in role seeking help from class as experts in waste disposal.
- Class as factory workers given a choice between wage increase and installing expensive new waste recycling apparatus.

Working at various distances from the material – (see The dramatic frame, Chapter 4)

- Aliens from another planet coming to earth to discover how we use our raw materials.
- Time travellers coming back to the present day from the future.
- An investigation into a disaster – perhaps a waste site has leached chemicals into the water supply.
- Explorers trying to discover why a large town has been abandoned.
- Teacher in role (as farm/factory worker) goes to class (as detectives/journalists) requesting their assistance in investigating inexplicable illness.
- Advertising agency:
  - improving the image of a polluting company
  - developing a campaign to promote recycling.

Before making a decision about which of the above to use I need to consider my likely aims. I now need to start thinking carefully about the specific class I'm going to be working with on the project. My aims will be provisional, but I shall use them to start refining and focusing the material generated so far. Much of it will inevitably be discarded; I now need to be realistic in terms of what's appropriate, achievable and relevant to the needs of the specific group of children.

Possible aims

Content

To explore and examine:

1. Conflicts of loyalties: personal/group; family/personal.
2. When do people feel principles are more important than material reward?
3. When might short term necessities override long term consequences?

4. When might financial gain override personal safety?
5. What we mean by the words – loyalty, courage, sacrifice.
6. The responsibilities we have to those who work with us.
7. From whom do we take orders and why?
8. What are the rights and wrongs of allowing people authority over others?
9. Are there occasions when we might be justified in plundering the resources of others?

Form

In formulating the aims of the project which relate to theatrical form I need to consider:

1. How I can build on the group's strengths?
2. What needs developing?
3. What aspects of theatrical form do they need to understand more fully?
4. What concepts and dramatic forms might be introduced?

Social

These aims will always relate to a specific group. In formulating the aims I draw on my knowledge of the children, thinking realistically how I might use the drama to improve their social health, trying to be as specific as possible, and referring to individual children and/or groups of children where appropriate.

I make my decision to use the following frame:

The children are the inhabitants of a remote island. A large company wants to buy up land on the island to build a factory to recycle dangerous waste.

I have answered the basic questions – Who? What? Where? I now know the roles, the situation and the issue – but not yet in enough detail. It is best if much of it is filled in by the children. To plan in too much detail will make the project yours, not the children's. You want to be able to say to them:

I know where the drama starts, but I don't know what's going to happen. That's what we're going to find out together.

An experienced drama teacher, confident in her questioning skills, would probably proceed from here in collaboration with the children. In order to clarify the process I shall pose the questions, and briefly suggest some of the answers you might be given:

1. Who?

The children are islanders, *but*

- Who are the islanders?
- What's the most important work on the island?
- How important is their work to them?

They might be involved in:

- farming – tending crops, animals
- fishing – at sea, on fish farms, on lakes and rivers
- coral or sponge diving
- pearl fishing
- forestry, wood carving, carpentry
- mining.

What sort of problems do these people face? The answers to this question will lead to possible initial challenges which will create early tension, interest and give a focus to small group improvisations which would otherwise tend to become rambling.

Possible problems
- mastering new machinery
- introducing new species of tree
- less than full employment
- inadequate harbour facilities
- no title deeds to the forest. It is common land
- a storm: • accounting for the damage in the aftermath
              • saplings destroyed, endangering future crop
              • boats damaged, trade and fishing implications.

And if the teacher is to use the teacher in role strategy,

- Who is the teacher?

Possible roles that the teacher might take on
- a tourist
- a member of the community (low or high status)
- messenger
- company representative
- company manager
- government official
- intermediary (PR)
- investigative journalist

- fisherman who arrives on the island in the storm, and has heard rumours (the stranger or traveller)
- a neighbouring islander (from an island where the company has already set up a similar plant).

2. What?

What does the company do?

Recycles batteries: importing used household batteries, and then separating these into raw material components for re-use. If the drama is to involve a dilemma, the company proposals must at least have the potential to split the island community.

Possible attractions of the company proposals

- trading improvements
- improved employment prospects – bringing new jobs and teaching new skills, and wealth for those employed directly and indirectly
- major improvements to the harbour
- perks for company employees
- new housing and associated developments for employees
- new roads
- new transport to mainland
- airfield to be built.

Possible dangers/drawbacks of the company proposals:

- pollution
- health
- many trees will have to be cut down
- many islanders will have to change their jobs
- loss of autonomy
- the island exporting vast quantities of mercury and hydrochloric acid
- how are the dangerous chemicals transported to and from the island?
- how are they stored on the island?

3. Where?

- What sort of island is it?
- Climate?
- Geographical location and attributes?

Much of this will have been decided by the children as they agree on the details of their work.

Research

- climate
- location
- contour lines.

Other work

- making a ritual, a community celebration
- thanksgiving ceremony
- making a model of the island, the port.

THE WORK IN PRACTICE

Now that the pre-planning has been done, how do we go about translating that into a scheme of work and putting it into practice?

The Topic: Pollution and Toxic Waste Disposal

Pre-conditions:

Age of children	– •	8 and 9 year olds (Years Four and Five)
	•	equal number of boys and girls, mixed race
Space and time	– •	school hall one hour per week
	•	classroom
	•	small A/V room two hours per week
Content/theme	–	part of school topic for the term on environmental problems
Potential audience?	–	parallel class of same age
Performance spaces	–	school hall and classroom

Possible dramatic starting points

- Journalist arrives on island to make TV programme about effects of the storm.
- Company plans to develop recycling plant discovered in brief case washed up on a beach.
- A notice board, on which is posted the company's request for planning permission.

Possible preliminary activities – leading up to the *dramatic starting point.*

Creating the island community, giving the children a stake in what's going on; deciding on:

- responsibilities
- creating interdependent groups
- working groups, family, friendship groups
- census return or population register.

Map-making

- geographical map, including resources, small groups feeding into large, displayed on classroom wall
- emotional maps
- subjective maps.

Building up storm – out of role

- music, sound pictures
- classroom artwork and writing about the storm
  - feelings, descriptions, specific details
  - what destruction has the storm caused?
  - listing storm damage.

Small group improvisation

- repairing houses, nets, boats and other equipment
- logging fallen trees
- bartering before the storm.

Additional relevant information

In planning this project I assumed that the children have no prior experience of performing to an audience; that the school is *not* open plan, and does not work an integrated day but that there is a degree of flexibility within the timetable and that some cross-curricular work is encouraged.

Intentions and rationale

Many of the strategies, techniques and activities suggested here should by now be familiar. This project, however, attempts to take the work one stage further than those documented in Part Two: by editing, shaping and structuring the work into a piece of theatre and presenting it to another class considerable benefits accrue to both performers and audience – in terms of theatrical understanding and curriculum content.

After the extensive initial brainstorming I choose to look at *Treating and Recycling Dangerous Materials* because children can respond to it on a very simple level (from their own direct experience – newspaper collecting, bottle banks, etc.); the issue is central to the environmental/ecological debate and it exemplifies the sort of *dilemma* which is central both to good drama in education and to the production of good theatre.

As described above, the aims and objectives are intended to indicate both what I'm hoping to *teach* the children and what I hope we will discover and explore. Having considered a variety of possible aims, I narrow them down to the following which I believe are realistic, useful and relevant to the needs of the children. The stated aims and objectives are those for drama, and do not include those for other curriculum areas which would in practice be placed alongside these.

Aims

Content

1. To develop understanding of the problems of waste disposal and the concept of recycling.
2. To explore conflicts of loyalties between individuals, small groups and large groups.
3. To examine what is the nature of our responsibility to those who work with us?
4. To motivate research in related curriculum areas.

Formal

1. To develop understanding of simple theatrical forms.
2. To create an opportunity for the children to use the methods and practices of an educational drama project as the basis for a piece of work which is shared with another class.
3. To encourage and develop movement skills.
4. To develop the skills involved in creating and analysing still images.

Social

To build the children's confidence in their own abilities as researchers and performers.

Key organising question

Unanswered Question

How do we reconcile the apparently conflicting demands of short term solutions to problems with their long term consequences?

Objectives

The children will:

1. • develop the following linguistic skills:
   • listening
   • conveying messages
   • describing
   • persuading
   • participating in discussion
   • developing clarity of argument and in verbal and in written form
   • summarising a series of events
   • sequencing a narrative
   • developing a connected narrative.
2. • develop understanding of the following conceptual vocabulary: loyalty, courage, consequence
3. develop understanding of the needs of an audience and how that affects our representation of ideas
4. develop understanding of dramatic structure, in particular cause and effect linear narrative
5. develop skills in using and analysing evidence.

Narrative summary

It's usually advisable not to preconceive a story line. To prejudge a class's response is always to remove any possibility of real decision-making and to dilute their experience of dramatic tension. For the purposes of this example, however, I have assumed the following to be the story/scenario that the *class* develops in collaboration with the teacher. Within the limitations of space I have taken account of alternative directions that the class *might* choose to follow.

Back story

An island community, dependent upon fishing and forestry for its livelihood suffers a major storm. On this island there is a large rubbish dump which has been used indiscriminately by islanders and people from the mainland for a number of years. Material from the dump has become scattered across the island during a major storm, which has also done great damage to the harbour, boats, trees and housing. The islanders have to take stock of the situation, tidy up and make plans for reconstruction.

A television journalist arrives to make a documentary about the effects of the storm. He discovers a briefcase which has been washed ashore.

It is full of waterlogged papers which indicate that a large company is planning to build a factory on the island for recycling household batteries. This is likely to create a dilemma for the islanders, who might welcome the prosperity brought in by such a development, but could well resist the changes to their lifestyle.

The class, in role as islanders, then make the decision about whether or not to accept the development. Whatever they decide to do, the islanders create a *presentation* for the company hoping it will influence their decision.

In school the class make their presentation to an audience – the parallel class, who take on the role of company representatives.

After the presentation the drama continues with the class examining the consequences of the decision they have made. The project could be completed by presenting a second performance piece in the form of a Documentary Drama about the recent history of the island.

Note that the presentation has clear educational and narrative purpose. It is an important part of the project in its own right. It is much more than a way of showing 'This is what we've been doing in our drama.'

REALIZATION OF THE PROJECT

Important note: Throughout the following account of the project reference is made to strategies and techniques which are described in detail in Part Two, 'Drama in Practice'.

The Storm

Starting with the storm means that the project begins with an event that is powerfully dramatic. Although this is not itself the dramatic starting point, it is likely to engage the children from the outset. It would be possible to start by creating and building up a community and *then* introducing a problem, but this is a lengthy process and without some dramatic tension (e.g. the community threatened in some way) it would be likely either to lack impetus and or to become focused on a very different area than the one planned for.

Ways of 'creating' the storm

1. Photographs of actual storm damage shown to children. Children's responses then shared through discussion, movement and improvisation.
2. Sequences of still images created by the children in small groups, showing effects of storm damage.

3. Children respond to pre-recorded music and/or sound effects.
4. Children create a sound picture of their own – with or without movement.
5. Collaborative class painting to cover a wall.
6. Classroom questioning with the whole group gradually building up a word picture, possibly leading to a story or collaborative narrative.
7. Teacher narration:
   • using extracts from published prose or poetry
   • using children's writing
   • teacher's own narrated responses to the children's work in progress.

Many of these activities could be used in combination.

We would now move on to some initial work on establishing our island community.

Dramatic starting point

A television journalist arrives (the teacher in role). The teacher can use the role to add information to that already provided by the children. In this instance it might include comments and questions about:

1. Damage to houses, forestry, harbour, boats, nets, etc.
   • 'As I was getting here I saw . . .'
   • 'How many people have lost their boats? What does that mean to you?'
2. The more general problems faced by the island community such as: unemployment; poverty; trading and transportation problems. 'What will that mean for your jobs?'
3. Specific comments focusing on the litter from the rubbish dump now strewn all over the island.

The dramatic frame becomes evident

The journalist will do everything he can to help the islanders, but he would like their assistance in making a TV programme about what has happened, so that the outside world can know of the extent of their problems. This is the dramatic frame. Here it functions to initiate documenting the damage.

Suggestions as to how this work could be done
1. • The children's own writing – in role as islanders.

- 'Can you make a list of all those things you've lost in the storm.'
2. 'Can you describe what you saw when you woke immediately after the storm.'

Map-making

The teacher gives outline maps, one to each small group, showing the coastline and identifying one key area (e.g. the harbour, the rubbish dump, etc.). The children, in role as islanders, then complete their maps, noting the worst damage in their area. These are then pieced together and displayed.

In small groups, the children create 'photographs' (i.e. still images) of people dealing with the immediate effects of the storm damage.

Building commitment to the community

'What was the community like before the storm?'

This could be done out of role, in the classroom (art work, written stories, comic strips) or in-role in the Hall. It's effectively a 'flashback', moving back in time in order to build belief in the situation and commitment to the community, looking at how the islanders lived before the storm threatened their way of life.

Organisation of groups

Having already established their roles within the whole group, they can now develop those roles through improvisation, mime, writing and art work. The small working groups could be organised through

- work (e.g. fishermen, foresters, carpenters, sculptors)
- family and/or friendship
- geography (where they live on the island).

The activities might include

1. Story telling:
   - individually on paper (as written stories or storyboards)
   - in pairs one to another verbally
   - in groups collaboratively.
2. Creating the myths and legends of the island and its inhabitants.
3. Making or drawing (representing) something very precious to them: a place, an artifact, an icon.
4. Small group improvisations.
5. Sequenced still images.

Suggestions for sequenced still images and/or improvisations

- the daily routine (a problem overcome)

- 'making' what the work group makes
- buying/selling goods (fish, wood, furniture)
- conflict over land
- conflict between members of group, some of whom wish to stay on the island, others to leave for better employment prospects
- dealing with inadequate medical facilities
- celebrating a special event (birthday of an elderly inhabitant).

It is important to remind them at this stage, as they're looking at each others' work, of the context of their presentation work thus far, which has been for the journalist's TV programme. This will give the teacher and the class a framework within which to comment.

'I can see how hard life must have been for you, even before the storm. But there must have been joys, too, for you to have stuck at it, as you did.'

'These pictures are very powerful; but I'll need to write a commentary to link them together.'

Return to the present (i.e. in the aftermath of the storm)
Working initially in small groups to create a celebration/ritual to

- consecrate a new planting area
- thanksgiving for surviving the storm.

The small group work can feed into a whole group activity.

Reflection in and out of role on the events so far. The teacher might:

- ask questions, wonder, comment
- read in-role as if from from the journalist's diary, or speak as if to a camera: 'When I first arrived the islanders seemed still in a state of shock. Although the damage is terrible and they have very little money, these people are strong and resilient: they have allowed me to see rebuilding work, and they have shown me old photographs and home videos of the way the island used to be.'

The children might:

- write their own journals
- collaborate to make newspaper articles.

Heightening the dramatic tension

Drama lessons and projects need to be structured around key dramatic moments; moments which heighten tension and hold the work together

– tension is the spine upon which any drama is built. The same is true of any work which is to be shared with an audience. By this stage in the project I would expect the children to be engaged in the project and interested in the work in related curriculum areas. But it needs to be more *dramatic*.

The journalist (teacher in role) finds a document bag washed up, full of waterlogged papers relating to a large company's proposals to build a factory on this *or* a neighbouring island for recycling household batteries. The documents give details of the likely nature of the operation, and imply concrete *advantages* to the community.

Much of the power of any drama lies in the strength of its imagery and symbolism. The document bag, with its waterlogged papers, is mysterious, intriguing and threatening. It is likely to become pivotal both in motivating the class's work and in holding the attention of the audience in the presentation.

Interpreting the documents
- community meeting (teacher present in-role as journalist)
- classroom work – individual or small group.

Individual/group responses to the documents
- emotional maps
- journals
- vocalising feelings and thoughts.

Improvisation work
- *Small groups, forum theatre:*
  Conducting interviews on the journalist's behalf –
  – using real or imaginary video equipment
  – using audio cassette recorders.
- *Whole group* meeting:
  'Televised' meeting in which the journalist focuses on the issues raised by the discovery of the company proposals.

The role chosen allows the teacher to play low or high status, to feed in information (he might have had dealings with the company elsewhere) and to play Devil's Advocate – the intention being all the time to *open up* the issue.

If the factory were sited on the island the existing way of life would be substantially changed but there would be many short-term benefits: improved harbour and transportation facilities, better employment prospects, improved leisure facilities and greater personal wealth.

Decision making
The islanders must decide whether to welcome the company's

proposals or dissuade it from siting the factory on the island. This is a *branching moment* – if they do want the factory, the presentation to the parallel class is intended to sell the island's attractions to the company; if they don't want the factory, the presentation will show how unsuitable the island is for a factory site. Either way this first presentation is in the form of a piece of propaganda. The discussion which informs this decision-making will need to be organised so that the less verbally articulate children can be given a voice. In order to ensure productive discussion, the teacher should make certain that the children are aware of the various dilemmas the islanders face. These include:

- building the factory might damage the environment
- if the islanders lose the factory they lose investment
- recycling has to be done somewhere
- how might the proposals affect them – individually, and communally?

At the end of these 'discussions' – which could take various forms, including visual presentations of ideas – a decision must be reached.

SHARING THE WORK

Whatever is decided, the class now have to start thinking about making representations to the company. The function of the teacher's role as TV journalist now subtly shifts. S/he can become a coordinator and can assist the class in their work, although s/he can still challenge as necessary.

Presentations

Because our audience, the parallel class, is itself playing a part (i.e. company representatives) the *intention* in making the presentation is clear. This enhances the work in two quite specific ways:

1. Any writing – or art work – in role has a clear purpose.
2. It facilitates the development of those skills which are an essential theatrical requirement, namely:
   - the selection of appropriate material
   - editing that material
   - structuring and shaping that material in a purposeful and dramatic way
   - clarifying its content for an audience who have no prior knowledge of it.

Suggested ways of developing these skills

1. Storyboard of the drama so far.
2. Written list of all the events.
3. In each small group decide upon three reasons for siting the factory on the island, then decide upon three events which demonstrate the suitability of this island as a factory site. Share and justify decisions. Groups could present these events in still image form or through improvisation.

The results of these activities all need to be shared at some point among the whole class and this can be done in a number of ways:

- use of the black/whiteboard
- diagrams on card, flipchart, overhead projector
- small group to large group presentations
- use of video (see appendix).

Any of the above activities could easily be adapted should the class have decided to oppose the factory scheme.

How is the presentation to be staged?

1. A visit to the island by the company representatives –
   the parallel class comes to the hall, or a section of the school field or playground becomes the island.
2. The islanders go to the company –
   our class performs in parallel classroom.
3. The islanders take the company to see a 'lecture demonstration' –
   video and audio tapes used as part of the performance.

In any of the above there are a variety of possible permutations of the audience/performer relationship:

- small groups to small groups – taking groups physically to specific areas of the island;
- small group to whole group;
- whole group to whole group;
- Forum theatre and 'hot seating' – i.e. the company representatives ask questions after the presentation.

Follow up work

After the presentation the two classes might work together, the teachers working as a team, or independently. There is, however, no *necessity* for the parallel class to be involved in the work.

The project is not complete at this stage: the class must confront the *consequence* of the decision which led to their first presentation.

In effect the exploration of the issues now arising is the real meat of the project. It could well lead to a second presentation, which takes the form of a 'documentary'.

Here are two of many possible directions it might take:

1. The factory *is* sited on the island. The benefits begin to accrue. After a short time, however, someone discovers that the recycled products from household batteries include cadmium and mercury and that due to cost cutting they are beginning to leak into the sea – with devastating effects on the environment.
2. If the islanders reject the factory proposal, they return to their island and try to re-establish their old way of life but the dump contains a lethal cocktail of toxic chemicals – not least household batteries – and many waste materials which could have been recycled productively.

This 'documentary drama' could be presented to the parallel class, to another class, or to the whole school in an assembly.

A brief indication of the *work in other curriculum areas* that might accompany this project:

Science

*   How batteries work; how can batteries be recycled? What other uses are there for the chemicals used in batteries?
*   Researching the usage of batteries. What requires batteries?
*   Ask the children to list those things they'd like to find out about.

Geography

*   Placing our island on a map of the world. Where, given what we know about its climate, economy, etc., could it be situated?
*   Relating our island map to Ordnance Survey maps.
*   Where on the island would the recycling factory be best situated? What factors do we need to consider in expanding the port, building new roads, etc.?

Maths

*   Rebuilding their own community: calculating areas, volume, wages.
*   Scales: understanding the company scale drawings.

APPENDIX: General Advice

Research
Materials
The drama room
Drama policy guidelines
Using video in drama work
Rehearsal schedules
Story books recommended for use in drama
Select Bibliography and comments
Useful names and addresses

RESEARCH

When children are engaged in good drama projects they develop a desire for authenticity in their work. This will sometimes involve them in making their own documents (as exemplified in Chapter 5), but good drama projects should also create a necessity for research.

It's sometimes assumed that children can only engage in secondary research – i.e. using material that summarises someone else's findings (TV programmes, books, etc.). In my experience, children get very excited about dealing with primary sources; and the learning that takes place when they successfully seek out and shift through information for themselves is of a very high quality.

This research can take many forms. It will range from going to look at an encyclopaedia in the school library, to interviewing their own grandparents.

Consider the various ways we might research 'How people lived in the 1930s'.

Secondary research

*   school library, public library
*   viewing relevant television programmes
*   slide and audio-visual information packs.

Both documentary material and fiction are useful. Many of the children's novels of Robert Westall, for example, are set during the Second World War and give a strong flavour and accurate picture of wartime Britain. But research doesn't have to be limited to material specifically produced for children. An appropriate extract from an adult novel can be photocopied and enlarged. *Saville*[1] by David Storey, for example, contains some wonderful and very funny scenes as Colin, then a young boy, observes his father's attempts to build an Andersen shelter in the garden.

Researching primary sources

- Examining historical documents in local libraries: including maps, census, parish register, factory regulations, letters, old newspapers, advertisements.
- Interviewing members of the local community – parents, grandparents, relatives. Finding out about life in the 1930s in other countries. Most people really enjoy talking about their own lives.
- Looking round houses, buildings in the neighbourhood.
  It's always surprising how many interesting buildings there are: domestic and places of work. There are those famous places you might visit on a school trip, but quite 'ordinary' places can be just as fascinating – even old schools, their brick work frequently scored with the names of children who might now be great grandparents.
- Visiting museums – preferably ones where the children can get 'hands on' experience, where they can rummage and clamber. They do exist. But always prepare for a visit by ensuring that: the children are seeking information, their visit is purposeful; they have clear tasks; they know what they are trying to find out; the museum has what they need; and the museum staff know you're coming!

That is only a selection for one particular topic. It's extraordinary how much more interesting the neighbourhood becomes for everybody (children, parents and teachers) once they get into a local history project of this kind – which then feeds into their practical drama work.

And the key to all this is the drama. By making the research an essential part of the drama project, they need the information they're seeking, the drama enables them to make it their own; they gain ownership of this material in a way which happens regrettably rarely in school life. And in my experience the resulting research is not only of a very high quality, but begins to become important in itself and is long remembered.

Jonathan Cape Ltd used to publish an excellent series known as *Jackdaw Publications*. They took the form of a folder, each on a particular subject – e.g. The Gunpowder Plot, Newton and Gravitation, Columbus and the Discovery of America – and contained: facsimile documents (letters etc.), drawings, charts and maps; pictures, photographs; broadsheets summarising the relevant issues. Although they are now unfortunately out of print, many college, polytechnic and university libraries still contain many of them – usually filed away in audio-visual aids. They are well worth seeking out.

MATERIALS

Drama teachers are always on the scrounge; at least they should be! Get hold of hats and other items for dressing up; cut off lengths of fabric, of varying weights, colours and textures. You can usually get these from parents, factories, markets, where people are often surprisingly willing to give things away if it's for school use.

Look through magazines for pictures; collect mysterious objects which become intriguing focal points in the drama: crystals, old maps, Victoriana, old postcards . . .

Prints of antique maps are fascinating to adults and children. Many towns have a shop which sells framed and unframed prints. They frequently have a selection of antique maps, which (if unframed) can be very cheap. How cheap? In 1992 I bought a set of five maps for £10. Facsimiles of the first series of Ordnance Survey maps are readily available. In 1992 you can buy replicas of seventeenth century maps printed on parchment for less than £2 from:

The Olde Map Company
Sennen Cove
Penzance
Cornwall
England TR19 7DF

It's well worth having an antique map of the local area. If we're off time travelling to the nineteenth century, it's good to have a guide.

Reproductions of posters (such as 'Smuggling', reproduced on p.22) are available from: Bounty Arts, Dartmouth, Devon, or from the copyright holder Don Campbell and Co., 80 Penn Hill Avenue, Parkstone, Poole, Dorset BH14 9NA.

A central store for use throughout the primary school is also worth having – too often it is assumed that dressing up clothes are only useful for children in the early years. In addition to those things already mentioned (including fabric, textiles and costumes) it would be useful for it to contain some of the following:

- picture frames
- scrolls
- parchment-like paper for old documents
- suitcases, bags, rucksack
- purses, wallets
- a variety of keys, to include the largest you can find
- walking stick
- hats
- spectacle frames
- rope

- camera (including old still cameras and, if possible, a working polaroid)
- jewellery and jewellery box
- telephones
- baskets
- handbell, Indian bells, simple percussive musical instruments.

Disused parachute

There are numerous games one can play using parachutes, but they also look really good under light, especially when lit from behind and the side. Excellent as a screen for shadow puppets. Wonderful for set dressing. Creating a neutral backdrop for an Assembly or the school play simply by hanging it over the wallbars.

How to get hold of one? What do you think the Army, Navy and RAF do with theirs when they are torn, worn and dangerous to know? Throw them away – unless you get in first and ask.

THE DRAMA ROOM

There are primary schools which have purpose-built drama rooms. I think it's a worthwhile investment. When drama becomes important in a school, there is certainly a need for a space in which drama has priority. This in no way contradicts my assertion that good drama can and should take place in the classroom.

The benefits of setting aside a space in which the teaching of drama takes priority:

1. It makes the subject special; it shows clearly – to children, to staff and to parents – that the school values drama, accords it status. If the school values drama, the children are far more likely to take it seriously.
2. It makes the space we are working in special. There are times in drama when we need a clear act of commitment from the children. Crossing the threshold into a space specifically allocated to drama makes it much easier to demand that commitment.
3. Equipment. If we're working in the school hall (with assemblies, dinners, wet breaks and PE vying for use of the space) it's difficult to leave equipment as we'd like to return to it, or even to set it up in advance.
4. A drama room enables us to use lighting, sound, video, musical instruments, overhead projector.
5. The drama room gives our work more privacy – where that is needed.
6. Work produced by one class can be displayed for use by another.

Equipping the drama room

Furnishing

The floor should be carpeted in a light neutral colour (grey or fawn). It's much more comfortable sitting on a carpeted floor than a wooden one. The reason for the neutral colours is to give you maximum control over the way you light specific areas. A spotlight onto a grey carpet lights that particular area; the rest of the room remains dark. If you do the same on a polished wooden floor, the light reflects all over the room.

In order to ensure a good blackout all windows should have black curtains or blinds.

Equipment

- Lighting: – a *minimum* requirement would be:
  a lighting control board, two lighting stands, five Fresnel lights (with gel frames and coloured gels), one Parcan, pinspot or profile spotlight.
- Sound: – cassette recorders for use by the children
  – CD player, audio cassette recorder, amplifier and speakers
  – musical instruments, to include Indian bells, tuned and non-tuned percussion
- Video: – a Camcorder, playback VHS machine and TV monitor
- Pinboards: – for display
- A whiteboard or flip chart
- An overhead projector

DRAMA POLICY GUIDELINES

The following is a set of policy guidelines for drama which might be adopted by a primary school. They are loosely based on the policy document used by Redlands School, Reading, formulated by Lindsay Beaton, Liz Pye and myself in 1990.

Preamble: Drama is an essential part of the educational process within the school. It is a learning environment for both teachers and pupils. Working together we are able to develop our knowledge and skills and our understanding of the world we live in. Good practice in drama is essentially cross-cultural.

Drama is a vital part of the English National Curriculum. Its usefulness is not confined to the development of speaking and listening skills nor to the language development of the pupils, although it is of great benefit in these areas. It is cross-curricular and as such is incorporated in all our termly plans. It is not only a subject in its own right, but also a method; it is both a creative art form and a learning tool.

The three activities which constitute the subject of drama in schools are *making, performing* and *responding*. It is possible to engage in more than one of these activities at the same time. Pupils improvising, for example, are simultaneously making, performing and responding.

Making drama is the ability to generate and shape dramatic forms in order to express ideas.

Performing drama is the ability to engage and communicate with an audience in a dramatic production.

Responding to drama is the ability to express understanding, discernment and appreciation of drama in all its forms.[2]

Our work in drama will be in three main areas: *role, narrative, language* (*verbal* and *non-verbal*). These cannot be taken in isolation but are all interlocked. The children work within these areas according to their age, experiences, and ability. In each area they will be using drama to explore ideas, learning about dramatic forms and learning to respond appreciatively to the work of others.

Throughout the creative processes of drama, children are actively involved in developing skills of synthesis or *making* (e.g. putting together a series of still pictures to tell a story) and analysis (e.g. considering how the meaning of the story is communicated).

We should not lose sight of the fact that the vast majority of children arrive in school with a wide experience of dramatic fiction through television. In addition to the intercurricular work we are advocating here, we would want children to become active participants in a creative art form with which they are very familiar.

The following sections should be seen as interactive. It is, for example, impossible to do work on narrative or role without considering the use of space or dramatic form.

We would want to create opportunities whereby the children could undertake the following:

Role

1. Understand and take pleasure in the differences between pretence and reality.
2. Have the opportunity and experience of moving in and out of role.
3. Identify with characters and actions through role playing, singly, in pairs or groups or as a spectator of active performance.
4. Explore a variety of roles, from working through their own life experiences, to stepping into unfamiliar roles and projecting into other people.

5. Develop the skills and ability to step in and out of role confidently.
6. Take moral decisions appropriate to the character, and be able to step out of role to examine why a decision was made and what its consequences will be.
7. Have the opportunity to consider the formative experiences which go to make up a character (both social and psychological).
8. Use role beyond the immediate experience of the drama lesson (e.g. writing, drawing, designing and making).

Narrative

1. Develop an understanding of cause and effect.
2. Examine the consequences of making decisions.
3. Use dramatic forms to enact, create and develop stories.
4. Experience and manipulate dramatic tension.
5. Consider the meanings and implications of the narratives they have generated.
6. Develop their skills of prediction (considering probabilities and likely outcomes).
7. Identify and use a variety of narrative forms e.g.

    (a) straightforward cause-and-effect narrative (linear – moving forward in time at a steady pace)
    (b) flashback (including investigations and reconstructions)
    (c) flash forward
    (d) multiple narrative
    (e) thought tracking/monologue
    (in which characters are given the opportunity to speak their thoughts aloud or have others speak for them).

Language

Verbal language

1. Develop listening skills in a variety of situations.
2. Develop fluency and confidence in expressing feelings and ideas in both verbal and non-verbal linguistic forms.
3. Explore the meaning of abstract linguistic concepts through drama (e.g. bravery, loyalty, poverty, etc.).
4. Develop and extend a vocabulary which will assist in their understanding of drama as an art form (e.g. comedy, character, scene, improvisation).
5. Appreciate the aesthetic possibilities of language.

In using drama to develop verbal language we would wish to ensure that opportunities are created for children to:

- describe
- persuade
- negotiate
- plan and predict
- report
- narrate
- challenge
- confront
- question
- use different vocal registers.

In all the above we would wish to encourage and develop a multi-lingual process whereby children can use their mother tongue and appreciate the richness of cultural diversity.

Non-verbal language

Throughout our work in drama we would create opportunities for children to experiment with:

- eye contact and eye movements
- facial expression
- body language
- movement
- mime
- mask.

We would want to place all the above work in the broad context of non-verbal language having possible different meanings in different cultures. Throughout the work on non-verbal language we would encourage children to experiment with and develop an understanding of how the use of space can itself create meaning (e.g. proximity, distance).

The dramatic art form

These guidelines are offered in the context that all drama work necessarily involves performance at some level. We see the concept of performance as one which falls on a spectrum ranging from one-to-one through a class presenting work to another class, to assemblies and scripted plays.

The children will:

1. Experience a range of dramatic forms including role-play, whole group drama, improvisation, forum theatre and performance.
2. Be able to use artefacts or properties as symbols in dramatic action.

3. Experience ritual as both participants and observers in order to understand its purposes and meanings (e.g. watching a video of Chinese New Year Celebrations or the children devising and performing a creation myth as ritual).
4. Select and use costume in order to clarify and enhance characterisation and/or narrative.
5. Appreciate drama in performance both as participants and spectators.
6. Experience and develop an understanding of the relationship between games and drama (i.e. ritual, repetition, narrative content and role).
7. Appreciate and explore the power and possible meanings of silence.
8. Employ and develop skills which will enhance the relationship between the audience and participants (to include considerations of staging, audibility, positioning).
9. Comment on their own and others' contributions in a positive manner.
10. Accept and make use of the critical comment of observers .

USING VIDEO IN DRAMA WORK

The National Curriculum documents for English give some prominence to both Drama and Media Studies. While this brief section does not look at Media Studies as such, it does suggest a few ways in which you might consider using playback and/or recording equipment in your drama.

Using playback equipment only:

Just as antique maps, local parish records, photographs or children's own work can be used as part of a drama, so one can use pre-recorded video material: as an initial stimulus, as research material or as evidence. Here are some brief suggestions.

Current News items

Crop circles

The class as a group of investigators, who have to set up an experiment to discover the true cause of the phenomenon, or catch a group of hoaxers; any similar story of an unusual phenomenon (a sighting of the Loch Ness Monster or the Yeti) could be used in this way.

Take a major news item, which is known to be of interest to the children – perhaps a rail crash. Look at the communities affected by it: possibly a hospital. This is fascinating even to very young children; they often see the news and have strong desires to work through their feelings and anxieties. If this seems too risky, take an item such as a successful rescue from a shipwreck and build a drama around the rescue services.

Advertisements

Using the current trend for advertisements as mini-sagas, storyboard one, let the children make their own alternative storyboard (for a real or an imagined product) and enact it.

Alternatively, take a current advertisement (with a highly condensed and often rather fragmented narrative) and develop the lives of those characters who only appear peripherally – who is X or Y, how do they live?

Old newsreels

The class as time travellers, studying the material carefully before going back in time to live in that period – maybe to conduct an investigation or an experiment. The class could be subdivided into groups looking at: clothing and styles of dress, transport, housing, work, leisure.

Old films

The class as aliens who have picked up transmissions from earth (radio waves take several years to reach their planet, so these old movies are the most up-to-date material they have showing the earthlings' way of life); they are studying them in preparation for a (friendly?) mission of First Contact.

Using camera and recording equipment:

Consider why one might want to record any piece of drama; what purpose a recording might have within the context of the dramatic fiction.

Some brief suggestions:

- Interviews, creating a record of a council meeting, a statement made directly to the camera for broadcast.
- A message sent from one group to another (perhaps a ransom demand, an SOS message, a communication from a spaceship to earth or vice versa).

- The video as evidence – perhaps the teacher in role as the Pied Piper now arrested and being interrogated by the Hamelin Police!

A camera can be used simply to record, but that on its own is not likely to develop the children's understanding of the media, nor of their own drama work. Try to make the way the camera is used an issue in itself – possibly by giving instructions in role:

- What happens if you shoot from an unusual angle – directly overhead, from below?
- What happens if you let the camera take on the role of a character – so children speak to it directly as if it were an active participant in the drama?
- 'How can we create a sense of the confusion in this meeting without showing the whole of the meeting?'
- 'We've only got 30 seconds for this whole item. How can we use the camera to create a sense of the sheer hard work these people have to endure?'

If the use of video becomes part of the drama, it is given a specific context. It can be a very useful way of learning actively about the media and a very helpful tool in communicating between one class and another.

Access to equipment

A few schools now have a video camera as well as playback equipment; if your school does not, it's increasingly likely that parents might have a Camcorder which they might be willing to lend. Colleges of Further and Higher Education and Universities with Departments of Education might well be interested in setting up a project with students using video. The same might well apply if your local secondary school offers Drama, Theatre Studies or Media Studies at exam level.

REHEARSAL SCHEDULES

If you find yourself in the position of taking responsibility for the school play, one of the organisational tasks you'll need to tackle early on is constructing a rehearsal schedule. It might sound terribly formal, but it will save a great deal of unnecessary acrimony if everyone involved knows what is required of them and by when. It's one thing to take on a commitment, and something quite different to find out half way through that it involves three times as much work as you'd agreed. A good rehearsal schedule which is realistic and sensible is as

continued on page 242

Staging diagrams

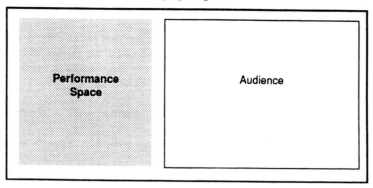

Diagram 1: 'End on' staging

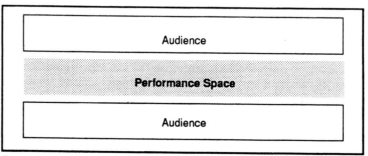

Diagram 2: Audience on two sides

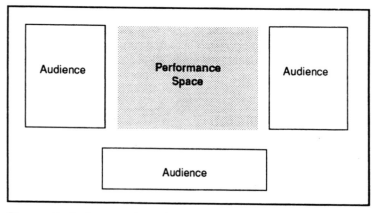

Diagram 3: Audience on three sides

Staging diagrams

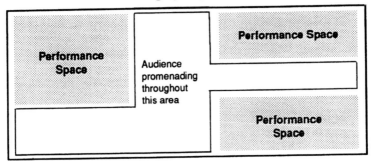

Diagram 4: Audience promenading
[Note that the performance spaces need not be all the same size]

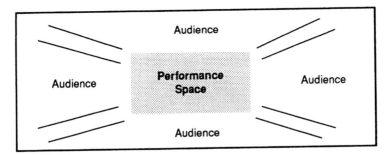

Diagram 5: Arena style or ['in the round']
Note - the spaces in the corners, which could be reached by gangways
between the audience, might be used to store props and costumes

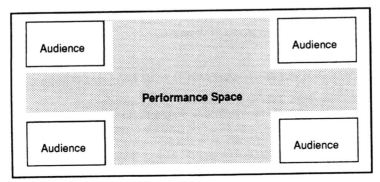

Diagram 6: Traverse
Note - this traverse performance space could equally well run diagonally
between the corners

vital to the smooth running of a production as a timetable is to the smooth running of a large school.

The simplest piece of advice in constructing any rehearsal schedule is start at the end and work backwards. When is your first performance? What are the key dates? How does the performance fit in with all the other things that are going on in the school?

So a typical rehearsal schedule might include the following headings:

- action
- people involved
- dates and times
- other activities going on in the school.

Under the heading of action you would include such things as:

- check licence and fire regulations, make appropriate arrangements
- preliminary staff meeting to discuss the project and agree priorities
- attend PTA meeting to request volunteers
- meeting with parent volunteers to assign tasks and responsibilities, e.g. lighting, costume
- teachers working with classes as part of timetabled lessons
- drama club meetings
- run through of whole play
- costumes to be finished
- borrowed lights to be in place
- dress rehearsal
- first performance
- last performance
- hall to be cleared.

The other headings are self-explanatory.

STORY BOOKS RECOMMENDED FOR USE IN DRAMA

Aiken, Joan. 1974. *Tales of Arabel's Raven*, BBC/Jonathan Cape.

Berry, James. 1988. *Anancy-Spiderman*, Walker Books.

Browne, Anthony. 1980. *Look what I've got*, Julia Macrae Books.

Browne, Anthony. 1983. *Gorilla*, Julia Macrae Books.

Browne, Anthony. 1989. *The Tunnel*, Julia Macrae Books.

Bragg, Mike. 1986. *The Pet Cellar*, Methuen Children's Books.

Corrin, Sara and Stephen. 1988. *The Pied Piper of Hamelin*, Faber and Faber.

Hallworth, Grace. 1990. *Cric Crac, a collection of West Indian Stories*, Heinemann.

Hedderwick, Mairi. 1984. *Katie Morag Delivers the Mail*, The Bodley Head.

Hedderwick, Mairi. 1985. *Katie Morag and the Two Grandmothers*, The Bodley Head.

Hedderwick, Mairi. 1986. *Katie Morag and the Tiresome Ted*, The Bodley Head.

Hoban, Russell. 1974. *How Tom Beat Captain Najork and his Hired Sportsmen*, Jonathan Cape.

Hughes, Shirley. 1981. *Alfie Gets in First*, The Bodley Head.

Hughes, Shirley. 1983. *Alfie Gives a Hand*, The Bodley Head.

Hughes, Shirley. 1977. *Dogger*, The Bodley Head.

Hughes, Ted. 1968. *The Iron Man*, Faber and Faber.

Jones, Terry. 1981. *Fairy Tales*, Pavilion Books.

McKee, David. 1980. *Not Now Bernard*, Andersen Press.

McKee, David. 1970. *The Magician who lost his Magic*, Abelard Schuman.

McKee, David. 1981. *Magician and Double Trouble*, Abelard Schuman.

Muller, Jorg and Steiner, Jorg. 1982. *The Sea People*, Gollancz.

Van Allsburg, Chris. 1986. *The Polar Express*, Andersen Press.

Wiesner, David. 1991. *Tuesday*, Clarion Books, New York.

Wilde, Oscar. 1888. *The Selfish Giant*, (originally published in 1888 – available in several editions).

Williams, Jay. 1978. *The Practical Princess*, Hippo Books/Scholastic Press.

SELECT BIBLIOGRAPHY

Books

Arts Council of Great Britain. 1986. *Policy for Theatre for Young People*, ACGB.

Arts Council of Great Britain. 1992. *Drama in Schools – Arts Council Guidance on Drama Education*, ACGB.

British Film Institute. 1988. *Picture Stories*, BFI Education.

British Film Institute. 1989. *Primary Media Education: A Curriculum Statement*, BFI Education.

Boal, A. 1979. *Theatre of the Oppressed*, Pluto Press.

Boal, A. 1992. *Games for Actors and Non-Actors*, Routledge.

Bolton, G. 1984. *Drama as Education*, Longman.

Brecht, B. (translated and edited by Willett J). 1982. *Brecht on Theatre*, Methuen.

Bruner, J. S. (ed.). 1976. *Play: Its Role in Development and Evolution*, Penguin.

Burgess, R. and Gaudry, P. 1986. *Time for Drama*, Open University Press.

Davies, G. 1983. *Practical Primary Drama*, Heinemann Educational Books.

Department of Education and Science (DES). 1989. *English for Ages 5 to 16*, HMSO.

Department of Education and Science (DES). 1990. *Aspects of Primary Education: The Teaching and Learning of Drama*, HMSO.

Donaldson, M. 1978. *Children's Minds*, Fontana.

Fines, J. and Verrier, R. 1974. *The Drama of History*, New University Education.

HMI Series. 1989. *Drama from 5 to 16 – Curriculum Matters 17*, HMSO.

Hornbrook, D. 1989. *Education and Dramatic Art*, Basil Blackwell.

Johnson, L. and O'Neill, C. (ed.). 1984. *Dorothy Heathcote – Collected Writings on Education and Drama*, Hutchinson.

Johnstone, K. 1981. *Impro*, Methuen.

McCaslin, N. 1990. *Creative Drama in the Classroom*, (5th edn), Longman, New York.

Morgan, N. and Saxton, J. 1987. *Teaching Drama*, Hutchinson Education.

National Curriculum Council. 1991. *Drama in the National Curriculum*, (poster), NCC.

O'Neill, C. and Lambert, A. 1982. *Drama Structures*, Hutchinson.

O'Neill, C., Lambert, A., Linell R., and Warr-Wood, J. 1976. *Drama Guidelines* Heinemann.

National Association for the Teaching of Drama (NATD) et al. 1986. *Positive Images*, 1985 Conference Publication Joint Committee NATD, NATFHE Drama, NAYT, NADECT, NADA.

Nixon, J. (ed.). 1982. *Drama and the Whole Curriculum*, Hutchinson.

Parsons, B., Schaffner, M., Little, G. and Felton, H. 1984. *Drama, Language and Learning*, NADIE, Tasmania.

Redington, C., (ed.). 1987. *Six Theatre in Education Programmes*, Methuen.

Wagner, B-J. 1976. *Dorothy Heathcote, Drama as a Learning Medium*, Hutchinson.

Periodicals

The Drama Magazine (formerly *London Drama*) is published three times a year and is obtainable from:

Holborn Centre for the Performing Arts
Princeton Street
LONDON WC1R 4AZ

2D

2D subscription office:
AB Printers Ltd
(*2D* subscription office)
33 Cannock Street
LEICESTER, LE4 7HR

2D Publications also publish a number of useful teachers' packs providing specially chosen source material and suggestions how to use it in drama.

A BRIEF DISCUSSION OF SOME OF THE BOOKS REFERRED TO

ACGB, *Drama in Schools*

An important report which argues strongly that drama should be taught as a subject in its own right alongside its use as a learning medium. The report offers a programme of study for each key stage and highlights the relationship between drama in education and professional theatre. Copies have been made available free of charge to every school.

Boal, A. *Theatre of the Oppressed*
The second section of the book, where the idea of forum theatre is described in detail (Boal first coined the term) is the most useful section for primary school teachers.

Boal, A. *Games for Actors and Non-Actors*
Very useful sequences of exercises and games based work. An intelligent discussion of the underlying principles of Forum Theatre.

Bolton, G. *Drama as Education*
A useful historical overview of the development of Drama in Education.

Burgess, R. and Gaudry, P. *Time for Drama*
Some excellent ideas here – but it's heavily weighted towards work in secondary school. Teachers at the top end of Primary might also find it useful.

Davies, G. *Practical Primary Drama*
A small book which is a very easy read – full of good ideas. There is an excellent chapter on drama and story/topic work.

Fines, J. and Verrier, R. *The Drama of History*
It's getting on for 20 years since this was published, and it's been out of print for a good while – but it remains one of the best books on drama ever written. It's delightfully entertaining and as useful to the non-specialist as to the specialist. It's specifically about using drama to teach history, but it contains a wealth of wisdom about teaching drama (and indeed teaching itself). If you can get hold of two copies, send me one for Christmas!

O'Neill, C. *Dorothy Heathcote – Selected Writings*
Dorothy Heathcote writing about her own practice. There's a great deal of very sound and thought-provoking material here.

HMI Series. *Drama from 5 to 16*
The HMI document. Useful to have in the staffroom.

McCaslin, N. *Creative Drama in the Classroom*
An American publication – now available from Longman in the UK. Very thorough. An enormous amount of material here, including some excellent ideas for use with Infants (for whom there is very little published) and lots about drama as performance.

Morgan, N. and Saxton, J. *Teaching Drama*
Excellent. Useful for Primary and Secondary alike. Full of good sound practical advice, usefully combined with good theory to give a strong sense of direction. Particularly useful are the chapters on Planning and Questioning.

NATD, etc. *Positive Images*
A practical workbook suggesting drama work to combat Racism,

Sexism and stereotyping. Still available from NATD (contact address below).

O'Neill, C. and Lambert, A. *Drama Structures*
An excellent book aimed specifically for use in secondary schools – but the rigour and clarity of the thinking make it a valuable resource to have available for the top end of the primary school. Good sections on teacher in role, etc. Very detailed breakdowns of topics of work taught over a lengthy period of time – e.g. Victorians, The Way West, etc.

O'Neill, C. et al. *Drama Guidelines*
Written more than fifteen years ago – still very useful. A series of lessons described and analysed. Age of children taught in the seventeen examples of lessons ranges from 5 to 17. Good sound practical advice underpinned by very helpful theory. A4 format.

Parsons, B. et al. *Drama, Language and Learning*
The book attempts to analyse in detail the very positive effects of using drama in language teaching.

Wagner, B-J. *Dorothy Heathcote, Drama as a Learning Medium*
A great deal of excellent practice described in this book. Particularly useful for its chapters on planning, working in role and on drama with the handicapped.

USEFUL NAMES AND ADDRESSES

Drama Associations

At the time of writing there are two drama associations (although discussions are under way to effect a merger). They each provide support for drama teachers of all age groups and offer regular in-service courses for teachers at regional, national, and international level – at very reasonable cost. They are: National Drama and The National Association for the Teaching of Drama (NATD).

NATD:
 Janet Cassford (NATD)
66 Margaret Avenue
Bedworth
Nuneaton
WARWICKSHIRE CV12 8ED

National Drama:
The Secretary
56 Empress Avenue
Wanstead
LONDON E12 5EU

Theatre in Education

This an extremely valuable resource for schools. Theatre in Education (often referred to as T.I.E.) is a broad term; it's beyond the scope of this book to attempt a precise definition. Throughout the country there are professional Theatre in Education companies producing programmes of work which they tour to schools. These range from plays intended for large audiences to participatory programmes for small groups lasting for a whole day. What the different companies share in common is their desire to use theatre in an educational way, often raising serious issues in entertaining but thought-provoking ways. Most of the programmes are accompanied by teachers' packs and sometimes workshops. Many of the companies seek out advice from teachers in the planning stages and all of them welcome regular liaison with schools.

If you would like to discuss the possibility of a 'Theatre in Education' company visiting your school (some of them are still subsidised by local education authorities) either contact the Drama Officer at your local Regional Arts Board (addresses listed below) or write to:

ASSITEJ GB
Unicorn Theatre
6/7 Great Newport Street
LONDON WC2H 7JB

ASSITEJ is the British Centre of the International Association of Theatre for Children and Young People.

Writers/artists in residence.

Several of the Regional Arts Boards offer schemes whereby they will fund an artist or a writer working in residence with a school for a period. Schemes like this could well enable you to get a playwright to come and work with the children in the school.

Regional Arts Boards

Contact either the Drama Officer or the Literature Officer:

Eastern Arts Board	East Midlands Arts Board
Cherry Hinton Hall	Mountfields House
CAMBRIDGE CB1 4DW	Forest Road
	Loughborough
	LEICESTERSHIRE
	LE11 3HU

London Arts Board
Coriander Building
20 Gainsford Street
Butlers Wharf
LONDON SE1 2NE

Northern Arts Board
9–10 Osborne Terrace
Jesmond
NEWCASTLE UPON TYNE
NE2 1NZ

North West Arts Board
12 Harter Street
MANCHESTER M1 6HY

Southern Arts Board
13 Clement Street
Winchester
HANTS SO23 9DQ

South East Arts Board
10 Mount Ephraim
Tunbridge Wells
KENT TN4 8AS

South West Arts Board
Bradninch Place
Gandy Street
EXETER EX4 3LS

West Midlands Arts Board
Brunswick Terrace
STAFFORD ST16 1BZ

Yorkshire and Humberside Arts
  Board
21 Bond Street
DEWSBURY WF13 1AX

Notes

1.   Storey, D. 1976. *Saville*, Jonathan Cape.
2.   Taken from: Arts Council of Great Britain 1992. *Guidance on Drama Education*, ACGB, p. 10.

I N D E X